Anthropocene Theater and the Shakespearean Stage

Anthropocene Theater and the Shakespearean Stage

WILLIAM H. STEFFEN

OXFORD
UNIVERSITY PRESS

OXFORD
UNIVERSITY PRESS

Great Clarendon Street, Oxford, OX2 6DP,
United Kingdom

Oxford University Press is a department of the University of Oxford.
It furthers the University's objective of excellence in research, scholarship,
and education by publishing worldwide. Oxford is a registered trade mark of
Oxford University Press in the UK and in certain other countries

First Edition published in 2023

Impression: 1

Published in the United States of America by Oxford University Press
198 Madison Avenue, New York, NY 10016, United States of America

British Library Cataloguing in Publication Data

Data available

Library of Congress Control Number: 2022947811

ISBN 978-0-19-287186-2

DOI: 10.1093/oso/9780192871862.001.0001

Printed and bound by
CPI Group (UK) Ltd, Croydon, CR0 4YY

For Anna, Oscar, and Calliope,
my muses, who never let me down.

Acknowledgments

This book began as an undergraduate thesis about Shakespeare's Roman plays and transformed into a dissertation about Shakespearean ecologies. Parts of this book were inspired by my own ecological encounters with Shakespearean performances in western Massachusetts, and I feel extremely lucky to live in a community with so many fellow Shakespeareans and scholars. I remember attending a summer evening outdoor performance of *The Winter's Tale* in 2012 presented by the Hampshire Shakespeare Company in Amherst. At one point, the actor playing Leontes turned to the audience (weathering the 92-degree July sunset) and wiped real sweat from his brow as he complained that it was indeed, "Too hot, too hot!"

There are many people to thank, without whom this project never would have come together. First and foremost, I would like to thank Jane Degenhardt for her years of dedicated and unwavering support. I am grateful to L. Brown Kennedy for her early support. Malcolm Sen's generous guidance into the environmental humanities has also been invaluable to me. Thank you as well to Adam Zucker, Brian Ogilvie, and Daniel Sack for their feedback. I am grateful to friends and colleagues for their considerate comments on different parts of this project as well—Neelofer Quadir, Ashley Nadeau, Lauren Silber, Michelle Brooks, David Katz, Sean Gordon, Annaliese Hoehling, Benjamin Zender, Jenny Krichevsky, and Catherine Elliot.

I also wish to thank Miles P. Grier, Lisa Barksdale-Shaw, Matthieu Chapman, and other participants on the 2017 Shakespeare Association of America (SAA) panel on "Race and the Materiality of Early Modern Performance" for their feedback and encouragement. Thanks to Robin Bates, Andrew Bretz, and Charisse Willis for their organization and feedback during the 2018 SAA panel on "Sites of Resistance." Thank you to Chris Barrett, Sarah Higinbotham, Alison Chapman, and Kyle DiRoberto, and other participants on the 2019 SAA panel on "Environments of Justice," for their facilitation and comments. Thanks to Amy Tigner and Jennifer Munroe for their organization and flexibility during the "Ecologies and/of Resistance" SAA panel during an unforgettable spring of 2020. I am indebted to the editors and to the anonymous referees for *The Journal for Early Modern Cultural Studies*, *Renaissance Drama*, and Oxford University Press who helped to shape this project into something worthy of publication. I am also grateful to the judges of the 2020 SAA J. Leeds Barroll Dissertation Contest, who bestowed a tremendous honor upon me, and without whom I would not have considered publishing this project in its current form.

Thank you as well to the Special Collections librarians at the University of Adelaide, Marie Larsen and Cheryl Hoskin, for digitizing Allan Wilkie's autobiography at my request. Thanks to Ellen Jane Hollis at the Bermuda National Library for helping me find information on a spectacular performance of *The Tempest*.

I am also grateful to all of my friends and family who helped me marinate, digest, and regurgitate these ideas. I would not have been able to write a word of this manuscript without the love and support of my wife, Anna-Claire Simpson, whose own work never ceases to inspire me. I am also indebted to Lloyd Steffen, Lori Paige, and June Schlueter for their assistance and support during this publication process.

Contents

If by your art, my dearest father, you have
Put the wild waters in this roar, allay them.

William Shakespeare, The Tempest (1611)

Introduction

Early Modern Drama and the Anthropocene

In 1613, when the Globe Theater caught fire and burned to the ground, the end of the world seemed overdue. Despite England's nascent efforts to colonize what was still seen as a "New World" across the Atlantic, English culture was steeped in the idea that doomsday was imminent. God had already destroyed the earth with water once; he might easily do it again. The time allotted for the human species on earth was thought to be as finite as life itself, and rapidly approaching its quietus. Each of the popular temporal schemes for imagining the breadth of human history on earth—which were broken into three, four, six, seven, and even twelve distinct "ages"—placed the "present" of the early modern period in the final age.[1] In *As You Like It* (1599), Shakespeare's somber clown Jaques articulates one such seven-age scheme. Each "age of man" corresponded macrocosmically to a different stage in an individual's life, to a different planet in the Ptolemaic solar system, and to a day of God's creation of the earth.[2] Reflecting on Orlando's suffering, Adam's starvation, and his own age, Jaques anticipates an impending oblivion for himself, if not his species:

> Last scene of all,
> That ends this strange eventful history,
> Is second childishness and mere oblivion,
> Sans teeth, sans eyes, sans taste, sans everything.
>
> (2.7.170–3)[3]

By comparing the seven "ages of man" to seven acts or scenes of a play, Jaques turns the duration and form of the play he inhabits into yet another microcosm for collective and individual human existence. Our play, he reminds us,

---

[1] John Anthony Burrow, *The Ages of Man: A Study in Medieval Writing and Thought* (Oxford: Clarendon Press, 1988), 2.

[2] Burrow, *The Ages of Man*, 52, 72.

[3] William Shakespeare, *As You Like It*. Edited by Barbara A. Mowat and Paul Werstine (New York: Washington Square Press, 1997).

Anthropocene Theater and the Shakespearean Stage. William H. Steffen, Oxford University Press.
© William H. Steffen 2023. DOI: 10.1093/oso/9780192871862.003.0001

is almost over. But he also situates the early modern stage within its own apocalyptic parameters. Early modern theater and performance history, as Ellen MacKay reminds us, is fraught with anecdotes of disaster, accident, and death.[4] Theaters themselves became the loci of cataclysm on several occasions. On 6 April 1580, for example, long before the building was disassembled, carried across the Thames, rebuilt, and renamed the Globe, the Theater was rocked by an earthquake during an afternoon performance, which prompted several frightened spectators to leap from the balcony.[5] Though it would endure earthquake and plague, Shakespeare's wooden O would not survive fire. The Globe burned. But the world did not end.

The idea that humans are inhabiting their final stage on earth has not faded with the last 400 years of theater history. The medieval temporal schemes used to describe the "age of man" in terms of Biblical history or astronomical correspondence have translated into the less human-oriented narratives offered by geology and natural history. Human life on earth, we now know, has been relatively brief compared to the 4.5 billion years the earth has existed (though it has also far exceeded the 6,000-year timeframe promoted by early modern antiquarians and scholars). Geologists today will discuss earth's history in periods, eras, and epochs rather than "ages." The term "Anthropocene" ("human era" or "age of man") continues to gain traction among scientists and scholars for describing our current geologic era. The Anthropocene names the era in which humans have gained geologic agency and influence over the earth's climate and environment without necessarily meaning to. In the twenty-first century, the Anthropocene seems remarkably compatible with an early modern understanding of humanity's borrowed time on earth. Just as early modern English writers were preoccupied with identifying how their own behaviors (sins) indirectly caused storms, floods, earthquakes, and other seemingly "natural" manifestations of God's wrath, scientists today are continuing to uncover how human behaviors are to blame for a host of similar and seemingly "natural" events. Anthropogenic climate change may be responsible for the intensification of weather events, like the particularly devastating hurricane season during the fall of 2017. Anthropogenic climate change is also the primary culprit in global sea-level rise, and it is contributing to the increasing acidification of the earth's oceans. Floods are becoming more frequent and more intense, in part due to the increased amount of

---

[4] See Ellen MacKay, *Persecution, Plague, and Fire: Fugitive Histories of the Stage in Early Modern England* (Chicago, IL: University of Chicago Press, 2010).
[5] Thomas Churchyard, *A warning for the wise, a feare to the fond, a bridle to the lewde, and a glasse to the good* (London, 1580), B2r.

moisture in the air. Wastewater injections from oil and gas drilling operations have been shown to induce earthquakes in parts of the central United States. Global commerce and the unwitting introduction of invasive species to foreign environments are driving the earth's sixth mass-extinction event. The COVID-19 pandemic has even been cast as a disease cultivated in the petri dish of global commerce and the resulting interspecies relationships.[6] Today, the greatest threat to the continuation of life (human or not) on earth is not Almighty God. Nor is it a six-mile-wide asteroid barreling toward the Yucatan Peninsula—though our threat is likely just as dangerous. It is just us. Human behavior by itself is innocuous enough; our species has existed for millennia without altering the earth's climate. But human behavior within a system of global commerce—since Columbus inaugurated the globalization of the earth's biota—has proven to be an irrevocable geologic force of ecological devastation. Early modern European colonialism was not the first world system of capital exchange.[7] But its beginning may have marked the dawn of the Anthropocene, our last "-cene" of all.[8]

Our late rude awakening into the dawn of an "age" where humans are suddenly conscious of the geologic agency they possess has not eradicated or even minimized apocalyptic thinking. Dwelling on the end of days did not die out in the cinders of the Globe—nor with the execution of the English monarch, or even with the great fire of London. The secular culture of the twenty-first century is no less preoccupied with doom and gloom than early modern English culture was. We are just as willing to draw conclusions from a starving polar bear as Hamlet is to read an end in the fall of a sparrow. Early modern "catastrophizing"—what Gerard Passannante calls "the imaginative and often involuntary creation of speculative disasters"—served some of the same utilitarian purposes that it does today in the age of anthropogenic climate change.[9] Speculating on disaster, for example, can render an imperceptible phenomenon (like climate change) tangible, however terrifying. It can remind us "of something that should seem obvious but rarely is: that we've had a hand in making the disaster we feel befalling us."[10] It can also compel us to act

[6] Cristina O'Callaghan-Gordo and Josep M. Antó, "COVID-19: The Disease of the Anthropocene," *Environmental Research*, Vol. 187 (2020), 109683.

[7] See Janet L. Abu-Lughod, *Before European Hegemony: The World-System A.D. 1250–1350* (Oxford: Oxford University Press, 1989).

[8] Simon L. Lewis and Mark A. Maslin, "Defining the Anthropocene," *Nature*, Vol. 519 (2015), 171–80.

[9] Gerard Passannante, *Catastrophizing: Materialism and the Making of Disaster* (Chicago, IL: University of Chicago Press, 2019), 1.

[10] Passannante, *Catastrophizing*, 243.

responsibly and productively in response to an impending disaster (if it does not induce us into a state of nihilistic paralysis first).[11] The Anthropocene narrative easily conforms to an apocalyptic mindset, especially given how it "indicates that the cosmic insouciance that was the basis for historical forms of human being-in-the-world has come to an end."[12] The Anthropocene narrative even risks reinforcing a hard distinction between the modern categories of "Nature" and "Society," which propels the binary politics of either "sustainability or collapse."[13]

As our planet faces a future of ecological uncertainty, *Anthropocene Theater and the Shakespearean Stage* turns to early modern drama for a reevaluation of a period that was once regarded as the final "Age of Man." I argue that the English stage—where the modern distinction between human and nature was still emerging, and where commercial properties on stage accentuated the agency of the natural world in facilitating colonial expansion—provides a material counternarrative to the history of the first phase of biological globalization, one that can help modern audiences come to terms with our own uncertain future shaped by climate change.

From Shake-scene to Anthropo-cene

The thesis of this book is simple: the early modern stage laid the groundwork for what I want to call a "theater of the Anthropocene." This theater might be broadly defined by three characteristics.

First, a theater of the Anthropocene regards performance as a fluctuation between human intention and unplanned accident in the context of European globalization. While it may be tempting to grant Shakespeare credit for inventing our solace to global deluge, for discovering a dramatic haven from the so-called "natural" disasters that are the consequences of anthropogenic climate change, it would also be irresponsible to put Shakespeare at the center of this discourse. A theater of the Anthropocene recognizes the ecological nature of theater, that any performance is a culmination of several different competing and collaborating human and non-human actors. A playwright might write a play with the intention that it will be sold or performed, that it

---

[11] Passannante, *Catastrophizing*, 237, 241.
[12] Peter Sloterdijk, *What Happened in the 20th Century?* Trans. Christopher Turner (Cambridge: Polity, 2018), 9.
[13] Jason W. Moore, *Capitalism in the Web of Life: Ecology and the Accumulation of Capital* (London: Verso, 2015), 19.

will entertain and delight, that it will become popular and make money. But a playwright has no control over the rowdiness of the audience, the drunkenness of the actors, the condition of the stage, or the foulness of the weather. Theater is always an ecology, and the ecology of the early modern theater was more global than any performance space had ever been before. Elizabethan and Jacobean drama fashioned the horizons of a nascent English empire for London audiences, and could not have done so without material stage properties of foreign provenance and commercial investment made possible by English economic expansion.

Second, a theater of the Anthropocene upholds the unpredictability of live theater, and makes room for ecological factors to influence the meaning of a given performance. I am indebted to the work done to analyze Shakespearean performance in the context of a changing global environment by Randall Martin and Evelyn O'Malley, whose special issue of *Shakespeare Bulletin* (36.3) in 2018 began by asking how Shakespearean performance can address or "mitigate…threats to human and nonhuman life in the Anthropocene."[14] They frame their issue around three propositions that remain relevant to the value that a theater of the Anthropocene places on performance as an unpredictable ecology. Martin and O'Malley underscore first the "conceptual frameworks and material relations that can reshape Shakespeare as our eco-contemporary in performance." Second, they invite analysis of "past and current productions for ways of modelling Shakespearean performance as an interactive platform among non-human actants and human performers." As I hope to show in Part II of this book, the material relations that have shaped Shakespearean performance in a colonial context have produced the curious effect of both centering and decentering Shakespeare from colonial discourse. Finally, they hope "to theorize community relations in locally-situated performances with a view to rethinking Shakespeare environmentally as a metacontextual playwright."[15] Granted, some will argue that any attempt to examine the impact of environmental or non-human factors on the meaning of a specific performance will smack of speculation, if not outright anachronism. Who is to say what an audience watching an outdoor performance of *Romeo and Juliet* during a late nineteenth-century gold rush in South Africa would glean from the timing of the rain? In attempting to shine a spotlight on the non-human actors that populate a theater history of Shakespearean

[14] Randall Martin and Evelyn O'Malley, "Eco-Shakespeare in Performance: Introduction," *Shakespeare Bulletin*, Vol. 36, No. 3 (2018), 377.
[15] Martin and O'Malley, "Introduction," 378.

performance, I seek to uncover an ecological archive that has remained dormant for too long. If this project seems speculative, it is because our global crisis requires us to be speculative. Scholars in the humanities would do well to follow the examples of climate scientists who have been forced to speculate about what another decade without a carbon tax might mean for the American economy, or what five more decades of sea-level rise might mean for the earth's coastal populations. We are in good company with biologists who have been tracking the earth's sixth mass-extinction event, and who have been forced to speculate about which species have a shot, and which are done for. If it is anachronistic to turn to the early modern stage for a lesson about the relationship between globalization, climate change, and its consequences, then so be it. Living in the Anthropocene means inhabiting anachronism. Historicism can only get us so far.

Finally, a theater of the Anthropocene acknowledges that the material traffic of the stage—whether a stage property, a costume, a racial or gender prosthetic, an artificial or even an authentic weather effect—not only transforms during a given performance; it also underscores the extent to which theater itself is a resource for audiences. Anthropocene theater and a good deal of early modern drama both offer strategies for confronting ecological crises during the supposed final "Age of Man"—strategies that can be useful to modern audiences who are also confronting a rapidly changing global environment.

Provincializing the Anthropocene: Theater as a Resource

This third characteristic of Anthropocene theater needs some elaboration. As the term "Anthropocene" continues to gain traction in both the sciences and the humanities, it also continues to generate a considerable amount of debate. Climate scientists, geologists, and biologists agree that the term defines our current geological epoch, where "humankind has become a global geological force in its own right," altering the earth's carbon and nitrogen cycles and terrestrial water cycles (including "water vapour flow from the land to the atmosphere"), and driving the earth's sixth major extinction event.[16] Scholars are in less agreement about when this epoch began, or whether

---

[16] Will Steffen, Jacques Grinevald, Paul Crutzen, and John McNeill, "The Anthropocene: Conceptual and Historical Perspectives," *Philosophical Transactions of the Royal Society*, Vol. 369 (2011), 843.

"Anthropocene" is the best term to describe it.[17] The term privileges human beings as the primary agents of change, and risks essentializing the behavior of all humans into a narrative about the species rather than individual human behaviors.

Kathryn Yusoff, professor of inhuman geography at Queen Mary University of London and author of *A Billion Black Anthropocenes or None* (2018), articulates a valuable critique of the Anthropocene's essentializing narrative. For Yusoff, the homogenization enacted by the species narrative performs a violent continuation of European colonialism and its extractive geology:

> If the Anthropocene proclaims a sudden concern with the exposures of environmental harm to white liberal communities, it does so in the wake of histories in which these harms have been knowingly exported to black and brown communities under the rubric of civilization, progress, modernization, and capitalism. The Anthropocene might seem to offer a dystopic future that laments the end of the world, but imperialism and ongoing (settler) colonialisms have been ending worlds for as long as they have been in existence.[18]

Yusoff problematizes the catastrophizing impulse of the Anthropocene by evaluating the racial politics of geology. European settler colonialism was an extractive ecology that sought to replace indigenous bodies with dehumanized Black laborers, and the genocide catalyzed by the slave trade constitutes a catastrophe the Anthropocene narrative seems to overlook. Catastrophe is post-racial in the Anthropocene's ethos.[19] Furthermore, in attempting to universalize the agency of the human species under a dubious "we," the narrative of the Anthropocene erases the power dynamics that drove colonial resource extraction and necessitated an ideology of race: "To be included in the 'we' of the Anthropocene is to be silenced by a claim to universalism that fails to notice its subjugations, taking part in a planetary condition in *which no part* was accorded in terms of subjectivity."[20] The call to action that the Anthropocene's catastrophizing is meant to awaken in human beings as citizens of the earth is, for Yusoff, yet another pitfall of the narrative. The takeaway that "we" must become better stewards of the environments we

---

[17] Steve Mentz's attempt to "pluralize the Anthropocene!" has generated such alternatives as: the Neologismcene, the Capitalocene, the Chthulucene, and the Naufragocene. Steve Mentz, "The Neologismcene," *Arcade: Literature, the Humanities, & the World*, 1 July 2018. https://arcade.stanford.edu/blogs/neologismcene.

[18] Kathryn Yusoff, *A Billion Black Anthropocenes or None* (Minneapolis, MN: University of Minnesota Press, 2018), xiii.

[19] Yusoff, *A Billion*, 3.   [20] Yusoff, *A Billion*, 12.

inhabit is a thinly veiled attempt to "absolve the positionality of Western colonial knowledge and extractive practices, while simultaneously reinforcing and resettling them in a new territory." Arming ourselves with the knowledge of our geologic agency in order to become better protectors of mother earth "indicates a desire to overcome coloniality without a corresponding relinquishing of the power it continues to generate in terms of who gets to formulate, implement, and speak to/of the future."[21]

Yusoff's critique is also valuable for the scrutiny it aims at the debate over the origins of this novel "-cene." Geologists require a global stratotype section and point, also known as a GSSP or a "Golden Spike," to mark the boundary between two geologic time periods. The Anthropocene, in other words, must be recorded in the rock record to qualify as a new geologic era. But the three most popular starting points of the Anthropocene in the scientific community are not without their problems. Each "spike" constitutes a "geotrauma" for Yusoff, "where flesh is the medium of exchange that organizes and modifies the Spike," and where "the Golden Spike is something that spikes or impales."[22] The Orbis Spike, proposed by Lewis and Maslin, identifies 1610 as the start date of the Anthropocene. On the one hand, this Spike casts Europe's extractive geology as responsible for the decrease of atmospheric carbon dioxide that resulted from the die-off of indigenous Americans (a keystone species of their ecologies) when the "Columbian Exchange" inaugurated a wave of genocide, slave trade, and globalization of the earth's biota. But on the other hand, insofar as this "exchange" identifies not so much a two-way exchange as a westward-moving Old-World-to-New-World "colonial violence of forced eviction from land, enslavement on plantations, in rubber factories and mines, and the indirect violence of pathogens through forced contact and rape," the narrative it offers is incomplete.[23] The Anthropocene emphasizes a narrative about an agency that focuses on atmospheric changes and seems to ignore the brutal human-to-human relationships that make our geologic agency recordable in the first place. The Orbis Spike "naturalizes European colonial relations and their epistemological and ecological transformations."[24] Similar objections can also be leveled at the proposed 1800 start date, which emphasizes the increase in atmospheric carbon dioxide emissions inaugurated by the Industrial Revolution, and the "Great Acceleration" narrative, which identifies 1950 as a potential start date, and which uses Plutonium as a stratigraphic trace, whose proliferation as a result of the nuclear weapons

---

[21] Yusoff, *A Billion*, 27.   [22] Yusoff, *A Billion*, 59.
[23] Yusoff, *A Billion*, 30.   [24] Yusoff, *A Billion*, 32.

testing during the arms race of the Cold War will be legible in the rock record for millennia.[25]

Dipesh Chakrabarty provides a similar critique of the Anthropocene by reminding us that "we" as a species neither contribute to nor bear the consequences of geologic agency (such as climate change) equally across the globe.[26] And while I agree that the essentializing narrative of the Anthropocene occludes a discussion about the violent inequalities that have fostered the conditions for both capitalism and climate change, I also think this narrative is valuable for the way it frames human geologic agency as accidentally or unwittingly acquired. Chakrabarty insists that we (*Homo sapiens*) "have stumbled into" the Anthropocene without intending to.[27] As the history of capitalism, European colonialism, and globalization demonstrate, the global North's "stumbling into" the Anthropocene looks very different from the global South's. Although individuals cannot be held accountable for producing natural disasters or causing extreme weather events—like hurricanes Harvey, Irma, and Maria, which devastated Florida, Puerto Rico, and parts of Texas during the fall of 2017—the Anthropocene has increased awareness of human geologic agency, and has raised new ethical concerns about accountability and blame in the wake of certain disasters. In July 2021, for example, a San Bernardino couple was charged with thirty crimes, including involuntary manslaughter, for using a smoke bomb at their gender-reveal party, which sparked the 2020 El Dorado wildfire. The fire killed a firefighter and injured thirteen others. The couple could face up to twenty years in prison.[28] Is such a punishment warranted? Is it just? The couple may have lit the spark, but can the justice system hold them accountable for creating the conditions of the

---

[25] Yusoff emphasizes that the 1800 date problematically spins a "tale of entrepreneurship of a few white men transforming the world with their ingenuous creations or of a political economy that is aggressively sutured to the earth's processes via the lifeblood of fossil fuels" (39). The Industrial Revolution also relies heavily on slave labor and on the extractive geology of the primitive accumulation of capital that European colonialism made possible. The Great Acceleration narrative also conveniently erases the disproportionate effect that nuclear weapons testing had on the brown bodies of the Pacific Islands where the US carried out a majority of their tests: "This nuclear colonialism in the Pacific and Marshall islands used a brown strata of bodies to mitigate and absorb its geochemical shocks" (47).

[26] Dipesh Chakrabarty, "The Climate of History: Four Theses," *Critical Inquiry*, Vol. 35, No. 2 (2009), 214, 218. Chakrabarty insists that "species cannot be thought of in essentialist terms" (214) and that "to speak of species thinking is not to resist the politics of 'common but differentiated responsibility' that China, India, and other developing countries seem keen to pursue when it comes to reducing greenhouse gas emissions" (218).

[27] Chakrabarty, "Four Theses," 217.

[28] Martin Estacio, "Couple Charged with Involuntary Manslaughter in Southern California Fire Sparked by Gender Reveal," *USA Today*, 20 July 2021. https://www.usatoday.com/story/news/nation/2021/07/20/couple-charged-involuntary-manslaughter-southern-california-gender-reveal/8036779002.

fire as well? In the age of climate change and geologic agency, a more distributive sense of justice is needed.

Similarly, the emerging field of "weather event attribution science," which studies anthropogenic climate change as a causal agent for specific weather events, even suggests that storms should no longer be thought of as purely "natural" phenomena. As Kevin E. Trenberth argues, "the atmospheric environment is now warmer and moister than it was prior to about 40 years ago. All storms develop in this changed environment."[29] The task of attributing the intensification of weather events to carbon-surplus nations brings with it a host of political issues. As the climate scientist Myles Allen points out, it is not just citizens of climate debt nations who wonder if they are victims of climate change, and who have incentive to seek compensation for relief from natural disasters: "In the absence of agreed standards of attribution, many countries and communities are claiming to be adversely affected. Which of these claims are valid? And whose interests are being ignored, simply because they do not have the science base or political nous to complain?"[30] Allen's observation highlights a trend where people are more interested in seeing themselves as victims of climate change than they are in recognizing their role as contributors to a changing climate.[31]

So how can we discuss the Anthropocene without essentializing human geologic agency, without ignoring the "geotrauma" of early European colonization, and without overlooking "our" unexpected arrival in a new geologic era? And how do early modern performance practices offer a resource for treading this razor's edge? In attempting to reframe the anthropocentric narrative of globalization around nature and its material agents, there are a number of materialist frameworks from which we might draw, including Gayatri Spivak's theory of "planetarity," Jane Bennett's "vital materialism," Andrew Pickering's "mangle," Bruno Latour's "actor-network theory," Stacy Alaimo's

---

[29] Kevin E. Trenberth, "Attribution of Climate Variations and Trends to Human Influences and Natural Variability," *WIREs Clim Change*, Vol. 2 (2011), 929. Mike Hulme identifies Trenberth's "philosophical" approach to weather event attribution as one of four methods for attributing human influence to weather events. The other three include (1) physical reasoning, (2) using classical statistical analysis of meteorological data as a kind of control with which to compare more recent extreme weather events, and (3) establishing the Fractional Attributable Risk (FAR) of an extreme weather event. Mike Hulme, "Attributing Weather Extremes to 'Climate Change': A Review," *Progress in Physical Geography*, Vol. 38, No. 4 (2014), 502–4.

[30] Myles Allen, "In Defense of the Traditional Null Hypothesis: Remarks on the Trenberth and Curry *WIREs* Opinion Articles," *WIREs Clim Change*, Vol. 2 (2011), 933.

[31] Allen, "In Defense," 933. Allen's observation demonstrates some of the political debates of attribution studies. He adds, "For almost anyone I talk to who is not a climate scientist or environmentalist, the question of whether they are being adversely affected by climate change today is far more interesting than the question of what the climate will be like in 2100."

"trans-corporeality," Deleuze and Guattari's "assemblages," Timothy Morton's "mesh," or Karen Barad's "agential realism."[32] These material frameworks are useful for the way they resist the universalizing narrative where all humans share the same amount of agency over a global environment. Instead, they emphasize ecological relationships that work to flatten Enlightenment hierarchies and to emphasize the distributive agency between human and non-human actants that produce events such as climate change. Jason Moore's theory of an *oikeios*, or the "creative, generative, and multi-layered relation of species and environment," is particularly useful for our purpose of trying to read the early modern stage as an exhibition of the Anthropocene.[33] Moore takes issue with the nature/society binary, which was solidified by the early

---

[32] Gayatri Chakravorty Spivak, *Death of a Discipline* (New York: Columbia University Press, 2003); Jane Bennett, *Vibrant Matter: A Political Ecology of Things* (Durham, NC: Duke University Press, 2010); Bruno Latour, *Reassembling the Social: An Introduction to Actor-Network Theory* (Oxford: Oxford University Press, 2005); Karen Barad, "Posthumanist Performativity: Toward an Understanding of How Matter Comes to Matter," *Signs: Journal of Women in Culture and Society*, Vol. 28, No. 3 (2003); Serpil Oppermann, "Feminist Ecocriticism: The New Ecofeminist Settlement," *Feminismo/s*, Vol. 22 (December 2013); Timothy Morton, *The Ecological Thought* (Cambridge, MA: Harvard University Press, 2010).

Gayatri Spivak's theory of "planetarity" proposes an alternative to an essentializing globalization, or the "imposition of the same system of exchange everywhere" (72). Planetarity seeks to "embrace an inexhaustible taxonomy" of alterity, which includes "mother, nation, god, nature"; planetarity asks us to "imagine ourselves as planetary subjects rather than global agents, planetary creatures rather than global entities" so that "alterity remains underived from us" (73). Jane Bennett's theory of "vital materialism" is similarly aimed at emphasizing the alterity of matter that constitutes the human subject. But Bennett can also help us to think past the anthropocentricity of the Anthropocene. Through recognizing the "thing power" of nonhuman actants, Bennett privileges a focus on Latourian "events" (Bennett 27) or Deleuzian and Guattarian "assemblages" (Bennett 23) rather than focusing on human or nonhuman subjects. It is the interaction between the human and the nonhuman that counts. Accounting for the distributive agency of these events, where causality is "more emergent than efficient" (Bennett 33), forces us to pinpoint provincial human or nonhuman actions that contribute to the unfolding of a particular event. A vital materialist, then, turns anthropogenic climate change into a narrative about the accumulation of individual emergent events over the centuries rather than a narrative about what the human species has stumbled into. Through emphasizing the emergent status of agency and the distributive agency of events, vital materialism is interested in provincial rather than species narratives. Serpil Oppermann compares the related concepts of Andrew Pickering's "mangle," Bruno Latour's "actor-network-theory," Stacy Alaimo's "trans-corporeality," and Deleuze and Guattari's "assemblages" with Jane Bennett's "vital materialism" as useful ontological tools for deflating anthropocentric hierarchies, each of which may prove useful in moving the Anthropocene away from a species narrative (Oppermann 73). To this list, we might add Timothy Morton's concept of the "mesh" (Morton 28). Karen Barad's theory of an "agential realism" also seems particularly useful for emphasizing the inequalities inherent in a project of naming the Anthropocene a species narrative. Barad relies on the post-humanist idea of performativity and understands discourse itself as a material rather than a representational practice: "Discursive practices are specific material (re)configurings of the world through which local determinations of boundaries, properties, and meanings are differentially enacted" (Barad 821); for Barad, a discursive practice is "not what is said; it is that which constrains and enables what can be said" (Barad 819). Through characterizing discourse as a performative material practice, Barad undermines the ontological reasoning responsible for perpetuating a history of what Bennett terms "earth-destroying fantasies of conquest and consumption" (Bennett ix). At the same time, Barad accounts for the human beings who are excluded from a shared geologic agency when Chakrabarty names the Anthropocene a species narrative.

[33] Moore, *Web of Life*, 4.

modern Cartesian revolution, and which has served the impulse of late modernity to view nature as a storehouse of limitless resources, but whose resources also exist primarily to serve human beings and to facilitate the accumulation of wealth.[34] Moore's alternative is to view capitalism as a way of organizing a nature that already includes the category of humans: "in this double internality, everything that humans do is *already* joined with extra-human nature *and* the web of life: nature as a whole that includes humans."[35] In suggesting that we need to deconstruct the human/nature binary to better understand the ecological crisis we face in the era of late capitalism, Moore echoes a move made by early modern scholars who share his concern about the ontological barrier that a modern distinction between humans and nature generates for solving our ecological crises.[36]

To help negotiate "our" accidentally acquired geologic agency as a species with "our" intentional agency as individuals, I turn to the Shakespearean stage as a place where we might begin to *provincialize*—rather than "pluralize"— the Anthropocene.[37] I mean to invoke the postcolonial scholarship of Dipesh Chakrabarty by identifying this project as an undertaking of "provincializing." Not only do critiques of the Anthropocene (such as Yusoff's) owe a tremendous debt to postcolonial scholarship, but they are also largely a continuation of the same endeavors. Just as Chakrabarty sought to "decenter" European Enlightenment ideals from the historiography of global relations of power, provincializing the Anthropocene involves a similar awareness of historiography.[38] But instead of excavating European thought, which operates as both "indispensable and inadequate" for understanding experiences of political modernity in Southeast Asia, the question we must answer is, "how does nature work for capitalism?"[39] Instead of showing how European historiography resigned "Indians, Africans, and other 'rude' nations to an imaginary waiting room of history," our task is to excavate the agents—human, non-human, inhuman, or post-human—of global environmental change that are subsumed by the Anthropocene narrative and evaluate their dynamic ecological relationships.[40] As Yusoff reminds us, the racial logic of colonial discourse

---

[34] Moore, *Web of Life*, 19, 16.   [35] Moore, *Web of Life*, 5.
[36] Jean E. Feerick and Vin Nardizzi, eds, *The Indistinct Human in Renaissance Literature* (New York: Palgrave Macmillan, 2012).
[37] Mentz, "The Neologismcene."
[38] Dipesh Chakrabarty, *Provincializing Europe: Postcolonial Thought and Historical Difference* (Princeton, NJ: Princeton University Press, 2000), 4.
[39] Chakrabarty, *Provincializing*, 6. I am also paraphrasing Moore's articulation of this question: "Instead of asking what capitalism *does* to nature, we may begin to ask how nature *works for* capitalism" (Moore 12).
[40] Chakrabarty, *Provincializing*, 8.

that coincided with humanist rhetoric allowed for an easy slippage between human and object; the agency of human, nature, and object runs the risk of being conflated by the Anthropocene narrative.[41] In short, we need to provincialize not history or geography but agency in the complex ecology of capitalism.

Because the Anthropocene has made it much more difficult to distinguish between human and natural agency—especially where both climate and weather are concerned—we might theorize a theater of the Anthropocene by attending to the interplay between human intention and extra-human agents that create meaning during a performance. More specifically, by focusing on Shakespearean representations of the weather that intersect with *real* atmospheric phenomena during performance (as I do in Part II of this book), I hope to make three observations about a theater of the Anthropocene. In addition to demonstrating how theater can be a resource for navigating the Anthropocene, I hope these observations (which are given more attention in Chapters 4 and 5) might also be fruitful for determining the implications of a human agency in the epoch of human-induced catastrophe.

First, when live theater intersects with actual weather, the atmospheric scale of the performance can challenge the artifice of the theater, and Shakespearean representations of the weather embrace this phenomenon. Prospero is *meant* to have control over his storm and his theater; they are one and the same thing. But in a real storm, his stage-managing becomes unmanageable, as a history of outdoor performances of *The Tempest* demonstrates. At the same time, a theater that involves real weather events reinforces the ecological unpredictability of live performance. In this sense, the early modern stage itself might be thought of as a theater of the Anthropocene.

Second, the performance of live weather on stage showcases the ethical dilemma with seeing weather as the product of a homogeneous human agency. Anthropocene theater positions the audience as both knowing participants in the act of weather on stage and passive recipients sharing in an atmospheric phenomenon that exceeds human control. And though an audience might share the same experience of weather and theater during a given performance, they will likely not share in what that experience means, or in understanding how they have participated in its creation.[42] The Anthropocene

---

[41] Yusoff, *A Billion*, 9. Yusoff writes, "The language of materiality and its division between life and nonlife, and its alignment with concepts of the human and inhuman, facilitated the divisions between subjects as humans and subjects priced as flesh (or inhuman matter)."

[42] Gretchen E. Minton, "'The Season of All Natures': Shakespeare in the Parks' Global Warming *Macbeth*," *Shakespeare Bulletin*, Vol. 36, No. 3 (2018); Evelyn O'Malley, "'To Weather A Play': Audiences,

narrative offered by attribution science suggests that humans exert some degree of influence on weather events; the stage suggests that humans can fully control the weather, or at least how it is intentionally represented. But while some may read a storm's performance as a felicitous conflation of humans and nature performing together, others may see it as an unhappy evening, a reason to keep Shakespeare indoors. Furthermore, actors ultimately possess *more* agency than audience members in choosing how to engage the weather during a given performance, which highlights the unequal distribution of human agency in the production of a theatrical or non-theatrical weather event.

Finally, directing our attention to real weather events in a live space of performance grounds each Shakespearean performance in a particular place, time, and context, where the weather carries on with or without Shakespeare. In Chapter 5, I offer two examples of how we might read Shakespearean performance through the lens of a more provincial, less homogeneous, geologic agency. A stormy performance of *The Tempest* in colonial Bermuda during hurricane season draws attention to the island's colonial history, while simultaneously underscoring the limits of Prospero's—and by extension Shakespeare's—colonial authority on the island. A rainy performance of *Romeo and Juliet* in Cape Town, 1892, similarly signals the failure of colonial power to subdue the weather, while also pointing to the enduring environmental legacy of letting it rain where Romeo exchanged gold for poison. As we continue to come to terms with the geologic agency that has been thrust upon us as a species, a theater of the Anthropocene can be a useful tool for provincializing that agency, especially as we begin to see the history of British colonialism, Shakespearean performance, and our future as a species on this planet in a new light.

Nature's Empire

Of course, weather is not the only non-human actant capable of performing on stage, nor is it the only non-human entity imbued with a new-found significance since our collective awakening in the Anthropocene.

Outdoor Shakespeares, and Avante-Garde Nostalgia at The Willow Globe," *Shakespeare Bulletin*, Vol. 36, No. 3 (2018). Gretchen E. Minton and Evelyn O'Malley model a useful methodology by interviewing audience members of outdoor productions of Shakespeare performances. In the case of the Minton's evaluation of the Montana Shakespeare in the Parks tour of 2017, a performance of *Macbeth* endorsed "the terrifying possibility that we are all implicated in a violent culture that has been and continues to be destructive to the ecosystem" (Minton 436).

During a stroll through Kew Gardens in London, Antiguan novelist Jamaica Kincaid once mistook a cotton flower for a hollyhock. Her misidentification summoned an epiphany of the plant's historical resonances:

Cotton all by itself exists in perfection, with malice toward none; in the sharp, swift, even brutal dismissive words of the botanist Oakes Ames, it is reduced to an economic annual, but the tormented, malevolent role it has played in my ancestral history is not forgotten by me.[43]

Nature is not innocent. Kincaid names the plant's "tormented, malevolent" staying-power, and its ability to "play a part" in shaping her identity as a Black woman, "long after its role in the bondage of some of [her] ancestors had been eliminated."[44] Kincaid thus identifies cotton's agency, its culpability in slavery, empire, and modernity. Furthermore, she demonstrates that knowing what a plant *is* is just as important as knowing what it *does*, and what it has done. In the age of late global capitalism, the entire cotton species shares in this "temporality of conjunction," where the past and present can hold congress in a single object or natural commodity.[45] Before cotton, there was sugar, and before sugar, gold. My own project takes up the sixteenth-century commercial networks surrounding galls and corkwood in a context of English deforestation. I suggest that understanding the history and agency of the natural commodities on which European empires were built has become increasingly important, especially as the effects of climate change continue to be disproportionately felt in the global South, and as climate scientists overwhelmingly identify human agency (rather than passive nature) as a culprit.

By placing non-human nature at the center of this book, I build on the work begun by environmental historians such as Alfred Crosby, Henry Hobhouse, and Richard Grove.[46] We—scholars of English literature, scientists of climate, and anyone living in 2023 concerned about a sustainable future— need to understand how the natural world made European empire a possibility, for two reasons. First, grasping nature's agency allows us to consider how

---

[43] Jamaica Kincaid, *My Garden* (New York: Farrar, Straus, Giroux, 1999), 150.
[44] Kincaid, *My Garden*, 150.
[45] Jonathan Gil Harris, *Untimely Matter in the Time of Shakespeare* (Philadelphia, PA: University of Pennsylvania Press, 2009), 16. Though Harris is more focused on human-made objects and texts, I think his temporal frameworks are useful for thinking about a history of natural commodities as well.
[46] Alfred W. Crosby Jr., *The Columbian Exchange: Biological and Cultural Consequences of 1492*, 30th anniversary edition (London: Praeger, 2003); Henry Hobhouse, *Seeds of Change: Six Plants That Transformed Mankind* (Washington, DC: Shoemaker & Hoard, 2005); Richard H. Grove, *Green Imperialism: Colonial Expansion, Tropical Island Edens, and the Origins of Environmentalism, 1600–1860* (Cambridge: Cambridge University Press, 1995).

non-human objects, species, and environments contributed to both the early construction of and later dissolution of Enlightenment hierarchies—human over nature, man over woman, White over Black—which are foundational to colonial and postcolonial discourse.[47] This is not to say that nature played a more primary role than humans in establishing these hierarchies. Rather, I aim to read nature's agency as distributive—that is, as participating in a network of interdependent relationships between human and non-human actors, which together produce the material conditions of European empire. Kincaid's cotton flower does not exist all by itself in perfection, and its perceived "malice" is a symptom of its agency, which is complexly intertwined with human appetites and aspirations. Secondly, we need to understand nature's active role in the production of European empire because we need to continue to think of nature not as a resource to exploit further but as one to rely on as an ally in diminishing global, ecological, and climate-related crises.[48]

In *Anthropocene Theater*, I turn to the early modern English stage as a site where nature's agency speaks with most miraculous organ, and where the repercussions of that agency resound offstage. By representing the oscillating potential of imperial power, the English stage ultimately limits for its audience the number of causal agents—human and non-human actants—that can participate in the production of an empire. I begin with the premise that the early modern stage constitutes a unique site for showcasing how the agency of non-human things motivates and determines the outcomes and consequences of economic and colonial expansion. At the same time, I am also interested in recovering the ecological narrative—and the non-human dramatis personae, which are the protagonists—of this first phase of globalization.[49] By tracing a series of object histories, I hope to frame the early globalization of the earth's biota in context with its postcolonial and ecological legacy in the

---

[47] Elizabeth DeLoughrey and George B. Handley, "Introduction," in *Postcolonial Ecologies: Literatures of the Environment*, edited by Elizabeth DeLoughrey and George B. Handley (Oxford: Oxford University Press, 2011), 24–5. DeLoughrey and Handley foreground how the "Enlightenment dualisms of culture/nature, white/black, and male/female were constituted through the colonial process" and subsequently show how both postcolonialists and ecofeminists seek to disentangle "the hierarchies that derive from these interpellations of non-European nature."

[48] For example, Meera Subramanian looks to the Staten Island Bluebelt for a model of how ecological infrastructure can help manage sea-level rise: "The extensive system of engineered ponds, creeks, and wetlands naturally provides flood control by absorbing storm surges across ten thousand acres and sixteen watersheds that span the southern end of the borough, Oakwood Beach among them." She also advocates for repopulating New York City's lost oyster reefs, "which could naturally help shield the city from future storm surges" in the event of another hurricane. See Meera Subramanian, "The City and the Sea," *Orion Magazine*, 2015. https://orionmagazine.org/article/the-city-and-the-sea.

[49] In this sense, I share Steve Mentz's concern with exploding and exploring the competing potential narratives of early globalization. See Steve Mentz, *Shipwreck Modernity: Ecologies of Globalization, 1550–1719* (Minneapolis, MN: University of Minnesota Press, 2015).

Anthropocene. This book, by extension, attempts to reframe a few key objects or phenomena of the stage within a more *oikeios*-oriented Anthropocene. In the same way that Kincaid acknowledges cotton's role within the brutal economic network of the slave trade, I hope to investigate the natural commodities upon which the early modern stage depended, and to shed them of their seemingly passive innocence. The natural commodities that made early modern theater possible became the imperial materials that built the British Empire.

Oops: Nature's Distributive Agency as Accident

While the chapters of this book concentrate on different natural objects, phenomena, and plays, there are four main throughlines I would like to identify at the outset. First, each of the plays and performances I am most concerned with either represent or demonstrate the distributive agency of "nature." Although I use the word "nature" to distinguish the category of the non-human from the modern category of the human, my aim is to destabilize this modern binary and to historicize an ontological lack of distinction between human and nature in the early modern period. Through privileging accident within (or *as*) the history of the English stage, British colonialism, and the global climate, my intention is to expose the porousness of modern boundaries between subject and object, between human and "nature," between intention and outcome. The ontological muddiness that failed to distinguish early modern humans from the non-human "natural" world or environment has been explored by other ecologically-minded scholars of the stage.[50] But more than simply reiterating the primacy of "nature" in an early modern understanding of the "human," I am interested in analyzing how three types of events—performing a play, colonizing an environment and its human inhabitants, and changing the climate—do not occur by virtue of human intention alone; they occur within a network where non-human "nature" has some role in determining the play's tragic ending, the colony's rise or decline, and the rate at which carbon dioxide emits into the atmosphere. In *Bonduca* (c. 1614), for example, the Roman army makes a decisive victory over the British rebels, but not without being cursed by a host of metaphorical pathogens. At the same time the play was being performed in

---

[50] See Jean Feerick and Vin Nardizzi, eds, *The Indistinct Human in Renaissance Literature* (New York: Palgrave Macmillan, 2012).

England, those same pathogens were significantly aiding European settler colonialism in the Americas, all while quietly yielding credit to European discourses of might, right, and Whiteness. I turn to "nature" neither to apologize for nor to deflect the very real human violence that British colonialism engendered. Instead, I seek to highlight the ways in which human empire exploits—and perhaps even mimics—nature's ecology. The benefit of reading empire as an ecological endeavor where "nature" is neither entirely passive nor wholly responsible is that it retains the potential to be an active ally in catalyzing a more sustainable future for humans today. Both on and offstage, non-human "nature" is always tied up with human affairs. Under a rubric of "accident"—as opposed to a more historicized early modern narrative of pre-destination or divine explanation—I hope to reorient the anthropocentric histories of British colonialism, the Shakespearean stage, and the Anthropocene around a more distributive and ecological "nature."

One avenue for exploring non-human agency in a context of performance, colonization, or even climate change is to evaluate human intentions and their productive failures. The rubric of "accident" may be anachronistic for an early modern culture that would have all events explained by divine providence. But on the other hand, as Michael Witmore points out, " 'accidents'—sudden, lamentable, happy, doleful, wonderful—occur in abundance during the period and are regularly described as such."[51] It is a word Shakespeare used often to explain tragic circumstances—the undelivered letter to Romeo that would have prevented his suicide, or Othello's enslavement (and redemption), for example. At the same time, Shakespeare just as often associates accidents with pretense and performance, which is how they are shaped in the mouths of Iago, Prince Hal, or Claudius. Despite the providential bias of English Protestant culture, accidents became powerful vehicles for discovering the truth in the context of a scientific revolution, especially on stage.[52] Accidents, at least within the plot of a play, emphasize that an intention is not going according to plan; they "result when certain narrative conventions (what we usually describe as plot) come into contact with communal beliefs about what is likely, valuable, or purposive."[53] Because they are also "a prime occasion for the recognition and expression of communal values which shape

---

[51] Michael Witmore, *Culture of Accidents: Unexpected Knowledges in Early Modern England* (Stanford, CA: Stanford University Press, 2001), 2.

[52] Witmore, *Culture of Accidents*, 3. Witmore writes, "accidents and experiments require an unusual disposition of circumstances, which is what makes both a powerful engine of discovery."

[53] Witmore, *Culture of Accidents*, 11.

narrative representations of 'what happened,' " accidents are extremely useful in analyzing performance, where things do not always go as rehearsed.[54]

But a lens of accident is also useful for examining the Anthropocene. Yusoff's critique of the Orbis Spike hypothesis as the start of the Anthropocene, for example, seems unwilling to acknowledge anything accidental in either European settler colonialism or in the attempt to "stress the enormity of humanity's responsibility as stewards of the Earth."[55] When framed as a "spike of brutality, sadism, and death, coupled with the subsequent dispossession of indigenous peoples from their land and the beginning of industrialized global slavery," there is nothing accidental about the start of the Anthropocene. And yet, climate change, much like the Orbis Spike itself—which pinpoints a rise in atmospheric oxygen and a decrease of carbon dioxide—was never the intention of Europeans engaged in a dehumanizing, genocidal, and extractive colonialism. To address the role of accident in this early phase of globalization is not to apologize for or to dismiss the damage inflicted by European settler colonialism and its accompanying racial ideology. On the contrary, accident allows us to view the narrative of climate change through a modern set of communal values that have been shaped by our awakening into the Anthropocene through science. If climate change is the unintentional consequence of unprecedented geotrauma, then accident endorses an even more scrutinizing view of early European colonialism and its tenacious legacies. In addition to destabilizing a narrative where European technology, intellect, and resources justified their dominion in the New World, a narrative of accident takes the wind out of these sails and allows us to look at which non-human agents facilitated the fulfillment of European desires and intentions. Accident should urge us to continue the work of deconstructing the barnacle imperial legacies that endure today—which include hierarchical thinking, racial ideology, and the perception that humans and nature are separate entities.

Imperial Materials

Another throughline in this book emphasizes that the materials of the stage are inextricably tied to the material expansion of the British Empire.

---

[54] Witmore, *Culture of Accidents*, 13.

[55] Paul Crutzen and Christian Schwager, "Living in the Anthropocene: Towards a New Global Ethos," 2011. http://e360.yale.edu/featuers/living_in_the_anthropocene_towards_a_new_global_ethos. Quoted in Yusoff, *A Billion*, 27.

The non-human objects, phenomena, and stage properties used in sixteenth-century (but also in nineteenth- and twentieth-century) performances were the same materials that drove British commercial and colonial expansion.

Timber is one material that had significance on stage and in the project of English economic and colonial expansion. Nine theaters were constructed out of wood in spite of the devastating shortage of timber in England, which was motivating colonial extraction of timber resources, particularly from Ireland and the Americas. Centuries earlier, yew trees—like the one central to Vittoria's dream in Webster's *The White Devil* (1612), and the one to which Tamora is allegedly threatened to be bound in *Titus Andronicus* (2.3.106–7)—provided superior bowstaves for the English army after the thirteenth century.[56] Yew bowstaves, which began to be imported to England from Ireland and Spain during the early fourteenth century, provided decisive victories for the English at Agincourt in 1415 as well as several other important battles over the next two centuries, which may have "helped to forge the Empire."[57]

From an ecological perspective, the English stage was a biological con-glomeration, a vantage from which spectators could discern the material scope of an emerging global marketplace. Actors wore face paint that used ingredients like cork from Portugal or gum Arabic from northern Africa. Galls were also likely used to make a black face paint, and brought to the stage the product of a parasitic insect ecology from the Ottoman Empire.

Some of the scarlet clothing and rouge cheeks worn by men playing women on stage likely used cochineal, the product of a Mexican prickly pear and insect ecology, brought to England through Spanish colonization and English piracy.

The expansion of the English Navy would not have been possible without hemp for rope, which the Muscovy Company began manufacturing in Russia in the mid-sixteenth century.[58] Plays like *A Christian Turn'd Turk* (1610), *The Two Gentlemen of Verona* (1589), and *Romeo and Juliet* (1597) rely on ladders of rope as stage properties. At the same time that the English were increasing the cultivation of hemp in the Americas, their exposure to New World com-modities such as tobacco may have also taught them new ways of consuming hemp, and of exploiting its psychoactive properties.

---

[56] Botanists have shown that yew trees actually do live their lives according to a cycle made up of seven distinct ages, a cycle that can repeat when new trees use the existing root system of a dead tree to begin life anew. See Fred Hageneder, *Botanical: Yew* (London: Reaktion, 2013), 69–70.

[57] Hageneder, *Botanical: Yew*, 105.

[58] See Martha Morris, "Naval Cordage Procurement in Early Modern England," *International Journal of Maritime History*, Vol. 11, No. 1 (1999), 81–99.

Shakespearean performance itself eventually became a commodity of its own in the Victorian era of the British Empire, the value of which would increase with the unwitting aid of ecological elements.

Anachropocene

The third throughline weaving the chapters of *Anthropocene Theater* together concerns my method, which invites readers to return to early modern drama through the lens of the Anthropocene. If the analysis I offer seems anachronistic, it is because anachronism has been normalized by climate change. Human behaviors are rapidly acidifying the oceans and raising them to heights not seen in thousands of years, for example. The multitude of invasive species thriving in the Americas as an accidental or intentional consequence of European colonialism and globalization has turned the globe into a land- and waterscape teeming with anachronism. To live in the Anthropocene means inhabiting anachronism. I attend to how Shakespeare and his contemporaries represent the process by which human agency and behaviors create imbalances in nature. But far from offering a simple comparison between the ecological crises faced by twenty-first- and sixteenth-century audiences, I aim to take a hopeful and pragmatic lesson from early modern dramatists, who, not unlike us, were facing a bleak ecological future. It is a lesson shared by some restoration ecologists today: trust nature as an ally in seeking to correct imbalances in nature caused by human behaviors. As I show in Chapter 5 on *King Lear*, the natural imbalance of water that Lear endures during the storm is linked to the economic imbalance he perceives in his kingdom. Lear's desire to "shake the superflux" as a strategy to "show the heavens more just" (3.4.40–1) bears an important postcolonial relevance in the Anthropocene, since natural and economic imbalances between the global North and South are the legacy of European colonialism. But rather than offer a clear-cut human solution to the problem of economic inequality, the play insists that, given enough time, the *oikeios* can correct its own imbalances, and can even provide secular economic retribution.

The attention I am lending to non-human objects (Chapters 1–3) and events (Chapters 4–5) in this book will build on recent materialist scholarship. The recent post-humanist turn in material approaches to literature has perhaps reached its limit with object-oriented ontology and alien phenomenology, philosophies that would hold Kincaid's cotton ransom "all by itself" in a vacuum of "perfection, with malice towards none."[59] I prefer to ground my project in materialist political ecology. In attending to the agency of non-human nature, I seek to flatten the ontological hierarchies reinforced by Western historical narratives of European empire in an attempt to wrest a voice from a silenced, subaltern nature. My project thus follows in the tradition of Bruno Latour's actor-network theory, Jane Bennett's vital materialism, and Karen Barad's agential realism, each of which uphold the distributive agency of non-human actants. But rather than shift the materialist discussion away from the human and toward the object as these scholars have done, my focus on the object is intended to historicize the confluence between human and nature during this period, and to trace that ecology to our present moment. Early modern culture did not privilege human categories above non-human ones, and consumers were far more willing than we are to accept the agency of non-human objects and nature in determining events. Astrology, witch trials, and the curious law of the deodand uphold stars, "familiars," and quotidian objects as determining and agential factors in risky pursuits of fortune, domestic mishaps, or even accidental death.[60] Regarding nature on the early modern stage, then, requires that we contextualize humans as a part of nature.

Furthermore, through attempting to reconstruct the history of globalization, or the Anthropocene, from the perspective of the "natural" world, I aim to remind readers that what we think of today as "nature" is not only far from natural, it is also irrevocably tied to an imperial history. The concept of "nature" cannot be divorced from human behaviors and accidents, especially not in the era of anthropogenic climate change. The "nature" that Thoreau was so eager for "us" to hurry back to may not even have been entirely "natural" in 1854 when *Walden* was first published, and it is certainly less so today. Thoreau's Concord has been forever altered by the biological side-effects of globalization; according to one study, 27 percent of the floral species noted by Thoreau in Concord are now missing from the area, and another 36 percent are on the brink of extinction.[61]

---

[59] See Ian Bogost, *Alien Phenomenology or What It's Like to Be a Thing* (Minneapolis, MN: University of Minnesota Press), 2012; Graham Harman, "The Well-Wrought Broken Hammer: Object-Oriented Literary Criticism," *New Literary History*, Vol. 43, No. 2 (2012), 183–203.

[60] For more on the deodand law, see William Pietz, "Death of the Deodand: Accursed Objects and the Money Value of Human Life," *Anthropology and Aesthetics*, Vol. 31 (Spring 1997), 97–108; for more on astrology, see Keith Thomas, *Religion and the Decline of Magic* (New York: Charles Scribner's Sons, 1971).

[61] Richard B. Primack, Abrahama Miller-Rushing, and Kiruba Dharaneesaran, "Changes in the Flora of Thoreau's Concord," *Biological Conservation*, Vol. 142, No. 3 (2009), 502.

Through emphasizing a material history of non-human-centric agency, I also seek to make an intervention into recent ecocritical investigations of the early modern stage. I do not mean to suggest that Shakespeare was an environmentalist or that a genealogy of environmentalism in the West can be traced back to early modern literature.[62] In fact, part of my investment in focusing on the early modern period is to understand how the ethics of modern Western conservationist and environmentalist movements are complicated by a genealogy that begins with European colonial exploitation. Long before "conservation" connoted the protection of land from corporate deforestation or oil drilling, it was a principle of European colonial management and capitalist production.[63] Scholars have foregrounded how various environmental crises impacted literary and dramatic production in the early modern period, though few have privileged the object as a primary text.[64] Vin Nardizzi's *Wooden Os* (2013) provides a unique exception through demonstrating how the "constitutive woodenness" of London theaters themselves offered audiences, who were feeling the effects of a crippling wood shortage, "the pleasures and the frights of being inside virtual woods."[65] By virtue of being a part of a performance space, Nardizzi shows, the wood from which the theater is made conjures in its audience a "rich array of eco-fantasies and nightmares about the shortage of wood" in England.[66] Nardizzi offers a useful model for how to imagine a material (and unprecedented) performance history of the early modern theater. Randall Martin offers another notable exception, whose work on ordnance manufacturing and saltpeter harvesting

---

[62] Some ecocritics skirt around this suggestion, like Steve Mentz, Daniel Brayton, and Gabriel Egan. As Boehrer convincingly shows through the playwright's habits as a landowner, Shakespeare was probably just another early capitalist. See Daniel Brayton, *Shakespeare's Ocean: An Ecocritical Exploration* (Charlottesville, VA: University of Virginia Press, 2012); Gabriel Egan, *Green Shakespeare: From Ecopolitics to Ecocriticism* (London: Routledge, 2006); Steve Mentz, *At the Bottom of Shakespeare's Ocean* (London: Continuum, 2009); Bruce Boehrer, *Environmental Degradation in Jacobean Drama* (Cambridge: Cambridge University Press, 2013).

[63] Richard Grove shows how the English developed a conservationist ethic through a history of trial and error on their early island colonies in the Atlantic. See Grove, *Green Imperialism*. Maximizing "yield potential while conserving our natural resources" is still a principle of modern capitalist production in the case of Monsanto. See Monsanto's Commitment to Sustainable Yield, 1 July 2018. http://www.aganytime.com/Documents/DemonstrationReportsPDFs/2013%20Demonstration%20Summaries/MON_GLC_MonsantosCommitmenttoSustainableYield.pdf.

[64] For example, Bruce Boehrer demonstrates how the environmental side-effects of London's urbanization influenced Jacobean dramatic production, while others, like Ken Hiltner, focus on how environmental issues impacted the pastoral genre. Daniel Brayton also shows how human activity affected marine life in the early modern period, and influenced Shakespeare's plays. See Ken Hiltner, *What Else Is Pastoral? Renaissance Literature and the Environment* (Ithaca, NY: Cornell University Press, 2011).

[65] Vin Nardizzi, *Wooden Os: Shakespeare's Theatres and England's Trees* (Toronto: University of Toronto Press, 2013), 20.

[66] Nardizzi, *Wooden Os*, 24.

situates this burgeoning English military investment, on display in Shakespeare's *Henriad*, in the context of deforestation and rural protest.[67] *Anthropocene Theater* similarly investigates how environmental degradation and exploitation influenced English stage performances on a global scale. I will explore how plays foreground the provenance of the materials they stage, and how wood imported from Portugal or Ireland might conjure a different "eco-fantasy" or "nightmare" than wood from England's own backyard.

Furthermore, through foregrounding English ecophobia as a driving force behind economic and colonial expansionary efforts—and through reading the stage's depiction of Moors as a construction of degraded European and colonial environments—my project takes a step toward theorizing ecocriticism: I recognize, as Simon Estok does, "that ecophobia, racism, misogyny, homophobia, and speciesism are thoroughly interwoven with each other and must eventually be looked at together."[68]

The Economy of Tragedy

As a fourth throughline, this book might be thought of as a meditation on the economy of tragedy. Most of the plays I focus on in this project—with the exception of *The Tempest* and *The Two Gentlemen of Verona*—are tragedies. A number of scholars—including Bradley Ryner, Linda Woodbridge, Valerie Forman, and Jonathan Gil Harris—have considered how a shift in economic thought amidst a flood of economic treatises from two camps of English mercantilists influenced the generic conventions of early modern plays.[69] Although Edward Misselden and Thomas Mun would not diagnose the upset "balance of trade" in England as a cause for the loss of English bullion until the 1620s, the notion of balance had been dictating the conventions of

---

[67] Randall Martin, *Shakespeare and Ecology* (Oxford: Oxford University Press, 2015).

[68] See Simon C. Estok, "Reading Ecophobia: A Manifesto," *Ecozon@*, Vol. 1, No. 1 (2010), 75. In his manifesto for "Reading Ecophobia," Simon Estok pushes ecocriticism toward theory by arguing that, in the same way that "Feminism shows up misogyny and sexism—as queer theory shows up heterosexism and homophobia," so should ecocriticism be "performing the same kind of disclosures about how ecophobia is embedded in our cultural artifacts" (75). He also suggests that the heart of this work requires a concentration on things: "Reading ecophobia means challenging the modus operandi of a profit-based system that requires the maintenance of ethically inconsiderable objects always available for exploitation" (77).

[69] Bradley Ryner, *Performing Economic Thought: English Drama and Mercantile Writing 1600–1642* (Edinburgh: Edinburgh University Press, 2014); Linda Woodbridge, *English Revenge Drama: Money, Resistance, Equality* (Cambridge: Cambridge University Press, 2010); Valerie Forman, *Tragicomic Redemptions: Global Economics and the Early Modern English Stage* (Philadelphia, PA: University of Pennsylvania Press, 2008); Jonathan Gil Harris, *Sick Economies: Drama, Mercantilism, and Disease in Shakespeare's England* (Philadelphia, PA: University of Pennsylvania Press, 2004).

tragedy for decades, if not centuries. In *English Revenge Drama* (2010), Linda Woodbridge notes the obsessive logic of debits and credits in revenge plays of the period, and the ubiquitous imagery of double-entry bookkeeping: "An operating company's books are never closed with a 'final balance': at any given moment, debts will be outstanding. And a vendetta is never complete while some are alive on both sides."[70] Though some of the plays I look at in this project are revenge tragedies that conform to Woodbridge's thesis, I am more interested in how the tragic form engages with the idea of an emergent balance of nature as a precursor to the scientific study of ecology.

King Lear provides the strongest illustration of how nature's ability to balance itself, or water's ability to find its level, can amend the play's economic imbalances, which have been generated by human faults and errors. John Fletcher's *Bonduca* represents foreign pathogens as balancing agents when the metaphorical diseases infecting the invading Romans turn their military triumph over the British into a Pyrrhic victory. The revenge tragedies *Titus Andronicus* and *Lust's Dominion* display the tragic economy that Woodbridge describes above, where blood repays blood. But in their original performance, the two hero-villain Moors who made these plays commercially successful also depended on the right balance of ingredients to make a White actor appear like a Moor, a theatrical type commonly associated with an internal humoral imbalance. Furthermore, because of the combined inadequacy of English galls and the absence of cork oak in England, theater companies had to import galls and corkwood to bring these characters to life on stage. Blood will have blood, these plays suggest, but only if England can correct its dearth of blackface materials. Finally, I show how the tragedy that Romeo catalyzes through purchasing poison from an apothecary not only characterizes an unfair exchange of money for death but also takes on a pressing ecological urgency when the play is performed in a rainy Cape Town during an 1890s gold rush.

Chapter Breakdown

Anthropocene Theater investigates the agency of natural and non-human players on the English stage at a moment when the ecological consequences of human agency in the Anthropocene are being reckoned with. This book is organized in a way to showcase how the early modern stage lays the

---

[70] Woodbridge, *English Revenge Drama*, 62.

groundwork for a theater of the Anthropocene, and each chapter attempts to characterize this theory of performance. To reiterate, Anthropocene theater acknowledges that agency in performance is not only shared between a human performer and a human audience but also includes non-human actants, which may be physical properties on stage or components unique to the performance space. The capacity for human and non-human agents to influence the meaning of a performance reflects the burden of the human species in the Anthropocene, which, though collectively responsible for anthropogenic climate change, does not bear that burden equally across the globe. Provincializing the Anthropocene means attending to the unequal distribution of this burden. Instead of seeking to privilege one specific thing by which geologists in the future might characterize our present "-cene"— which has been variably dubbed the Neologismcene, the Capitalocene, the Chthulucene, and the Naufragocene—I am more concerned with how the stage can illuminate the inequalities, the "carbon surpluses" and "carbon debts," that the Anthropocene narrative presents.[71] I follow Kathryn Yusoff's lead in this; rather than proposing yet another "alter-cene," I recognize a need for "a redescription of the Anthropocene through the racializing assemblage from which it emerged."[72] A theater of the Anthropocene subscribes to the "Orbis Spike" hypothesis, which views 1610 as the potential start date for the Anthropocene because it holds European colonialism and the "Columbian exchange" as the *primum mobile* for our current ecological crisis.[73] The history of the Shakespearean stage is also the history of the British Empire, and the history of anthropogenic climate change; a theater of the Anthropocene aims to hold these narratives together, and to see them as one. But at the same time that it accounts for inequalities in wealth and carbon generated by human behaviors, Anthropocene theater also values accident in performance. By training audiences to look more charitably on unplanned weather events, for example, or to regard unfavorable performance conditions as productive, Anthropocene theater recognizes that rehearsal and human intention hold a tenuous grasp over what a performance ultimately will mean to a human audience. Audiences who are aware of how human behaviors (and atrocities) have, for the past four centuries, unwittingly shaped our current global

---

[71] Mentz, "The Neologismcene."   [72] Yusoff, *A Billion*, 61.
[73] Lewis and Maslin, "Defining the Anthropocene," 175. I also follow Yusoff in acknowledging the problem with Crosby's notion of a "Columbian Exchange": "The 'collision of the Old and New' covers over the friction of a less smooth, more corporeal set of racialized violences. In the language of exchange it might be assumed that something was given rather than just taken. In that slippage of grammar, I want to shake the innocence of a language of description that assails this dehumanizing logic and masks its operations" (Yusoff 30).

environment should appreciate accident as a global force offstage as well as on. Human intention may have driven European colonialism and the proliferation of the Shakespearean stage, but accident is what brought us into the Anthropocene.

This book is organized into three parts. My first three chapters, which comprise Part I, "Eco-Materialist History," of this book, are concerned with some of the unique natural resources that found traffic on the early modern English stage. Together these chapters show how grafted biota, unseen pathogens, corkwood, galls, and hemp negotiate the *oikeios* through early modern performance practices and an expanding global marketplace. Chapter 1, "Grafting and Ecological Imperialism in John Fletcher's *Bonduca*," reevaluates how the early modern English understood their agency in determining colonial conquest. For contemporary horticultural writers, the practice of grafting was closely associated with colonial acclimatization and offered a means of either enhancement or debasement for graft and grafter alike. Drawing upon this horticultural discourse, this chapter investigates John Fletcher's *Bonduca* and its pervasive treatment of grafting as a meditation on the horticultural practices that were considered essential to early modern English colonialism. Through metaphorical imagery as well as physical gestures of grafting, *Bonduca* attends to the ecological repercussions of Britain's colonial history and explores the potential risks of colonial expansion. In addition, the play represents the Roman exposure to several metaphorical diseases, which registers an early understanding of disease transmission as pathogenic, and which imagines a reversal of the effect of Old World diseases on indigenous human populations in the New World. Rather than promoting a pro- or anti-imperialist agenda, these dramatized grafts sanction a more complex representation of empire formation, where non-human actants play a more prominent role in determining the outcome of a political, military, and colonial struggle than human agents. But rather than exonerate colonial conquerors, *Bonduca*'s focus on the non-human reveals an early modern understanding of colonial conquest as determined not by the inherent superiority of one group of humans over another, but by the will of the graft.

Shifting from stage metaphors and gestures of colonial domination in Chapter 1, Chapter 2, "Hewers of Wood, Drawers of Gall: The Wooden Economies of Race in *Titus Andronicus* and *Lust's Dominion*," emphasizes how the natural characteristics of the stage's physical materials create meaning and position race as a construction of degraded European environments. Both plays I analyze in this chapter were written at the peak of the Elizabethan timber crisis, and each relies on a different pun to link the material technology for representing racial difference on stage to an expanding economy of wood. "How every fool can play upon the word!" (3.5.38) laments Lorenzo, cringing at Launcelot's play on "Moor" in *The Merchant of Venice*; Shakespeare and Dekker were clearly not above racial wordplay, though these puns may have only made sense in their original performance context. In *Titus Andronicus*, Aaron's black "hue" both begets and justifies the physical, bodily "hews" he orchestrates against the Andronicii, which are figuratively aligned with the excessive consumption of timber. In *Lust's Dominion*, Eleazar's furious "gall" informs his audience how they should read his "Inky" face (1.2.191). Galls, as early modern playwrights would have known, were common wooden ingredients in ink and blackface cosmetic recipes of the period. As forgers, Eleazar and Aaron are two of several Moors on the early modern stage who manipulate ink for their own revenge or advancement. I investigate these material wooden puns—which conflate the hued skin of a Moor with a tree's hewn limbs, humoral gall with imported galls, and Black characters of the stage with Black characters of the page—in the context of England's timber crisis and economic expansion at the turn of the seventeenth century. By focusing on the wooden ingredients that constituted an embodied form of difference on stage, I investigate what happens when we view the emergence of hierarchical or early modern racial thinking in association with ecological materials moving through economic networks. Through reorienting our understanding of Aaron and Eleazar around the wooden commodities that may have constituted their black skin on stage—namely cork and galls—I hope to show how the performance of "race" on stage was mediated by the natural world and its commodification.

Chapter 3, "Hemp, Tobacco, and Hot Commodities on the English Stage," unpacks the formal, commercial, nautical, ecological, religious, symbolic, and even racial valences attached to "ladders of rope" when they appear on the English stage as a necessary prop. In plays such as *Romeo and Juliet*, *The Two Gentlemen of Verona*, and *A Christian Turn'd Turk*, ladders of rope are used in scenes where male suitors seek to access commodified female bodies without arousing suspicion from the woman's father or husband. These stage properties were likely made of hemp and are therefore implicated in a global assemblage of commercial expansion and consumption. As the English sought to expand its economic reach, hemp became an important commodity for the expansion of the English Navy. In each of the "ladder plays" discussed in this chapter, the ladder is in close proximity to a real or metaphorical fire. *A Christian Turn'd Turk* calls for the ladder to be set on fire, which stages the potential risks of adventuring for wealth on the high seas in a fire-and-brimstone image that would have resonated with anti-theatricalists and Puritans. Shakespeare's ladder scenes, on the other hand, both reference Phaeton's scorching of the earth, which I suggest implicates hemp in the same anti-tobacconist discourse that cautioned White English consumers against smoking tobacco. Smoking, it was thought, could turn one's White English body into something Black and Other. I suggest that Shakespeare's association between hemp ladders and Phaeton's infamous ride, which turned the skin of the "Ethiopes" black in the classical tale, further conflates industrial hemp with psychoactive cannabis and tobacco in this anti-smoking discourse. In short, these ladder scenes stage hemp's complex role in signaling the risks and punishments of economic expansion on the one hand, but in laying the groundwork of a racial ideology on the other. Hemp is one ingredient that makes the English breach into the slave trade possible later in the seventeenth century. Not unlike cork and galls, hemp on the English stage helps to create an inextricable link to the objectification of African bodies in the English imaginary.

If *Anthropocene Theater and the Shakespearean Stage* is in part an attempt to study the materials of the stage that drove British imperialism, then the material dissemination of Shakespeare's works throughout the Empire deserves our attention. Chapters 4 and 5, which constitute Part II of this book, center on "Eco-Global Performance," and demonstrate how the environments in which Shakespeare plays have been performed are crucial to understanding both Shakespeare's imperial legacy and its misappropriation. The narrative produced by this imperial cultural production—that Shakespeare was a genius, the national poet of England, or perhaps even the inventor of the human—is a problematic one, for several reasons. For one, it often overlooks Shakespeare's own biographical context. Shakespeare was no great celebrity in his time, but just another playwright who likely benefited from collaboration. When actors or even English departments today promote Shakespeare's "genius," they often overlook the imperialist overtones embedded within the pedagogical history of that claim. Shakespeare's "genius" and cultural iconicity are the products of British imperialism, though Shakespeare's stature as a literary figure has not faded with the Empire. He became a global commodity who had purchase all over the world in part because of the actors and actresses who carried their performances beyond the British Isles. Despite my own affinity for Shakespeare's works, my goal here is to interrogate the processes by which Shakespeare became a global commodity, and to qualify his imperial ascendancy as an accident in which nature played no small part. The emergence of a Shakespeare industry, I hope to show, depended in part on natural and even atmospheric elements that were beyond the control of human intentions as his plays were paraded through the colonies.

Chapter 4, "Monkeys, Floods, and the 'Immortal William': Enduring Nature and Playing Shakespeare in the British Empire," shifts from speculating on the agency of natural commodities of foreign provenance on the stage to viewing Shakespearean drama itself as a commodity capable of changing (and being changed by) colonial environments. I introduce readers to the performance conditions that a number of touring actors and actresses encountered when they performed Shakespeare plays throughout the British colonies, from the eighteenth through the twentieth centuries. I argue that the status and iconicity that Shakespeare enjoys today owes itself in part to the ecological and environmental hazards that actors and actresses were willing to endure in order to wave the flag of Shakespeare in every corner of the globe. I offer a survey of the various heat waves, floods, dust storms, thunderstorms, droughts, earthquakes, illnesses, bugs, animals, and other nuisances of nature that allowed touring performers like Daniel Bandmann, Allan Wilkie, Geoffrey Kendal, George Crichton Miln, Genevieve Ward, Matheson Lang, Frank Benson, and W. E. Holloway to perform Shakespeare in the British colonies, and thus to fulfill the civilizing mission of British cultural imperialism. I suggest that the performance conditions encountered by these actors and actresses allowed them to see themselves as martyrs for Shakespeare. But when compiled together, this theater history also places Shakespeare at the center of a theater of the Anthropocene, where accidents abound, and where human intentions are often productively undermined by unforeseen natural players.

Chapter 5, "Stolen Thunder: Performing Shakespearean Weather Events in the Anthropocene," focuses on atmospheric agency in Shakespearean performance as a way of theorizing a theater of the Anthropocene. Through analyzing specific instances of Shakespearean theater history where weather events have coincided with dramatic performances, I argue that the stage can provide a helpful tool for determining the implications of human agency in the age of anthropogenic climate change. For one, weather on stage exposes how any given performance is constantly fluctuating between human intention and unplanned accident. A real weather event on stage can undermine the built-in artifice of theater, which Shakespeare so often exploits in his representations of the weather. At the same time, a real weather event that occurs during a modern Shakespearean performance can also reinforce the ecological unpredictability of live theater, which early modern audiences likely took for granted. To spectators conscious of how human behaviors are impacting the climate (and by extension exacerbating certain weather events), an authentic storm on stage positions the audience as both knowing participants in a performance event and passive recipients of a weather event. This dual positioning is similar to the species narrative offered by the Anthropocene, which argues that all humans are culpable for changing the climate, even if the reality is that some are more culpable than others. A theatrical space where the weather performs thus models how we might provincialize this Anthropocene narrative by attending to how human actors and audience members possess different degrees of agency in choosing how to engage with a given weather event on stage. I provide two examples of site-specific Shakespearean weather events in order to demonstrate how an ecological analysis of Shakespearean performance can attend to a more provincial geologic agency. One occurred during a production of *The Tempest* in the segregated colonial setting of Hamilton, Bermuda in 1950; Prospero's failure to control the actual weather, I speculate, demystifies him before his audience, and demotes him from seeming sovereign ruler of his isle to little more than a soggy actor, impotently imploring the weather to behave.

Shakespeare's colonial authority is also undermined by the errant storm. Another Shakespearean weather event from an 1892 production of *Romeo and Juliet* in Cape Town, South Africa—which coincided with a gold rush in the Witwatersrand basin—similarly failed, in a spectacular way, to demonstrate Shakespeare's linguistic and cultural superiority to a Dutch-speaking population. Romeo's purchase of poison from the apothecary takes on a new significance in the rain, especially during a gold rush, where rainwater and the toxic method of extracting gold particles from the soil carried unforeseen hazards of ecological devastation and slow violence that endure today.

In the introduction to their book *Postcolonial Ecologies* (2011), Elizabeth DeLoughrey and George Handley note several areas of overlap between postcolonial studies and the environmental humanities. Among them, they notice that both disciplines recognize that "human political and social inequalities cannot be successfully and sustainably resolved without some engagement with the more-than-human world and with deep time."[74] While scholarship of the early modern stage has thus far avoided this transdisciplinary principle, I hope to show how a careful study of the English stage can excavate the history of social inequalities created by the mutually reinforcing powers of colonialism and climate change. At the same time, I also want to think about how we can situate early modern drama in a greater historical timeframe, one that

---

[74] DeLoughrey and Handley, *Postcolonial Ecologies*, 25.

can help explain the inequalities of our present and future in geologic times-cales, without ignoring the history of European colonialism.

Part III of this book, "Distributive Justice in the *Oikeios*," comprises Chapter 6 and a brief Epilogue. This final part brings together the eco-materialist history and the eco-performance history of the first two parts by demonstrating the redemptive potential of embracing a new ecological per-spective within the *oikeios*. Chapter 6, "Shaking the Superflux: Sin and Redemption Along Geological Faults in *King Lear*," views Shakespeare's trag-edy as a text that engages with deep time in order to seek out a sustainable resolution to social inequality. I suggest that the play overturns a religious model of redemption offered by the medieval flood plays—where human sin is punished with divine retribution and global deluge—in favor of a more sec-ular model of redemption, where self-correcting imbalances in nature pro-vide solutions to economic imbalances between kingly pomp and houseless poverty. Gloucester and Lear each seek redemption in this play. Lear, who hopes Goneril and Regan will pay him "subscription" for giving them "king-dom" and for calling them "children," seeks (like blind Gloucester) to atone for the "fault" (1.4.277) of doubting the credit of his faithful child. But whereas "faults" are recognizable as human sins in the flood plays, they are also in *Lear* the geological fault-lines by which nature achieves balance. Although Lear and Gloucester seek atonement through different avenues—Lear through a stormy flood, Gloucester on the edge of a cliff—they also each imagine a future in which the debtor/debtee paradigm of Christian redemption, the zero-sum scheme in which one's "pomp" (3.4.37) is necessarily another's "houseless poverty" (3.4.30), is replaced by a more distributive justice. As Lear realizes that he "may'st shake the superflux" and "show the heavens more just" (3.4.40–1), Gloucester hopes that "distribution should undo excess, / And each man have enough" (4.1.80–1). Through (not) representing the cliffs of Dover as the site of Gloucester's theatrical redemption, the play registers a contemporary antiquarian interest in an emergent form of "natural history," which developed in part when scholars began to supplement historical texts and documents with artifacts and evidence from the physical world. One antiquarian, Richard Verstegan, imagined that the white cliffs of Dover had formed as the result of a superflux finding its balance in nature, a theory that informs the white cliffs as the site of Gloucester's economic redistribution. Both storm and cliffs are central to the action of the play because they suggest that the play's economic imbalances might be restored not with God but with the help of the earth's restoration of natural imbalances. In the age of anthro-pogenic climate change, where science has proven the damaging global reach of in/human behaviors, Lear's lesson has never been more important: we need to learn to see economic imbalance as resolvable not through God's divine grace but through the distributive justice made possible by an alliance between human and natural agency. We need to take responsibility for the economic imbalances created by a long history of human (and geologic) "faults."

PART I

ECO-MATERIALIST HISTORY

In the final chapter of *The Periodic Table*, the Italian chemist and Holocaust survivor Primo Levi delivers a short but eventful story—a "micro-history"—of a single atom of carbon that travels from a deposit of limestone all the way into a nerve cell of the author's brain, which helps him to compose the final sentence and ultimate punctuation of his book: "this dot, here, this one."[1] Perhaps a period has never weighed so much. Levi's story is one that only a chemist can tell, and it conditions its audience to see things on a temporal and spatial scale that oscillates drastically between the macro and the micro. Eons are contained in the atom's first appearance: "Our character lies for hundreds of millions of years, bound to three atoms of oxygen and one of calcium, in the form of limestone: it already has a very long cosmic history behind it, but we shall ignore it."[2] The journey of this carbon atom is an appropriate starting place for us to begin to provincialize the Anthropocene and to analyze the *oikeios* and the relations that collapse the distinction between nature and society—for several reasons.

In addition to serving as a primer for the micro-histories that Chapters 1 to 3 contain, Levi's story imagines his minuscule traveler as being neither wholly dependent upon nor completely independent from human beings. It is a nineteenth-century man who releases the atom from its limestone sarcophagus with his pickaxe, and whose kiln enfranchises the atom into the atmosphere as carbon dioxide. It is another man who drinks the wine made from the grape where the carbon atom finally enters the life cycle of a plant, and the same man who expels it back into the world with a brief exhalation. Finally, it is the author himself who imagines consuming the atom once more, this time in a glass of milk, which stimulates his intellectual capacities once it makes its way to the nerve cells in his brain.

---

[1] Primo Levi, *The Periodic Table*, trans. Raymond Rosenthal (New York: Schocken, 1984), 224, 233.
[2] Levi, *The Periodic Table*, 225.

At the same time, the atom has just as many adventures that are not so anthropocentric. Levi imagines the atom entering the lungs of a falcon on the wing, becoming enshrined for decades in the bark of a cedar tree, and composing one of the eyes of a moth that consumed the atom in its larval stage. The story of a single carbon atom emphasizes the agency that non-human elements possess and exercise outside of the realm of human intention. Levi draws our attention (however hypothetically) to the invisible relations that compose what we call "nature." Through enhancing our focus on carbon, Levi flattens the ontology that would make humans the primary subjects of such a narrative. And yet, even in their marginal role, the humans featured in this story are situated economically as well as ecologically. Why is limestone being mined in 1840?, we are prompted to ask. And where is it coming from? What was the price of the wine consumed by the second man who is mentioned, and why does it only escape his liver when he expels a "sudden effort" on a Sunday when he is forced to chase a "bolting horse"?[3] What kind of milk does the author drink on his final page? How far did it travel from the animal to his mouth, and is it cold or warm when it gets there? In the Anthropocene, even the non-human players of ecology circulate in a "nature" that is organized by capital relations.

Another reason this experimental story offers a useful starting point for the work of provincializing the Anthropocene has less to do with Levi's profession as a chemist and more to do with his experience as a survivor of Auschwitz. At one point in the narrative, as if attempting to identify a "Golden Spike" for the Holocaust, Levi imagines the relative insignificance of the human race from a geological perspective: "our very presence on the planet becomes laughable in geometric terms: if all of humanity, about 250 million tons, were distributed in a layer of homogeneous thickness on all the emergent lands, the 'stature of man' would not be visible to the naked eye; the thickness one would obtain would be around sixteen thousandths of a millimeter."[4] Levi's reflection—composed a few decades before the proposal of the Orbis Spike, before scientists began to notice that human beings had in fact already left a measurable, durable, and significant imprint on the surface (and atmosphere) of the earth—ironically prioritizes the mass of human bodies as the metric for identifying our impact rather than *carbon* dioxide. We now know that carbon dioxide emissions are a much better metric, since they measure the consequences of the energy we use, rather than the space we

---

[3] Levi, *The Periodic Table*, 229.   [4] Levi, *The Periodic Table*, 228.

occupy.[5] And yet, Levi's thought experiment might betray a chilling memory of the crematorium chimneys he witnessed at Auschwitz, where human beings were literally being transformed into carbon dioxide, "the ultimate destiny of all flesh."[6] There is no Golden Spike for the Holocaust, perhaps because the Holocaust is a continuation of the racializing geology of an already identifiable Golden Spike. As Yusoff argues, "Humanity continues to persist in its current forms of inhumanity precisely because it is a humanity that is racially constituted and where racial difference is produced as an oppositional form on the outside, when it is really…through spacialized and subjective modes, internal to the formation of such humanity."[7] From a geologic perspective, the Holocaust might be indistinguishable from the genocides inaugurated by European settler colonialism. Provincializing the Anthropocene must not erase these atrocities from the rock record. On the contrary, pursuing the micro-history of an ecological artifact—whether it pertains to the stage, to the history of early globalization, or to climate change—means bringing this violent history and its legacy to the forefront.

Finally, Levi's tale of the carbon atom is also a useful starting place for this part of the book because the place where his micro-history ends—with "this dot, here, this one."—overlaps with a slightly different micro-history I aim to explore in Chapter 2. This first part of *Anthropocene Theater* explores the object histories of a number of stage properties which, upon much closer examination, not only exerted an ecological influence upon a given performance but also negotiated the terms of racial and imperial discourse for early modern English audiences. Among the properties I discuss in the following chapters are hemp rope, grafted biota, microscopic pathogens, corkwood, and galls. Galls are bulbous growths on plants that facilitate the life cycle of certain insects; they were also common ingredients for ink and blackface cosmetic recipes in early modern England.

So let us suppose that Levi's carbon atom was liberated from its limestone prison a few centuries earlier, and found its way into the leaf of an oak tree near Aleppo.

A little after dawn on a cold December morning in 1605, a cynipid gall wasp pokes her head out from a small spherical casket—one of several dangling vampire-like beneath a single oak leaf—and sees the sun for the first time. She—there can be no question of her sex, since all of her generation will

---

[5] According to the US Energy Information Administration, the global carbon dioxide for energy-related emissions for 2019 totaled 33.6 billion metric tons. See https://www.usgs.gov/faqs/how-much-carbon-dioxide-does-united-states-and-world-emit-each-year-energy-sources.

[6] Levi, *The Periodic Table*, 228.   [7] Yusoff, *A Billion*, 55.

be female—slowly escapes her husk, beats her wings once, and then takes off. She is somewhere between Iskunderun and Aleppo, and the oak leaf that had been her dormant home for the last several months casts its long shadow toward the western bank of the Afrin river. She flies north. She will not live long, and she will never meet another wasp. She does not need a mate; the wasps of her generation reproduce asexually. Before she dies, she will lay her eggs, immaculately conceived, on the budding leaf of a tree that will remind her of the one she flew away from that first morning. Then she will fly off to die. As the leaf grows, so will her progeny; a small brown gall will swell on the underside of the leaf, where a wasp larva will live for a few weeks, leaching food and nutrients from the host plant, before it too emerges. Unlike his mother, this wasp will be male, and will need to find a mate. And unlike his mother, this wasp will not live to see the light of day. A man's hand plucks the gall from the leaf a few days after it has formed. The man tosses it into a basket full of galls just like it. The basket is fastened to a donkey, which will carry the man and the galls to Iskunderun, where the man will sell his galls to a merchant. Money changes hands. The gall mixes with hundreds more in a wooden barrel, which in a few days' time is sold to a group of men, who load it onto a ship. Money changes hands. The gall travels below deck in the swaying darkness across the Mediterranean, through the strait of Gibraltar. It will touch the Azores, and narrowly escape annexation by pirates. Blood is spilled. It lies dormant below deck as the ship moves up the Thames, and finally lands at London, where it is unloaded and sold to an apothecary. Money changes hands. The wasp larva has long since died when it is sold again to a playwright, freshly released from debtor's prison. He may also purchase gum Arabic and vitriol from the apothecary, and if he has any money left, paper. Money changes hands. Once home, or perhaps back in prison, he will use these ingredients to make an ink, which he will use to write a play. He invents names and characters. His fingers turn black as he clumsily dips his pen, and paints his words on paper. His play features a Moor who advances himself through forging letters. After hours, days, weeks of work, he might sell his play to a company. Money changes hands. A man from the company that bought the play purchases ten galls from the same apothecary shop where the playwright bought his ink ingredients. On the afternoon of the play's performance, the actor uses the galls to concoct a face paint, which he applies to his face and hands to play the Moor. The play opens. Money changes hands.

Without meaning to be, Aleppo galls are suddenly implicated in the human affairs of representation, writing, and performance. *Anthropocene Theater* demonstrates how natural properties of the stage create meaning during a period of global expansion. Working against the view that Britain's superior naval or military power is responsible for its imperial dominance—and in order to trouble Shakespeare's status as the icon of British cultural and intellectual superiority—I contend that natural materials and unintentional accidents played a significant role in facilitating early English global expansion. I analyze how objects of the early modern stage contribute to emergent ideologies of power in early English colonial efforts. Focusing on plays by Shakespeare and his contemporaries, *Anthropocene Theater* seeks to reconcile a shifting early modern discourse about human and natural ontological categories with more contemporary concerns about human geologic agency, sustainability in the Anthropocene, and a changing global environment.

The play is a great success. It is printed and reprinted. Money changes hands. Copies of the play are sent to India and to Bermuda and to Australia. Money changes hands. The play is memorized and performed, debated and discussed, translated and adapted. Ink is spilled by old scholars and absorbed by new ones. More ink is manufactured, but with a new recipe. Eventually, there is little demand for ink at all, and all the ink spilled about this play becomes accessible through a vast new ecological network called the internet. Money changes hands. The conversation about the play continues, and a new discussion unfolds about what this play might mean for the *Anthropocene*—a new time period, which, though a period, functions more like a comma, anticipating something other than an end, deferring the full-stop for as long as possible, but which also embraces catastrophe and which cannot defer the end forever, until it comes unlooked for, looking nothing at all like a period in fact, nothing like this dot, here, this one.

1

Grafting and Ecological Imperialism
in John Fletcher's *Bonduca*

Accidents happen.[1] Living in the Anthropocene means coming to terms with accidents, and inhabiting the consequences of unintentionally acquiring an influence over the global climate. When the Globe caught fire and burned to the ground in 1613, it was an accident. And while accidents were likely frequent during performances of early modern plays, playwrights were also invested in deliberately representing accidents for comedic and tragic effect. John Fletcher's *Bonduca* (c. 1612) provides a meditation on accident that is noteworthy for its scale and proximity. Not only does the play undercut the strength of the military in establishing a "successful" colony; it also suggests that the attempt to establish a colonial foothold in the Americas was subject to forces that were outside of human control. Through staging the British resistance to the Roman occupation, Fletcher turns his audience's attention to the past in order to comment on the present colonial narrative unfolding across the Atlantic. And while other plays may offer a similarly implicit commentary on a burgeoning English colonial project, Fletcher's portrayal of the Roman occupation places a unique emphasis on the ecological players that could make or break the enterprise. *Bonduca* stages the globalization of natural resources as a deliberate consequence of Roman imperialism, but it is nature that determines colonial victory.

In the opening scene of *Bonduca*, a play that dramatizes the fall of ancient Britain to the Roman Empire, the British general Caratach underscores a similarity between his men and their Roman opponents by using a metaphor that compares humans and plants. After reprimanding the British Queen Bonduca for boasting of her recent victory over the Roman enemy, Caratach cautions her neither to love nor to hate the Romans. But he also issues a warning to his enemy of what they can expect from him:

---

[1] This chapter first appeared in *The Journal for Early Modern Cultural Studies*, Vol. 17, No. 1 (Winter 2017), 68–96.

Anthropocene Theater and the Shakespearean Stage. William H. Steffen, Oxford University Press.

> That hardy Romane
> That hopes to graft himself into my stock,
> Must first begin his kindred under-ground
> And be alli'd in ashes.
>
> $(1.1.171-4)^2$

Caratach's horticultural metaphor, which describes the Roman imperial project as a "graft," reveals his understanding that the Roman invasion of Britain is more than a military takeover. The menace of the imperial Roman graft in Britain threatens to contaminate Caratach's familial bloodlines and to debase the British "stock." But Rome's weaponized graft poses an even larger threat to the British ecosystem. The imagery of grafting that proliferates throughout the play engenders grafting as the literal and physical means by which Rome colonizes Britain. I read grafting as a central metaphor for imperial incorporation in Fletcher's play, but a metaphor that illuminates a diversity of literal gestures—of joining, swallowing, interring, planting, and transplanting—that the play stages. However, at the same time that grafting encompasses for Caratach the nefarious intentions of the hardy Romans, the horticultural practice also serves as his own weapon of choice for resisting unwanted colonial incorporation. Caratach demonstrates that grafting and planting are fundamental and complementary practices of both colonial domination and colonial resistance. His proposal for resisting the Roman graft is to "begin"—a verb whose archaic transitive form connotes entrapment—the Roman "kindred" as ashes underground; he aims to bury all the Romans together, as if to keep them from mixing with the ashes of British soldiers.[3] Ironically, his self-defeating effort at genocidal containment promises to accomplish the very incorporation of Roman and Briton as the proposed graft; whereas the Romans want to "graft" onto his British "stock" and penetrate British bloodlines, Caratach imagines that planting Roman bodies in the British earth is the best way to keep Rome and Britain separate. Thus, even when the British are resisting colonization, they are moving toward an inevitable and tragic incorporation with Rome. The play incessantly anticipates the fall of Britain, which early modern English audiences would have expected from a familiar historical tragedy. But Fletcher's play distinguishes itself from other early modern dramatizations of British colonial history by foregrounding the graft

---

[2] John Fletcher, *Bonduca*, edited by Cyrus Hoy, in *The Dramatic Works in the Beaumont and Fletcher Canon*, 10 vols. (Cambridge: Cambridge University Press, 1979), 4: 149–259.

[3] "† begin, v.2." *OED Online*. Oxford University Press, June 2015. Accessed 19 August 2015.

as a tool through which to mediate colonial conflict. Though Roman "hopes" clash with British ones in *Bonduca*, colonial victory is ultimately determined by which graft flourishes and which fails.

While it may be tempting to imagine early modern English audiences identifying with either their British or Roman ancestors in the play's colonial conflict, *Bonduca* ultimately discourages identification with both sides by framing colonialism as an ecological issue. Although the play seems to provoke contemporary theatergoers to perceive themselves as the ancient Britons resisting foreign invasion and defending a burgeoning nationalist sentiment, while simultaneously soliciting its audience to imagine the Roman expeditionary force as a model for the English to idolize (especially in light of England's recent economic and colonial expansion), the incorporation between the two powers at the play's end troubles an easy alignment with one side or the other. At the turn of the seventeenth century, the Roman invasion of ancient Britain was "cited as a key precedent for English imperialism" and was thereby upheld as "an unequivocally good thing."[4] However, because audiences would have been familiar with the history of Queen Boadicea—if only as an emblem "of that period's belief in savage excess as the inevitable consequence of female rule"—they would have been primed for the inevitable incorporation of Britain into Rome at the tragedy's conclusion.[5] Instead of offering a pro-British or a pro-Roman message—and instead of promoting a pro- or anti-imperialist agenda—*Bonduca* emphasizes that the Roman conquest of Britain (and by extension the eventual success of contemporary colonial ventures) had more to do with the consequences of the grafting and less with the intentions of the grafters. The tragedy of *Bonduca* ensures that almost all of the human intentions are undercut by unforeseen consequences, so that even the victors are victims of circumstance. But rather than apologizing for the unforeseen consequences of a colonial invasion, the play reminds audiences that the victors of colonial conquest are sometimes only accidentally so.

Though I follow scholars who have acknowledged the ways in which *Bonduca* links ancient Rome's colonization of Britain with Britain's contemporary colonization of Virginia, I seek to define the relationship between Britain's ancient and contemporary colonial history in ecological, rather than

---

[4] Gordon McMullan, "The Colonization of Early Britain on the Jacobean Stage," in *Reading the Medieval in Early Modern England*, edited by Gordon McMullan and David Matthews (Cambridge: Cambridge University Press, 2007), 119.

[5] Jodi Mikalachki, *The Legacy of Boadicea: Gender and Nation in Early Modern England* (London: Routledge, 1998), 12.

allegorical, terms.[6] Caratach's metaphor effectively grafts a horticultural discourse onto a colonial discourse in order to explore the ecological consequences of colonial expansion. In doing so, it reveals how the practice of grafting was closely affiliated with planting in the early modern imaginary. But late sixteenth- and early seventeenth-century horticultural discourse also associated grafting with the practice of transplantation or acclimatization— the introduction of a foreign species into a new ecology. Acclimatization was a common practice during the age of trans-Atlantic commercial development, though seemingly innocent transplantations resulted in devastating unforeseen consequences. The introduction of domesticated animals to the Americas and the globalization of New World foods resulted in "a swift, ongoing, radical reorganization of life on Earth without geological precedent."[7] While American foods brought new diets to other parts of the world, the diseases that Europeans introduced to the New World may have reduced the native human population by as much as 90 percent in the first sixty years of contact.[8] Simon Lewis and Mark Maslin have even proposed that this "Columbian Exchange" and the "geologically unprecedented homogenization of Earth's biota" may mark the beginning of the geologic epoch known as the Anthropocene—the period in which human activity significantly influences the global environment.[9] Their argument about the geologic agency that humans have unknowingly acquired through early modern commercial, colonial, and horticultural practices is useful for thinking about how the stage mediates transcontinental grafts as practical measures with unforeseen consequences. It is also useful for thinking about how those consequences are still being felt centuries later.

---

[6] Claire Jowitt, *Voyage Drama and Gender Politics, 1589–1642: Real and Imagined Worlds* (Manchester: Manchester University Press, 2003), 108; McMullan, "The Colonization of Early Britain," 137. Jowitt reads Fletcher's play as an allegory for the respective foreign policies of Elizabeth, James, and Prince Henry regarding Virginia. McMullan has noted the tendency in Fletcher's plays in particular to celebrate both the colonial origins of Britain and England's contemporary colonial achievements without even staging English characters, though he does not discuss *Bonduca* in this regard.
[7] Lewis and Maslin, "Defining the Anthropocene," 174.
[8] Lewis and Maslin, "Defining the Anthropocene," 175.
[9] Lewis and Maslin, "Defining the Anthropocene," 175. Lewis and Maslin propose what they term the "Orbis hypothesis," which marks 1610 as a possible start date for the Anthropocene epoch (175). Their criteria for defining a new geological epoch includes locating a Global Stratotype Section and Point, or GSSP, or "the location of a global marker of an event in stratigraphic material" (173). Their GSSP for the 1610 date derives from the trans-Atlantic movement of species, but also from the sharp decline in atmospheric carbon dioxide, which they suggest is a result of the devastating human depopulation in the Americas, which resulted in "the near-cessation of farming and reduction in fire use" as well as "the regeneration of over 50 million hectares of forest" (175). This carbon dioxide dip between 1570 and 1620, observed from "two high-resolution Antarctic ice core records," is "the most prominent feature, in terms of both rate of change and magnitude, in pre-industrial atmospheric CO_2 records over the past 2,000 years" (175).

Fletcher's play stages this colonial form of grafting in two major ways. First, through representing the Roman importation of foreign commercial goods and flora as a means of sustaining the expeditionary force, the play demonstrates how Roman colonization irreversibly altered Britain's ecological history when it introduced (through grafting) foreign species to British ecosystems. Second, *Bonduca* refers to a number of devastating diseases (which happen to be of European origin) that were carried by contemporary English and European settlers to the Americas, where they wreaked havoc on native human populations. The metaphorical transmission of these diseases in the play registers the coterminous trans-Atlantic movement of the diseases themselves and situates them within a discourse of colonial grafting. The play's literal and metaphorical grafts (or gestures of colonial acclimatization) reinforce, as I will show, the attitudes expressed in contemporary horticultural manuals. Early modern horticultural writers promoted the practice of grafting and the movement of a plant from one soil to another as a gesture of potential enhancement, especially in the colonial setting of Virginia. In fact, more than the other European colonial powers in the Americas, the English cited their use of the land, their engagement "in agricultural or pastoral activities," and their improvement of it—which could refer to both "grazing (domestic animals) and planting"—as the primary means by which they claimed possession of their colonies.[10] And although Fletcher's play participates in the colonial discourse of grafting, its representation of grafting as a means toward colonial conquest services the enhancement of neither the Roman "graft" nor the British "stock." Instead, the play's tragic conventions highlight the ways in which colonial grafts produce unforeseen consequences for both "graft" and "stock" that confound the intentions of the grafters. By considering *Bonduca* as a meditation on actual grafting practices, we are made privy to an early modern understanding of empire that precedes the racist imperialist discourse of "White makes right," and reveals an early modern awareness of the role played by non-human agents in determining the "success" of colonial conquest. In *Bonduca*, the intent to conquer yields to the outcome of the graft; Fletcher's characters capitalize on the consequences of transplantation, which drives the action of the play. As a result, the play foregrounds colonization as a tragic undertaking through staging the involved risks and outcomes. By privileging ecology as a primary determinant in the unfolding of both ancient and contemporary British colonial history, the play

[10] Patricia Seed, *Ceremonies of Possession in Europe's Conquest of the New World, 1492–1640* (Cambridge: Cambridge University Press, 1995), 25.

neither condemns nor endorses the military campaigns of either the Romans or the British. Instead, it stages the history of the Roman Empire in Britain as a catastrophe of incorporation, which British colonizers seemed bound to repeat in the New World.

Grafting and Colonial Incorporation

Fletcher's *Bonduca*, which was first performed by the King's Men between 1611 and 1614 and was first published in 1647, stages a tragedy that unfolds through a series of efforts to incorporate early "British" soil and citizens into the Roman body politic. These Roman initiatives can be read as metaphorical grafts that reinforce the literal grafting represented in the play. Caratach's eventual embrace of his colonial oppressor at the end of the play, where he identifies himself as "The man that makes her [Rome's] spring of glory grow" (5.3.196), marks the culmination of a long series of scenes staging Rome's absorption into Britain, and Britain's into Rome. Scholars have shown how the early modern stage rehearsed the colonial origins of Britain, which constituted an emergent national identity, and which "was understood to be the product of a series of invasions from overseas"—from the Normans, the Saxons, the Danes, and the Romans.[11] *Bonduca* endorses a narrative of British colonial history where the Romans can still constitute seventeenth-century British identity, but without penetrating British bloodlines. The play overwhelmingly disavows incorporation between Roman and British humans in order to sanction incorporating gestures that unite humans with earth. The "stock" that the Romans infiltrate through their occupation of Britain is thus botanic rather than related to a human or national genealogy.

Throughout the play, sex repeatedly threatens to unite Roman and Briton, first through Junius's infatuation with Bonvica and then through Petillius's necrophilic infatuation with her. But the play repeatedly disallows sexual congress across enemy lines. Junius realizes the error of his ways once Bonvica captures and nearly executes him. And Petillius, who spends so much time mocking Junius for being in love at the beginning of the play, falls in love with the same woman. But he only realizes he loves Bonvica as he witnesses her

---

[11] McMullan, "The Colonization of Early Britain," 122. McMullan follows Richard Helgerson in comparing the frontispieces from John Speed's *Theatre of the Empire of Great Britain* and Michael Drayton's *Poly-Olbion*. See De Grazia's third chapter for a discussion of how Shakespeare's career reflects an understanding of Britain as a composite of colonial invasions. See Margreta De Grazia, *Hamlet Without Hamlet* (Cambridge: Cambridge University Press, 2007).

noble suicide, committed alongside her sister's and her mother's. In *Bonduca,* love between humans procures only an unconsummated union. And though the rapes of Bonduca's daughters are part of what motivated the historical queen's rebellion in the play's source material, the play seems to privilege their chastity in its representation of their suicides.[12] Alison Calder is right to point out that "an awareness of the rape threat faced by Bonduca and her daughters is central to an understanding of *Bonduca.*"[13] Bonduca's daughters do seek "vengeance for our rapes" (3.5.70). But Calder also reads Bonduca's "eldest daughter as a Lucretia figure," since "her suicide occurs to avert rape, rather than as its consequence."[14] So although sex as a means of conquest is not altogether absent from the play, its disavowal underscores the role of the non-human in the play's presentation of colonial incorporation.

The examples of colonial incorporation that proliferate throughout the play actually depend on the rejection of love and sex between humans. The inevitable union of Britain and Rome relies instead on imagery that combines humans with the contested earth that one side defends and the other occupies. The distinction between human and earth in the play is deeply unstable because of the way one is always swallowing the other. Humans are also constantly incorporating earth into their own bodies—both literally and metaphorically. The Roman officer Petillius brags to his starving countryman Judas that his company "eat[s] Turf" without complaining (1.2.105). Similarly, Caratach's adolescent nephew Hengo boasts that he "can eat mosse" and "live on anger, / to vex these Romanes" (4.2.87–8). The willingness of both Romans and Britons to sustain themselves on inedible British earth unites these foes in their dietary practices. But the earth is also constantly eating human bodies. In the Roman camp, for example, the renowned general Penyus stubbornly maintains his anti-imperialist position and refuses to send his men "into this Britain-gulf, this quick-sand ruine, / That sinking, swallows us" (2.1.49–50). When his men mutiny and help to turn the tide of battle in favor of the Romans, Penyus decides to commit suicide in an effort to regain his honor. Caratach's dirge for Penyus acknowledges his incorporation into British soil, and he hopes that "in thy earth, / Some Lawrel fix his seat, there grow, and flourish, / And make thy grave an everlasting triumph" (5.1.62–4). Similarly, the British general's hope for Hengo—Britain's "Royall graft," (5.3.161) and "fair flower" (5.3.164)—whom Caratach fails to protect from his

[12] Mikalachki, *The Legacy of Boadicea*, 12.

[13] Alison Calder, "'I am unacquainted with that language, Roman': Male and Female Experiences of War in Fletcher's *Bonduca,*" *Medieval and Renaissance Drama in England*, Vol. 8, No. 1 (1996), 214.

[14] Calder, "Male and Female Experiences," 219.

Roman adversaries is that he shall receive "honourable earth to lie in" (5.3.186) from his Roman conquerors. With Hengo's burial and Caratach's surrender, British and Roman land become one.

The series of earthly incorporations represented in *Bonduca* reflect early modern English attitudes toward grafting, which was understood as a practice that could potentially enhance a baser graft through becoming a part of a nobler stock. However, because the results of a graft were not always favorable, a graft could also potentially debase the nobler stock. As other critics have shown, playwrights of the period often refer to grafting as a metaphor for an unstable social or racial hierarchy, where a sexual union could either enhance or debase its offspring. Rebecca Bushnell shows how grafting commonly functioned during the period as a "metaphor for the conjunction of disparate things."[15] In Shakespeare, for example, grafting frequently connotes the mixing of a noble blood with a lesser blood, and signals the potential for a noble blood to be debased, or for a lesser blood to be made nobler.[16] Shakespeare's use of the metaphor is unique considering how horticultural manuals of the period call for a similarity between scion and stock to ensure a successful graft.[17] And though scholars have noted the "competing early modern uses of the language of botany and grafting for bastardy, marriage, and new, improved

---

[15] Rebecca Bushnell, *Green Desire: Imagining Early Modern English Gardens* (Ithaca, NY: Cornell University Press, 2003), 148.

[16] Bushnell, *Green Desire*, 149; Jean Feerick, "Botanical Shakespeare: The Racial Logic of Plant Life in *Titus Andronicus*," *South Central Review*, Vol. 26, No. 1 and 2 (2009), 98; Miranda Wilson, "Bastard Grafts, Crafted Fruits: Shakespeare's Planted Families," in *The Indistinct Human in Renaissance Literature*, edited by Jean E. Feerick and Vin Nardizzi (New York: Palgrave Macmillan, 2012), 105; Vin Nardizzi, "Grafted to Falstaff and Compounded with Catherine: Mingling Hal in the Second Tetralogy," in *Queer Renaissance Historiography: Backward Gaze*, edited by Vin Nardizzi, Stephen Guy-Bray, and Will Stockton (Burlington, VT: Ashgate, 2009), 151; Erin Ellerbeck, "'A Bett'ring of Nature': Grafting and Embryonic Development in *The Duchess of Malfi*," in *The Indistinct Human in Renaissance Literature*, edited by Jean E. Feerick and Vin Nardizzi (New York: Palgrave Macmillan, 2012), 90.
Bushnell argues, "In Shakespeare's history plays, grafting is used as a negative metaphor for the mixing of classes and for social transformation, whether the bastard scion is being grafted on a royal stock or a better plant on a wild one." Similarly, Feerick notes, "If grafting was readily available to Shakespeare as an image of mixture, it most often described the mingling of bloodlines perceived to be disparate in kind because disparate in rank." Wilson, too, recognizes how Shakespearean metaphors of grafting "not only mark a (potentially welcome) challenge to traditional hierarchies of gender and rank" but also "describe the moment when the unnatural masks itself as the natural." Nardizzi also discusses grafting as the joining of disparate elements in his discussion of the sodomitical and procreative grafts in the *Henriad*. Finally, Erin Ellerbeck describes how the metaphor works as both potentially debasing and potentially enhancing in Webster's *The Duchess of Malfi*.

[17] Ellerbeck, "'A Bett'ring of Nature,'" 87. Ellerbeck offers a useful summary of what is necessary for a successful graft: "Typically, one plant is selected for the strength of its stock and roots, while the other, the scion or slip, is chosen for the value of its fruit, flowers, or leaves. Once placed in an incision made in the rootstock, the scion uses the nutrients provided by its host and becomes a distinct, yet integral, part of the new plant...In order for a successful graft to take place, the two combined plants must be closely related."

methods of creation in the period," only a handful of critics have explored the relation between the horticultural practice of grafting and the project of colonialism.[18] Gabriel Egan has analyzed the metaphor of grafting in *Henry V*, where it reinscribes the common ancestry between the French and the English. The grafting metaphor illuminates England as a site of colonial conquest for the Normans, which allows Henry's marriage to Catherine to produce yet another "cross-channel grafting."[19] Vin Nardizzi has similarly noted the sexual implications that color Henry's invasion of France, which seem to implicate the grafting metaphor in a colonial eugenic project.[20] Miranda Wilson, too, shows how "for both classical and early modern writers, grafting serves as a civilizing process, transforming the wild or unprofitable into something sweet, productive, and mild."[21] Fletcher's use of the grafting metaphor is unique, however, because the colonial context of *Bonduca* positions the graft as *both* a civilizing tool of colonization and as a means of resisting a hostile takeover. The play does not privilege one function of the graft over another; instead, the metaphor weighs the risks of colonization on an ecological scale. On both sides of the conflict, grafting provides the weapon of choice for defeating debased enemies through an enhancing incorporation. Whereas Caratach perceives the external Roman "graft" as a threat to his British "stock," Bonduca recognizes that the British are the ones equipped to enhance the Romans through their resistance. Standing over her daughters' suicides, as poison courses through her veins, Bonduca spends her last breath offering "counsel" to the Romans who seek to conquer her: "If you will keep your Laws and Empire whole, / Place in your Romane flesh, a Britain soul" (4.4.152–3). On the one hand, this couplet suggests that the Romans have already accomplished the incorporating gesture of putting a British soul into their Roman flesh by defeating Bonduca; these words, after all, are her last. But on the other hand, Bonduca argues here that the Roman Empire still has room for improvement, which is to be facilitated by adopting a British soul. By this logic, the union between "Britain soul" and "Romane flesh" is not yet complete; the "hardy Romane" has yet to "begin his kindred under-ground,"

---

[18] Ellerbeck, "'A Bett'ring of Nature,'" 94.

[19] Gabriel Egan, *Green Shakespeare*, 77. According to Egan, the Dauphin's dismissal of the English as French "scions, put in a wild and savage stock" (3.5.7) of their Anglo-Saxon ancestors overlooks the way grafting was viewed as a method of enhancement, rather than debasement (75–6).

[20] Nardizzi, "Grafted to Falstaff," 164–5. For Nardizzi, grafting in *Henry V* reveals a connection between rape, dynastic reproduction, and imperial motivations. Through "compounding" with Catharine, the king intends to "continue in the marital lineage of his father and ancestor Edward by invading 'Constantinople and take the Turk by the beard' (V, ii, 195–96)."

[21] Wilson, "Bastard Grafts," 109.

leaving Caratach's prerequisite for a pyrrhic Roman graft in Britain unfulfilled. Bonduca's paradoxical strategy of resisting incorporation through incorporation attempts to show how "Empire" is missing from the genetic makeup of the Romans but forms an inherent "soul" in the British.

Horticultural Grafting and English Colonialism

The grafting imagery that disseminates throughout *Bonduca* crystallizes contemporary views of the potential enhancement that grafting can realize. At the same time, *Bonduca*'s appropriation of early modern horticultural discourse reveals what is at stake when English gardeners graft. Some English grafters experimented with different plant combinations in order to turn a profit.[22] But as a commercial play, *Bonduca* attempts to profit from experimentation with colonial rather than botanical combinations in order to assess the risks of conquest. Furthermore, the play's appropriation of horticultural discourse discovers the limitations of conceiving of the graft as a political tool of colonization. English horticulturalists argue that the potential enhancement bestowed on graft and grafter derives from the movement of plants, but only so long as it is facilitated by (English) humans. The play, on the other hand, suggests that enhancement or debasement is not determined by humans, but by the graft itself. *Bonduca* shows how a graft may happen accidentally or without any human facilitation at all.

In addition to offering prescriptive advice for how best to improve a particular graft or produce a new flower or fruit, early modern horticultural manuals reveal a strong connection between the practice of grafting and the formation of British national and imperial identity. For example, some authors perceived grafting as a pastime that could enhance the grafter in addition to the graft. In the paratextual epistle to *A Book of The Arte and Maner, Howe to Plant and Graffe* (1572), Leonard Mascall praises the physical labor of planting and grafting as a practice that not only promises to prevent idleness and make one more honorable but also to put the English, both "riche and poore," on par with certain emperors.[23] "Cyrus a great king of the

---

[22] Bushnell, *Green Desire*, 141.
[23] Leonard Mascall, *A Book of The Arte and Maner, Howe to Plant and Graffe* (London, 1572), Aivr. In praising the ability of the act of grafting itself to enhance one's social status, Mascall offers grafting as an alternative to the pastime of the theater: "Therevpon many great Lordes and noble personages, haue left their theatres, pleasant stages, goodly pastimes, forsaking and despising their pleasures, not much regarding rich Diademes, and costly perfumes, but haue giuen themselues to Planting and Graffing, and such like" (AiiV).

Persians," he notes, "did so much delite in the Art of planting & graffing, (which did shew a great prayse and glorie vnto his personage,) that he had no greater desire or pleasure, than when he might occupy himselfe in Planting & Graffing to garnish the earth, to place and order thereon certaine number of trees."[24] Mascall suggests that it is not the amount of land one owns that makes one a "great king" over it but that one delights in "graffing," "garnish[ing]," and "order[ing]" it. Similarly, Mascall points out that Emperor Dioclesian "did leaue the scepter of his Empire for to remain continually in the fields."[25] For Mascall, grafting figures as a task preferable to managing an empire, though it also positions the common gardener as a potential emperor. John Bonoeil's *Gracious letter to the earl of South-hampton* (1622), a publication promoting the cultivation of imported silk worms in Virginia, also emphasizes the ability to graft as a foundational trait of English colonial identity. Echoing Mascall's rhetorical strategy, Bonoeil describes acclimatization as part of a "profitable and pleasing Art"[26] and positions grafting as a royal enterprise. He also creates a link between ancient Roman and contemporary British colonial identity:

> Let none be ignorant to sow, to set, to plant, to graft, to manure, to dresse, and order all plants, according to their kinds, and that in proper grounds and seasons fitting them. This is part of that skill, which Emperours, Kings, and Senators of *Rome* haue both writ of and practiced.[27]

Fletcher's Bonduca urges her conquerors to graft a British soul into their Roman flesh, and Bonoeil implies that the early modern English colonist must recognize the Roman origins of the imperial "skill" of grafting; Bonoeil thus identifies grafting itself as a cultural component incorporated into Britain as a result of the Roman occupation. To graft, Bonoeil suggests, is to place within their British flesh a Roman soul.

At the same time that English horticulturalists recognized a debt to ancient Rome for teaching them to graft and for providing them with a model for their own burgeoning identity as a colonial force in the early modern period, they also recognized a need for an English literature of grafting. Wendy Wall shows how the contribution of the prolific English horticultural author

---

[24] Mascall, *Howe to Plant and Graffe*, Aiiv.   [25] Mascall, *Howe to Plant and Graffe*, Aiiv.

[26] John Bonoeil, *His Maiesties gracious letter to the Earle of South-Hampton, treasurer, and to the Councell and Company of Virginia heere commanding the present setting vp of silke works, and planting of vines in Virginia* (1622), M2r.

[27] Bonoeil, *His Maiesties gracious letter*, L4r.

Gervase Markham to a national myth of English land was informed by his own context in an English book market that was being infiltrated by "foreign books and advice."[28] Though Markham "argues powerfully for the necessity of a discourse of English husbandry," his xenophobia ultimately drove his nationalist project of cleansing "English practices and books from foreign influence."[29] But other authors saw a foreign influence as potentially productive, something to be embraced. While Markham sought to separate English from all other forms of husbandry, Mascall's *Epistle* attempts to graft an emergent English discourse onto established foreign practices. Ideologically, Mascall imagines a specific community of gardeners from which "this Realme might thereby receyue no small benefite."[30] At the same time, he pragmatically speaks to a difference of English soil and climate from that of other realms:

> for euery one hath written according to the nature of his countrey. The Greekes for Greece, the Barbarians for Barbarie, the Italians for Italy, the French men for Fraunce &c. which writing without the order and practise, doth very small profite for this our Realme of England, the which I can blame nothing more than the negligence of our nation, which hath had small care heretofore in planting and graffing.[31]

Mascall underscores how a Greek book on grafting, even in an English translation, will hardly be useful to an English gardener, whose plants and soil belong to a different climate and ecosystem. But he also fashions the urgency for an English literature of grafting as an economic necessity for his nation; where Greece, Barbary, Italy, and France seemingly do "profite" from their respective grafting literatures, England is missing out.

Edward Williams also surmised that the enhancement brought to English grafters through grafting in a colonial context would be economic. Williams, author of a publication about Virginia whose title promised to educate its readers on "*the meanes of raysing infinite profits to the adventurers and*

---

[28] Wendy Wall, "Renaissance National Husbandry: Gervase Markham and the Publication of England," *The Sixteenth Century Journal*, Vol. 27, No. 3 (1996), 773.

[29] Wall, "Renaissance National Husbandry," 772.

[30] Mascall, *Howe to Plant and Graffe*, Aivr.

[31] Mascall, *Howe to Plant and Graffe*, Aiiiv. Mascall continues by describing grafting as a potential source of commodity exchange for England, especially if it succeeds in producing a new strain of fruit: "we might florish, and haue many a straunge kinde of fruit (which now we haue oftentimes the want thereof) that might greatly pleasure and serue manye wayes both for the rich and poore, as well as in Grece, Barbarie, Italy, or Fraunce, if our nation were giuen so well that way as they are" (Aiiiv).

planters" who lived there, theorized that any plant of a particular latitude could be acclimatized to a new continent on the same latitude. Reflecting on the similar climates between Virginia and Persia, he seeks to demonstrate "what Commodities Nations so planted abound with, which found wee shall discover in this excellent Virgin a disposition ingrafted by Nature to be Mother of all those excellencies, and to be equall (if not superior) as well in all their noble Staples, as in nearenesse to their particular enricher the perpetually auspicious Sunne."[32] Williams assumes the "excellencies" of Persia will be easily "ingrafted" to the climate of Virginia, where through their transplantation they will be "equall, (if not superior)" to the plant in its original climate. For Williams, acclimatizing Persian flora and fauna on "English" soil in Virginia could potentially eliminate an English dependence on foreign trade for exotic commodities. Sir Thomas Gates, whose report of the Virginia colony was published in 1610, shared Williams's sentiment. "There are innumerable white Mulberry trees," Gates asserted, "which in so warme a climate may cherish and feede millions of silke wormes, and returne vs in a very short time, as great a plenty of silke as is vented into the whole world from al the parts of Italy."[33] One incentive for trans-Atlantic acclimatization, then, was to eliminate the intermediary in England's global trade.

Above all, horticultural manuals that were meant for a colonial readership emphasize transplantation itself as the agent of enhancement. In the same way that Caratach closely associates grafting with planting in Fletcher's play, horticultural manuals further conflated grafting with the transplantation and acclimatization of plants, animals, humans, and diseases from one climate to another. For several early modern horticulturalists, grafting formed a foundational part of early English colonial practice. Bonoeil, for example, thought grafting improved the planter as much as the plant. But his argument resonates with Williams's enthusiasm because it stresses the mere physical movement of the plants from one location to another as the cause of enhancement:

> by the Arte of skillfull planting, grafting, transplanting, and remoouing, the bad wilde plants are wonderfully bettered. As one of the best Authors of Husbandry saith, that euery replanting or remooing [removing] of wilde

[32] Edward Williams, *Virginia, more especially the south part thereof, richly and truly valued viz. the fertile Carolana, and no lesse excellent Isle of Roanoak, of latitude from 31 to 37 degr. relating the meanes of raysing infinite profits to the adventurers and planters* (1650), D1v.

[33] Counseil for Virginia (England and Wales), *A true declaration of the estate of the colonie in Virginia* (1610), H2r.

plants (hauing regard to the fitnesse of the soile and season) is worth halfe a grafting: so as two remooues then, are worth a whole grafting.[34]

Bonoeil treats "planting, grafting, transplanting, and remoouing" as interchangeable gestures of enhancement in order to show that the more a plant moves, the more it improves. But his logic, which literally equates a "whole grafting" with "two remo[v]es" of a wild or native plant, not only concentrates seemingly disparate horticultural practices into a single colonial gesture; Bonoeil also compares humans and plants in order to explicate how both stand to benefit from travel. Drawing from Pliny's *Natural History*, Bonoeil argues:

> this remoouing and transplanting of wild plants, doeth wonderfully mitigate and ingentle them, whether it bee... because that the nature of plants, as of men, is desirous of nouelty and peregrination, or because that at their parting (from the former grounds) they leaue there that ranke wildnesse, virulence, and ill quality that is in them, and as wild beasts, so they become gentle by handling, whilst the Plant is pluckt vp by the roote.[35]

His argument for acclimatizing plants fosters an emergent colonial ideology by projecting his own human and English desire for "nouelty and peregrination" onto "wild" or native plants; for Bonoeil, it is the plants themselves that possess the desire to travel to new locations, and human intervention fulfills the plant's desires as much as the colonist's. Plants become "ingentle[d]" not only because they move but also because their movement is facilitated by human travelers. But Bonoeil suggests that Pliny's logic should extend to humans too; he recognizes that the removal of English citizens to the colonies has the potential to "ingentle"[36] them as well. At the same time, the suggestion seeks to justify the displacement of those Americans already at home in "Virginia," as if they too would benefit from leaving their "ranke wildenesse" behind them.

---

[34] Bonoeil, *His Maiesties gracious letter*, M1r–M1v.

[35] Bonoeil, *His Maiesties gracious letter*, M1v.

[36] Bonoeil also identifies a profit motive for grafting and transplantation, and uses the example of what the Spanish have done with the Sarsaparilla plant: "In the printed Booke of the valuations of the commodities of *Virginia*, Sarsaparillia wilde, is fiue pound the hundred, and Sarsaparillia domesticke, is ten pound the hundred: so as the *Spaniard* hauing no other but the wilde Sarsaparilla at first, yet by replanting and cultiua|ting it, that he made it domesticke, and so much thereby innobled it in worth and goodnesse, as raised it to a double price you see" (M1V).

Staging Ecological Consequences

Fletcher's play and early English horticultural manuals each promote grafting as a metonym for the colonial processes of social and biological incorporation. But whereas Bonoeil perceives the potential for the transplanted subject to improve because it moves, Caratach worries that the mobile graft threatens to debase his native and stationary stock. However, the tragic components of *Bonduca* further complicate the consequential binary of the colonial graft. Instead of either threatening to debase British subjects (whether they are humans or plants) or, conversely, promising to ennoble Roman subjects, grafting in *Bonduca* forces the audience to reckon with an alternative effect. In the process of grafting the discourse of early modern English colonialism onto ancient British history, Fletcher's play focuses the audience's attention on the consequences of the graft rather than on the intention of the grafters. In other words, Fletcher's play envisions colonial conquest as tragic, if not because of who is conquered, then because of *how* they are conquered. In *Bonduca*, human intention yields to non-human agents in determining colonial events.

The imperial resolution of *Bonduca* results from a disparity between the intentions of the grafters and the outcome of the graft. In the same way that neither Bonoeil nor Williams could have predicted that the project of importing silk worms to Virginia would fail, or that diseases unwittingly carried across the Atlantic would cost so many human lives, no one in the first act of *Bonduca* could have predicted that the Roman graft would be successful in Britain.[37] Grafters in the early stages of an experiment knew neither what new fruit the graft would produce nor how the stock should be debased or enhanced; the plight faced by the Roman soldiers in the first act augments this horticultural uncertainty into a colonial register. Even though Rome does eventually conquer Britain, this resolution seems to ensue in spite of (rather than because of) the intentions of the human characters. Neither Bonduca nor Caratach on the British side intend to lose the war (though some of Caratach's decisions are highly questionable), and Penyus in the Roman camp does not intend to win it. When Penyus refuses to supply reinforcements to

---

[37] Charles E. Hatch Jr., "Mulberry Trees and Silkworms: Sericulture in Early Virginia," *The Virginia Magazine of History and Biography*, Vol. 65, No. 1 (1957), 51. Hatch identifies a number of factors contributing to the failure of silk production in Virginia, which included "a lack of labor and settled communities...inadequate customs and tax protection...market and exchange difficulties...the proven wealth in tobacco and the need for quick profit to finance slave labor," and, perhaps most crucially, "inexperience and a lack of trained workers" (51).

the Roman counter-offensive, he imagines he is preserving the honor of his men, which he argues "Must not be lost in mists and fogs of people, / Noteless, and out of name, but rude and naked" (2.1.41–2). Penyus certainly does not intend for his otherwise loyal soldiers to turn "to disobedience" (2.1.83), which places him in a position where only his suicide may recover his lost honor. Similarly, Junius does not intend to love Bonvica, which is perhaps why he compares his affection for his enemy to a contagious disease (2.2.10–11). Petillius clearly does not intend to love Bonvica either; in addition to hailing ridicule onto Junius for loving the same woman, Petillius only falls for her after she has already committed suicide, and loves her despite the fact that her body, which "stinks by this time strongly" (5.2.2), has already begun to decompose. Caratach does not intend to get Hengo killed by failing to protect him from Judas, though he does accept responsibility for releasing Judas from captivity: "I'll answer all" (2.3.54). Bonvica does not intend to let Junius go once she captures him in her trap, but Caratach orders his release as well, since he does not intend to defeat the Romans by "setting snares for Soldiers" (3.5.77). Fletcher's play privileges consequence over intention by staging a military conquest where everyone appears to be on the losing side; as a result, the audience has a clearer understanding of how the Roman conquest of Britain owes more to undermined intentions than to any inherent Roman superiority.

Additionally, *Bonduca* highlights the importance of the role of the graft— and its unpredictable consequences—by staging the process of acclimatization. At the beginning of the play, the Roman soldiers rely on importing to Britain the native produce to which they are accustomed in Rome. Incapable of sustaining themselves on British soil, the Romans argue that the problem with Britain is that it is not Rome. As the influential environmental historian Alfred Crosby points out, transcontinental colonial invaders are not biologically equipped to sustain themselves in a faraway colony without their own biological allies and provisions.[38] When the play begins, the Roman soldiers are in a bad way. Most of them are starving. Swetonius orders Petillius to "Look to those eating Rogues, that bawl for victuals," and notes, "provision /

---

[38] Alfred W. Crosby Jr., *The Columbian Exchange: Biological and Cultural Consequences of 1492*, 30th anniversary ed. (London: Praeger, 2003), 64; Alfred W. Crosby Jr., *Ecological Imperialism: The Biological Expansion of Europe, 900–1900* (Cambridge: Cambridge University Press, 1986), 270. Crosby's thesis in *The Columbian Exchange* is that Europeans would not have been able to survive—let alone flourish—in the Americas without bringing Europe with them: "the successful exploitation of the New World by these people depended on their ability to 'Europeanize' the flora and fauna of the New World" (64). In *Ecological Imperialism*, Crosby uses the term "portmanteau biota" to define "the Europeans and all the organisms they brought with them" (270).

Waits but the wind to reach us" (1.2.162–4). But according to Petillius, the Roman soldiers are not just hungry; they object to anything but a Roman diet:

> Sir, already
> I have been tampring with their stomacks, which I finde
> As deaf as Adders to delays: your clemency
> Hath made their murmurs, mutinies, nay, rebellions:
> Now, and they want but Mustard, they're in uprors:
> No oil but Candy, Lucitanian Figs
> And Wine from Lesbos now can satisfie 'em:
> The British waters are grown dull and muddy,
> The fruit disgustful: Orontes must be sought for,
> And Apples from the happie Isles: the truth is,
> They are more curious now in having nothing,
> Then if the sea and land turn'd up their treasures:
>
> (1.2.164–75)

Much like the early English colonists who became disillusioned with life in Virginia, so too are the Romans fed up with drinking "dull and muddy" water and with eating what "disgustful" fruit the British landscape provides. Instead, they demand food to which they are already accustomed from the Mediterranean regions they have already conquered—the islands of Crete and Lesbos, and everything between Lusitania (or the Iberian peninsula) and the Orontes river. This scene stages the process involved in the creation of what Crosby, in his book *Ecological Imperialism*, describes as a "Neo-Europe" when speaking of the European colonization efforts after the fifteenth century.[39] Unwilling or unable to adapt themselves to the climate they seek to conquer, the Romans aim to reproduce their life in Rome abroad through shipping to Britain and then planting all of their favorite foods for sustenance, which of course disrupts existing ecological systems. But Fletcher also betrays a working knowledge of ecological history in the list of commodities that the Roman soldiers desire. According to Lukas Thommen, Britain did not have apples before the Romans invaded the island.[40] Petillius's description of an apple imported from "the happie Isles" or as a commodity from the "Orontes"

---

[39] Crosby, *Ecological Imperialism*, xv. Crosby demonstrates how the popular narrative among white American and European historians only a century ago credited the formation of Neo-Europes to the simple fact that "Europeans were the best people in the world."
[40] Lukas Thommen, *An Environmental History of Ancient Greece and Rome*, trans. Philip Hill (Cambridge: Cambridge University Press, 2012), 136.

should be read, then, as an attempt to exoticize for the ancient British setting what would have been a common "native" fruit in early modern England.[41] The ancient Romans also found the British soil unsuitable for wine and olives, and imported Mediterranean foods like figs—from Lusitania—and fish sauce.[42] Although the Romans cannot plant grape vines, wine seems to be the one commodity the soldiers do have enough of, since Petillius tempts pouting Junius with "new wine, new come over" (1.2.47). Petillius's list of commodities, then, which includes "Lucitanian Figs," "oil" from Crete or "Candy," and "Wine from Lesbos," is not only historically accurate; it also stages an early modern concern for knowing where one's commodities come from and speaks to the desire for economic enhancement through grafting in a colonial setting.

The Mediterranean origin of the biological imports listed by Petillius would have borne a more overt commercial significance to early modern English audiences as well. By the time that the Virginia Company was attempting to establish a colonial foothold in the Americas, other overseas trading companies, like the Levant Company and the East India Company, had already expanded their geographical reach to the South and East, and had access to several markets by way of the Mediterranean.[43] English merchants were profiting from importing and re-exporting commodities from the very regions Petillius mentions. The Levant Company, for example, had a monopoly on currants, which were imported to England from various Greek islands at an increasing rate during the first half of the seventeenth century.[44] And during the period just before English trading companies controlled their Mediterranean and Eastern markets, the Iberian—or Lusitanian—peninsula functioned as a key intermediary; it was through trade with Spain and Portugal that the English first acquired the precious commercial imports they sought from India and the Americas.[45]

---

[41] Plums were also introduced to Britain through Roman colonization, and are referenced in *Bonduca* as a metaphor for Caratach's arsenal of stones, with which he will defend himself from the Roman force surrounding him. When the Romans have trapped Caratach on his rock, Judas warns them that they shall find him with "His sword by his side, plums of a pound weight by him / Will make your chops ake" (5.2.126–7). The Roman import, Judas suggests, has been maliciously appropriated on British soil and can no longer provide sustenance to the Romans.

[42] In *Agricola* Tacitus reports that "The soil is productive of crops, except for olives, grapes and other natives of warmer climes, and rich in cattle." See Tacitus, *Agricola and Germania*, trans. Harold Mattingly (New York: Penguin, 2009), 10. Thommen notes that grapes were occasionally planted in the south of Britain, and that "new vegetables, such as cabbage, peas and carrots; fruits, such as apples, plums, cherries and walnuts; and flowers, including roses, lilies, violets and poppies, were introduced to the island" by the Romans (136).

[43] Robert Brenner, *Merchants and Revolutions: Commercial Change, Political Conflict, and London's Overseas Traders, 1550–1653* (London: Verso, 2003), 33.

[44] Brenner, *Merchants and Revolutions*, 25. According to Brenner, currant imports more than quadrupled between 1600 and 1640.

[45] Brenner, *Merchants and Revolutions*, 46.

But the entrance of the English into Mediterranean trade had as much to do with demand for foreign commodities in London as with the ecological consequences of other imperial pursuits in the region. In fact, the play makes use of yet another grafting image of incorporation that compares the colonial venture attempted by the Romans in the first century to the increased presence of English merchant vessels in the Mediterranean at the beginning of the seventeenth century. When Swetonius declares his intentions to turn the tide of battle in favor of the Romans, he describes how a tree felled by a storm can be repurposed as a ship's mast and thereby enable the transplantation of flora and fauna across a body of water:

> All shall be right again, and as a pine
> Rent from Oeta by a sweeping tempest,
> Joynted again, and made a Mast, defies
> Those angry windes that split him: so will I,
> Piec'd to my never-failing strength and fortune,
> Steer thorow these swelling dangers, plow their prides up,
> And bear like thunder through their loudest tempests:
> They keep the field still.
>
> (1.2.184–91)

Swetonious imagines appropriating an emasculated pine from Mount Oeta to sail against Bonduca's army and the very "angry windes that split him." The pine offers the Romans an opportunity to meet the British "tempests" with their own "thunder," and "plow" through the British "field" in order to complete their graft-like incorporation into the British soil. If *Bonduca* was performed at the Globe, then Swetonius's reference to a metaphorical pine may have evoked for audiences the material reality of the timber shortage plaguing England at the turn of the seventeenth century, in which London theaters directly participated; Vin Nardizzi demonstrates how the "constitutive woodenness" of the public theaters themselves allowed them to "revert to a former material condition" during performance, thus producing a "rich array of eco-fantasies and nightmares about the shortage of wood and timber."[46] But this particular grafting image of a felled pine from Oeta moving across the Mediterranean in the form of a ship would have borne other significances for English audiences as well.

---

[46] Nardizzi, *Wooden Os*, 23–4.

Spectators familiar with Ovid's *Metamorphoses* may have registered Swetonius's (perhaps unintentional) comparison of Bonduca to Astraea, the goddess of Justice whose swift departure from earth during the Iron Age leveled the mountain forests that flourished during the Golden Age; for Nardizzi, Ovid's version of the "fall," which marks civilization's movement from the Golden to the Iron Age with the transformation of forests into naval fleets, acknowledges that "the advancement of exploration (navigation) and the degeneration of sociopolitical stability (the loss of Astraea) are coincident."[47] But at the same time that audiences may have reflected on their own timber crisis, Swetonius's imagery also invites English spectators to reflect on how they were actually benefiting from the effects of deforestation abroad. The increased economic activity among English trading companies in the Mediterranean might not have been possible without the environmental degradation of southern Europe and northern Africa. The problem of deforestation, which Swetonius's felled pine evokes, was particularly acute. As Richard H. Grove shows, a growing need for ships during the fifteenth and sixteenth centuries had driven Venice's shipbuilding industry inland and had resulted in deforestation; Grove notes that "a general famine of timber was being experienced throughout the Mediterranean" by the turn of the seventeenth century, which is part of what allowed the English to penetrate Mediterranean trade routes.[48] To an early modern audience, then, Swetonius's pine that was "rent from Oeta" by a tempest, and then turned into "a Mast" through human initiative, speaks to the struggling shipbuilding industry and the ecological effects of deforestation being felt in the Mediterranean. For the English, that deforestation provided the economic opportunity to increase their "strength and fortune" in the region. Swetonius's grafting imagery conflates first-century Roman desires for the imperial conquest of Britain with seventeenth-century English desires to flourish in Mediterranean trade, and makes visible the ways in which the consequences of each colonial endeavor confound human intention.[49] In the same way that seventeenth-century

---

[47] Nardizzi, *Wooden Os*, 104.

[48] Grove, *Green Imperialism*, 27–8. While the Mediterranean timber shortage was one factor that allowed the English to penetrate the new market, it was by no means the only factor. Brenner emphasizes the importance of the Dutch War for Independence and Venice's war with Turkey as distractions for England's competitors (16). The English made their own entrance through piracy and privateering in the region as well.

[49] Swetonius's identification of a "pine" as the specific conifer used for the mast not only betrays a knowledge of early modern shipbuilding but also links Mediterranean deforestation with English colonial interests in Virginia. Karl Appuhn details the types of wood needed for the Venetian shipbuilding industry, which was completely dependent upon timber harvests from public reserves under Venetian control (Appuhn 6). According to Appuhn, firs, not pines, were used to construct masts in the Mediterranean: "Oak was used for the hull, main bulkheads, structural ribs, and knees, as well as

English trade in the Mediterranean was made possible and successful not through any particular ingenuity of the English—except perhaps their ability to capitalize on the environmental crises and political disputes of other economic powers in the region—Fletcher's play shows how some "sweeping tempest" outside of human control can be a blessing in disguise for the destitute Roman expeditionary force. The play offers a reminder to the early modern English that their economic expansion into the Mediterranean resembled the Roman conquest of Britain. The success of both endeavors depended on factors that were extra-intentional and non-human.

Though several critics have shown how *Bonduca* uses the colonization of pre-Christian Britain to comment on the early modern English expansion into Virginia, much less critical attention has been given to the differences— and the ecological differences in particular—between the two colonial situations.[50] Although the play's literal and metaphorical grafts have no meaning outside of the discourse of early modern English colonialism, I am interested in how Fletcher's representation of the Roman occupation of Britain rewrites rather than rehearses the unfolding narrative regarding the grafting of European pathogens onto the native human population of Virginia. Thomas Hariot's account of a "rare and strange accident" that befell the

---

the keel of galleys and round ships. The galley oars were made of beech, the masts of fir, the deck and minor bulkheads of larch, the spars of elm, and the rudder of walnut" (Appuhn 54). Unlike the Venetians, the English did have access to foreign reserves of wood—namely in the Americas—and used pine, in addition to firs, for masts (Nardizzi *Wooden* 57). Thus, assuming that Swetonius is not using "pine" and "fir" interchangeably here, the pine that he believes will form his mast shifts his metaphor from a Mediterranean context to a New World context; the staged provenance of his "pine" conflates the pines of Virginia with the firs from the depleting forests of the Mediterranean. See Karl Richard Appuhn, *A Forest on the Sea: Environmental Expertise in Renaissance Venice* (Baltimore, MD: Johns Hopkins University Press, 2009).

[50] While I resist the one-to-one correlation that Jowitt pushes for in her allegorical interpretation, she does note some important parallels between the play's representation of the Roman occupation of Britain and the English settlement at Jamestown, such as the "chronic shortage of food." Crawford also resists Jowitt's allegorical tendency, but follows her lead in identifying key parallels between Elizabeth and Bonduca, James and Caratach, and Henry and Hengo. Boling, Nielsen, and Neil have also shown how the play's representation of colonialism comments on other early modern English imperial interests and informs the audience's decision to sympathize with one side more than another. Boling has argued that the play is pro-British because it is not meant to endorse Caratach's behavior or misogyny. Nielsen reports that "according to all the play's interpretations excepting one, Bonduca represents an uncomfortably familiar Otherness, while the Romans and Caratach represent British audiences." Neil argues that the play stages a resistance to James's absolutist politics, which attempted to impose Scottish monarchical law onto England's common law and to join the two nations under his rule. See Jowitt, *Voyage Drama and Gender Politics*, 110; Julie Crawford, "Fletcher's *The Tragedie of Bonduca* and the Anxieties of the Masculine Government of James I," *Studies in English Literature, 1500–1900*, Vol. 39, No. 2 (2009), 357–81; Ronald J. Boling, "Fletcher's Satire of Caratach in *Bonduca*," *Comparative Drama*, Vol. 33, No. 3 (1999), 392; Wendy C. Nielsen, "Boadicea Onstage before 1800, a Theatrical and Colonial History," *Studies in English Literature, 1500–1900*, Vol. 49, No. 3 (2009), 599; Kelly Neil, "The Politics of Suicide in John Fletcher's *Tragedie of Bonduca*," *Journal for Early Modern Cultural Studies*, Vol. 14, No. 1 (2014), 90.

English while they were visiting the Powhatan in Virginia suffices to demonstrate the extent to which the English failed to understand their role in the spread of disease in the Americas.[51] At the same time, it exposes how the English manipulated the consequence of an accidental biological graft to serve their own colonial intentions. In *A Brief and True Report* (1588), Hariot takes note of the mysterious illness and death that descends upon the Powhatan population after the healthy English visitors depart:

> There was no towne where wee had any subtile devise practiced against us, we leaving it unpunished or not revenge (because we sought by all meanes possible to win them by gentleness) but that within a few dayes after our departure from everie such towne, the people began to die very fast, and many in short space; in some townes about twentie, in some fourtie, in some sixtie, & in one six score, which in trueth was very manie in respect to their numbers.[52]

While neither the Powhatan nor the English can accurately explain the phenomenon, Hariot offers two hypotheses to his readers that work to justify the continuation of the English colonial project in Virginia. First, he suggests that God is on the side of the English. Since Hariot perceives he is the innocent victim of many a "subtile devise practiced against us," and since the English do not seek "revenge" for any misdeed, the disease that visits only the Powhatan must be the hand of God favoring the English. Second, Hariot reports that the Powhatan think the Englishmen to be gods themselves: "this marvelous accident...wrought so strange opinions of us, that some people could not tel whether to thinke us gods or men, and the rather because that all the space of their sickenesse, there was no man of ours knowne to die, or that was specially sicke."[53] Although Hariot characterizes this event as an "accident," it is also "marvelous" because of how he tailors it to fit the needs of a burgeoning English colonial ideology. After all, Hariot does not discover his mortality to the mistaken Powhatan in his narrative; instead, he assumes his accidental apotheosis means that the Powhatan will be more easily "brought through discreet dealing and government to the imbracing of the trueth, and consequently to honour, obey, feare and love us."[54] So even though Hariot's

---

[51] Thomas Hariot, "A Description of Virginia," in *A Briefe and True Report* (1588), in *Captain John Smith: Writings with other Narratives of Roanoke, Jamestown, and the First English Settlement of America*, edited by James Horn (New York: The Library of America, 2007), 900.
[52] Hariot, "A Description of Virginia," 900.   [53] Hariot, "A Description of Virginia," 901–2.
[54] Hariot, "A Description of Virginia," 902.

introduction of an Old World disease to the Powhatan population in colonial Virginia was accidental, his failure to tell the truth—that he did not know why the Powhatan were dying in masses—manipulates the accident into a political tool. His white lie turns a graft into a weapon.

Neither the English nor the Powhatan could accurately explain why diseases were prone to attack certain populations more than others. Crosby's explanation, which relies on modern resources and a broader historical perspective, is that Europeans, who had more domesticated species of animals than the Amerindians, and therefore lived in closer contact with more animals and their diseases, had thousands of years to build antibodies to diseases they unknowingly bioengineered, and which in turn thrived on New World hosts who had no protection against the microscopic invaders.[55] And while Fletcher most likely did not know that Europeans were transplanting their own home-grown diseases to Virginia, his play registers a pathogenic understanding of disease, which was still emerging during the period. Jonathan Gil Harris marks the influence of transnational commerce on the development of shifting conceptions of disease transmission. For centuries, diseases were understood as miasmic and endogenous, resulting from "polluted air or vapors" that created a humoral imbalance within the body.[56] But in the early modern period, as Fletcher's play shows, pathogenic and exogenous understandings of disease emerged. Harris notes that "deviations from the Galenic mainstream never seriously undermined the humoural model; indeed, they were usually accommodated within it."[57] However, he also demonstrates how syphilis—which we now know was a disease carried *from* the Americas back to Europe—became implicated in the nationalization of disease in Europe: disease "had begun to be seen as not only a *state* of humoral disarray but also a *thing* that migrated across national borders."[58] The xenophobic associations fostered by the nicknames of syphilis—the English called it the "French pox," for example—were a symptom of global commerce, and the transmission of syphilis between nations turned disease itself into a commodity in the early modern imaginary: "Communicable disease...was increasingly seen as an exotic if dangerous commodity, shipped into the nation by merchants, soldiers, and other alien migrants."[59] Harris's focus on how disease could be "shipped *into* the nation" from without supports his argument about how

[55] Alfred W. Crosby, *Germs, Seeds and Animals: Studies in Ecological History* (Armonk, NY: M.E. Sharpe, 1994), 12.
[56] Jonathan Gil Harris, *Sick Economies*, 13.   [57] Harris, *Sick Economies*, 13.
[58] Crosby, *Columbian Exchange*, 123; Harris, *Sick Economies*, 17.
[59] Harris, *Sick Economies*, 17.

dramatizations of pathogenic and economic discourses shaped modern conceptions of an English national economy. But it also overlooks how the commodification of disease contributed to the fashioning of English colonial identity abroad.[60]

In *Bonduca*, rather than providing a justification for the conquest of colonial invaders like Hariot, disease instead threatens to infect those invaders. If disease was something that could penetrate national borders through commercial exchange, it was also something that could be acquired by travelers or colonists abroad. After all, syphilis was brought to Europe by Europeans, and while syphilis was a venereal epidemic in Europe, the effects of airborne Old World pathogens on New World human populations were far more devastating. In *Bonduca*, the diseases metaphorically afflicting Roman soldiers on British soil—pertussis, mumps, plague, and smallpox—are (we now know) all of European origin. And because these specific diseases that infect Fletcher's Roman camp were, at the same time the play was being written, wreaking havoc on human populations in the New World, Fletcher's tragedy about imperial grafts (regardless of the author's intention) registers European culpability in the depopulation of the Americas.

Whereas Hariot passively accepts the mysterious deaths of the Powhatan as a colonial advantage, *Bonduca* suggests that the English could just as easily have been the devastated population. Through representing the *invaders* as the ones who are most threatened by, rather than immune to, diseases native to the foreign soil they occupy, Fletcher's play reverses a still-unfolding historical narrative and stages an accidental (though no less real) graft. Unlike the deliberate moving of a plant from one latitude to another with the intention of improving both the plant and the planter, moving a pathogen grafts an organism from one human population—equipped with the antibodies to defend themselves—to another population where the disease has no natural predators. And unlike the deliberate acclimatization of a plant, disease probably traveled without any human intention at all, though it solicited consequences that were beyond the scope of human control.

The diseases with which the Romans become metaphorically infected on British soil reflect—with or without Fletcher's intention—the literal

---

[60] Harris's focus on English understandings of pathology also overlooks non-Western conceptions of disease transmission. Crosby suggests that some Amerindian slaves understood contagion in pathological terms. Crosby summarizes Antonio de Herrera y Tordesillas's *Historia Generalia*: "The Indians became so enraged by the invulnerability of the Spaniards to epidemic disease that they kneaded infected blood into their masters' bread and secreted corpses in their wells—to little effect" (Crosby *Columbian* 38).

acclimatization of Old World diseases in Virginia; pertussis, mumps, plague, and smallpox are diseases that would have been familiar to an early modern English audience. But they were also already familiar to indigenous Americans through contact with European settlers. Without ignoring the metaphorical significance of these diseases—many of which work to emasculate first Junius, and then Petillius, for being in love with a British woman when they are supposed to be in love with war—I want to acknowledge the reality of these diseases in the English colony of Virginia in order to show how the play registers and reverses their effects.[61] Because we now know that these diseases were brought by Europeans to the Americas, their presence on British soil in Fletcher's play makes sense. And though Fletcher may have been unaware of the provenance of these pathogens, his play does call attention to Britain as a site of origin. The Romans carry no diseases with them, and the metaphorical diseases that do infect the Roman soldiers are only meaningful in the context of a colonial encounter. Although the metaphorical status of these diseases seems to support a Galenic or humoral representation of illness (possibly produced endogenously within the borders of Britain), the colonial encounter staged in Fletcher's play promotes the emerging pathogenic understanding of disease transmission instead.

In *Bonduca*, disease is allied with the British. When Petillius is busy teasing Junius, tempting him with alcohol and sex workers to alter his melancholic disposition (or his humoral imbalance), he reasons, "No, it shall ne'er be said in our Countrey, / Thou dy'dst o'th'Chin-cough" (1.2.29–30). Petillius associates this particular disease with Junius's reputation back home, which suggests that rumors can be transported as easily as pathogens. More commonly known as "[w]hooping-cough" or pertussis, "chin-cough" was a highly contagious bacterial infection, and it was also unknown to the Americas before the arrival of Europeans.[62] Later, Petillius reports to Swetonius that Junius can be

---

[61] Several critics emphasize how heterosexual love in the play is deemed effeminizing and poses a threat to the homosocial imperial embrace that the play moves toward. While Jowitt argues that Caratach's sexual desire for Roman military bodies unmans him, Crawford argues that "male love for women is seen as threatening to male power" and shows how the play offers an alternative homoerotic model, of which the play is also critical. Green argues that heterosexual love in *Bonduca* is "treated as a negative commodity" and highlights "the potential destructiveness of passion." Calder identifies Junius and Petillius as transgressive military figures for loving Bonduca's daughters, thus confusing "the masculine discourse of war with the feminine discourse of love." See Jowitt, *Voyage Drama and Gender Politics*, 119; Crawford, "Fletcher's *The Tragedie of Bonduca*," 367; Paul D. Green, "Theme and Structure in Fletcher's *Bonduca*," *Studies in English Literature, 1500–1900*, Vol. 22, No. 2 (1982), 310–11; Calder, "Male and Female Experiences," 222.

[62] "chincough, n." *OED Online*. Oxford University Press, June 2015. Accessed 19 August 2015; Crosby, *Columbian Exchange*, 49. Crosby describes how it is likely that "several diseases were at work" during Cortés's attack on the Aztec capital of Tenochtitlán: "The Aztec sources mention the racking

found in his cabin, "sick o' th' mumps" (1.2.265). Though Petillius perhaps means this as an emasculating comment, since an early modern connotation for the "mumps" included a derogatory slur for an old woman,[63] he also implies that Petillius suffers from the inflammatory disease, unknown in the Americas before 1492.[64] Two scenes later, Junius tells Petillius that his torment in loving Bonvica is "like the plague" (2.2.3): "'Tis sure the plague, for no man dare come neer me / Without an Antidote: 'tis far worse; Hell" (2.2.10–11). Junius clearly comprehends the bubonic plague as highly contagious when he warns Petillius to stay away from him. And though plague devastated European populations throughout the sixteenth and seventeenth centuries, it was also one of the invasive diseases introduced to the Americas by Europeans. In fact, the bubonic plague was likely the disease attacking the indigenous population of the American coastline at the same time that Fletcher was writing *Bonduca*.[65] Junius's adoration of his British opponent Bonvica seems to be the pathogen causing each one of these metaphorical diseases, which suggests that these diseases only have meaning (even as metaphors) in the colonial context of this play, and are therefore contracted from the British soil, rather than brought from Rome. On the other hand, Caratach accuses Judas of being a "pocky villain" (5.3.129) after he shoots Hengo, which can reference either the New World disease of syphilis or the Old World disease of smallpox. Regardless of which disease the pox signifies, by representing the Roman invaders as the ones with *all* the diseases, the play encourages its early modern English audience members—who were more than capable of unwittingly transporting their diseases (but not their antibodies) to the Americas—to speculate about what might cause a disease to decimate one human population and not another. While the British in the play are biologically equipped to withstand the Roman invasion, the number of diseases— both real and metaphorical—that threaten the Roman invaders represents infection as a side-effect of colonial expansion. The play suggests that the non-human agents that participated in the European expansion across the Atlantic could have behaved differently and canceled the "success" or even the possibility of European colonial conquest.

---

cough of those who had smallpox, which suggests a respiratory complication such as pneumonia or a streptococcal infection"—or pertussis.

[63] "† mumps, n.1." *OED Online*. Oxford University Press, June 2015. Accessed 19 August 2015.

[64] Crosby, *Germs*, 12. Crosby notes, "The Valley of Mexico had fifty devastating epidemics between 1519 and 1810, including smallpox, typhus, measles, mumps, and pneumonia" (*Germs* 12).

[65] Crosby, *Germs*, 36. Crosby points out that "an epidemic of plague or typhus decimated the Indians of the New England coast immediately before the founding of Plymouth" (*Germs* 36).

Rather than promote an imperialist (or anti-imperialist) agenda, *Bonduca* sanctions a more complex representation of empire formation, which privileges the role of non-human actants in determining the outcome of a political, military, and colonial struggle. If early modern audiences had trouble identifying with either the British or the Romans in Fletcher's play, it was because the play paints a more complicated picture of empire. Penyus's foiled pacifism, the proliferation of native diseases among the Roman soldiers, and Swetonius's ancient Roman expression of contemporary English desires for economic and colonial expansion—each of these scenes discourages seventeenth-century English audiences from seeing themselves as the inheritors of Rome's imperial legacy. At the same time, Bonduca's graft-like resistance to colonial incorporation and Caratach's sincere embrace of his Roman adversary discourage contemporary audiences from nourishing an emergent nationalist sentiment. Instead, *Bonduca* urges audiences to recognize empire itself as an ecology in which human volition plays only a partial role. The foiled intentions of the British and Roman characters in the tragedy reveal an early modern understanding of imperial conquest that is very different from a modern one. Whereas European colonial discourse of the late seventeenth and early eighteenth centuries furthers a narrative where white skin, alleged superior intelligence, and advanced technology justify colonial exploitation, Fletcher's play reveals an early understanding of imperial conquest as an achievement that is seldom deliberate, and one that belongs more to things than to humans.

To lend our attention to the role of horticultural discourse and the agency of things in determining the formation of colonial states is neither to exonerate nor to apologize for the human European colonial invaders who inaugurated and catalyzed a long history of human violence and genocide in the American colonies. On the contrary, sixteenth- and seventeenth-century European colonial invaders appear more culpable than ever once we recognize their ability to take advantage of the biological events caused by their travels and transplantations. In *Bonduca*, the triumph of accident over intention mediates colonial conquest. As Hariot demonstrates and the play suggests, empire and human intention are seldom compatible. Hariot belatedly grafts his preposterous intentions to make the Powhatan "honour, obey, feare and love" the English onto an accidental epidemic, which was but one of the many consequences of the European trans-Atlantic biological and colonial exchange. And by staging an imperial victory where even the victors seem defeated, Fletcher's play reveals a process of colonial formation where the intention to conquer remains contingent upon the consequence of the graft. *Bonduca* highlights colonialism as a situation where intention follows consequence, rather than vice versa. Furthermore, the play works against justifications for colonial conquest that seek, as Hariot's does, to take advantage of accidents. I suspect that the play provides a cautionary tale to its early modern English audience. In particular, by imagining the Roman invaders as the party less equipped to handle novel pathogens encountered in Britain within a colonial context, *Bonduca* invites its audience to speculate about an alternative historical narrative that might have unfolded had the English "graft" in Virginia—or the Columbian graft in the Caribbean—produced a different ecological outcome. What if Europe had been devastated by deadly American pathogens—airborne, let's say, and more lethal than syphilis—as a result of trans-Atlantic contact? What if more aggressive American pathogens made their way back across the Atlantic, and compromised the established social, political, and economic structures of an entire continent? What if the rapid decrease in the European population along with the weakened political structures made conquest possible for some one hundred or so Incan or Powhatan warriors? Fletcher's play seems to entertain a possibility that the collision between the Old and New Worlds might have resulted in an outcome much less favorable for Europeans. But rather than apologizing for the Roman occupation of England, or for English settler colonialism in Virginia, *Bonduca* portrays an unpredictable ecological graft as a determining force of colonial conquest.

2

Hewers of Wood, Drawers of Gall

The Wooden Economies of Race in *Titus Andronicus* and *Lust's Dominion*

And the princes said unto them [the Gibeonites], Let them live; but let them be hewers of wood and drawers of water unto all the congregation.
                                                                    Josh. 9:21, KJV

In the opening scene of *Titus Andronicus* (c. 1594), the victorious Andronicus clan demand that the Goth Queen's eldest son Alarbus be seized, "That we may *hew* his limbs and on a pile, /*Ad manes fratrum*, sacrifice his flesh / Before this earthly prison" (1.1.100–2, emphasis added).[1,2] When Tamora's plea for mercy fails to assuage her captors, Lucius orders his brothers to "make a fire straight, / And with our swords upon a pile of wood / Let's *hew* his limbs till they be clean consumed" (1.1.130–2, emphasis added). When the Andronicus sons return a few moments later, Lucius draws attention to the offstage spectacle of smoke rising in the air:

> See, lord and father, how we have performed
> Our Roman rites. Alarbus' limbs are lopped,
> And entrails feed the sacrificing fire
> Whose smoke like incense doth perfume the sky.
>
>   (1.1.145–8)

Shakespeare's first revenge tragedy repeatedly conflates the hewing and consumption of bodies with the hewing and consumption of wood. The Romans characterize Alarbus's arms and legs in wooden terms; his "limbs" will add fuel to an already hewn "pile of wood," but not before they are "lopped" like branches from a tree. The Romans, however, are not the only ones to "hew"

---

[1] An earlier version of this chapter first appeared in *Renaissance Drama*, Vol. 48, No. 2 (2020), 157–81.

[2] William Shakespeare, *The Arden Shakespeare: Titus Andronicus*. Edited by Jonathan Bate (London: Routledge, 1995).

Anthropocene Theater and the Shakespearean Stage. William H. Steffen, Oxford University Press.
© William H. Steffen 2023. DOI: 10.1093/oso/9780192871862.003.0003

human limbs in this play. Aaron the Moor lends a hand in severing the hand of Titus, and Chiron and Demetrius, the licentious siblings of the fragmented Alarbus, later avenge their brother's death by raping and dismembering Titus's only daughter Lavinia. Upon beholding her ravished body, Lavinia's uncle Marcus asks, "What stern ungentle hands / Hath lopped and *hewed* and made thy body bare / Of her two branches?" (2.4.16–18, emphasis added). In addition to calling attention to his niece's disfigured body, Marcus's metaphor conflates the violence of cutting off her hands with the excessive hewing and consumption of trees.

Marcus's metaphor may have struck a chord with his Elizabethan audience, who were in the throes of a devastating wood shortage. As a result of overconsumption, timber prices more than tripled between 1500 and 1600.[3] Early modern England was heavily dependent on wood for fuel, building materials, and (among other things) theatrical properties. As Vin Nardizzi has shown, the woodenness of the nine theaters built in London between 1567 and 1614 underscored the theater's complicity in the ecological crisis, informing several plays that indulged an "array of eco-fantasies and nightmares about the shortage of wood."[4] *Titus* was by no means the only play to evoke the timber crisis on stage. But what is unique about the ecological "nightmare" of *Titus* is the way it offers a suggestive link between the destruction of wooden timber, brutal violence against humans, and emerging racial discourses.

This material and linguistic link juxtaposes two different kinds of "hewn" bodies in the play. Alarbus, Lavinia, and Titus lose their limbs in a literal way, though the play measures the weight of this loss through their metaphorical comparison to a shorn, limbless, woody plant. At the same time, the verb "hew" (used three times in this play) operates ambiguously in relation to Aaron's black "hue" (a noun used eight times in the play).[5] The linguistic and

---

[3] Nardizzi, *Wooden Os*, 10.   [4] Nardizzi, *Wooden Os*, 20.

[5] Despite the auditory confusion that might be caused by the homophones in performance, the spelling for the three instances of "hew" and the eight mentions of "hue" remains consistent across the three quartos and in the first folio. The slippage between "hue" and "hew" in *Titus Andronicus*, which I am suggesting links blackface cosmetics and the cutting of wooden or human limbs, also has purchase elsewhere on the English stage. George Peele, who collaborated with Shakespeare on *Titus*, rehearses the pun in *The Battle of Alcazar* (1589) when the usurper of the crown of Barbary, Muly Mahamet, congratulates himself on his alliance with the Portuguese army by celebrating his exploitation of their labor, which will involve the slaughter of Moors, and necessitate his cosmetic makeup: "Now have I set these Portugals awork / To hew a way for me unto the crown" (4.2.70–1). In Thomas Heywood's *The Fair Maid of the West Part 2* (c. 1630), Spenser describes the lengths to which he will go to return to Bess, and how many Moors he is prepared to cut: "Through twenty bashaws I will hew my way, / But I will see thee ere morning" (2.4.21–2). In John Marston's *Sophonisba* (1605), Jugurth, who commands one Lybian army, anticipates that Asdrubal's own Lybian faction will "hew vs all to peeces" (C4v). See Charles Edelman, ed., *The Stukeley Plays: The Battle of Alcazar by George Peele; The famous history of the life and death of Captain Thomas Stukeley* (Manchester: Manchester University Press, 2005);

material interaction between the play's hews and hues fosters a connection between environmentally destructive labor and the early modern racialization of African bodies. In the sixteenth century, Christian Europeans had already begun to use the scriptural "Curse of Ham," Noah's declaration that Ham's son Canaan and his descendants shall be "servant[s] of servants," to link black skin with enslavement.[6] By the eighteenth century, the Curse of Ham and the punitive condemnation of the Gibeonites to be "hewers of wood and drawers of water" became the most popular justifications for enslaving Africans on the basis of race.[7] By the nineteenth century, the epithet "hewers of wood and drawers of water" named a racialized workforce enslaved by terror, whose labor was "necessary to the growth of capitalism."[8] But in the sixteenth century, this link between racialization and the damaging environmental labor of "hewing" was largely still emerging.[9] Through the violence it stages against a

---

Thomas Heywood, *The Fair Maid of the West, Parts I and II*, edited by Robert K. Turner Jr. (Lincoln, NE: University of Nebraska Press, 1967); John Marston, *The vvonder of vvomen or The tragedie of Sophonisba as it hath beene sundry times acted at the Blacke Friers* (London, 1606).

[6] Gen. 9:25, KJV. As David Goldenberg points out, scripture makes "no mention of a curse of blackness; it knows only a curse of slavery." Goldenberg shows that seventh-century Arabians are the first to link the curse's reference to servitude with Blackness, and that the curse eventually became "*the* ideological cornerstone for the justification of Black slavery" at the height of the English and American slave trade. Paul Freedman provides a useful discussion of the various interpretations of Ham's offense toward Noah, and affirms that while Ham has been historically interpreted as "the progenitor of the unfree of whatever race," he was viewed as the "ancestor of black slaves, as commonly argued from the sixteenth to the nineteenth century." See David Goldenberg, *The Curse of Ham* (Princeton, NJ: Princeton University Press, 2003), 168, 170, 175; Paul Freedman, *Images of the Medieval Peasant* (Stanford, CA: Stanford University Press, 1999), 93.

[7] See Mary Floyd-Wilson, *English Ethnicity and Race in Early Modern Drama* (Cambridge: Cambridge University Press, 2003), 10; Peter Linebaugh and Marcus Rediker, *The Many-Headed Hydra* (Boston, MA: Beacon Press, 1992), 42.

[8] Linebaugh and Rediker, *The Many-Headed Hydra*, 41–2.

[9] The "emergent" status of "race" in the early modern period is certainly debatable. In the same way that medievalists are accused of anachronism when discussing early forms of racism or racialization in medieval Europe, some early modern scholars are reluctant to use the term "race" when discussing the early modern period for the same reasons: "Medieval time, on the wrong side of rupture, is...shunted aside as the detritus of a pre-Symbolic era falling outside the signifying systems issued by modernity, and reduced to the role of a historical trace undergirding the recitation of modernity's arrival" (Heng 21). For some early modern scholars, the *early modern* period is simply not yet modern enough to bear the history and context for a discussion of "race." But on the other hand, the work done by medievalists like Cord J. Whitaker and Geraldine Heng makes a convincing case not only for using the term "race" in the premodern historical context of medieval Europe but also for rejecting its anachronistic connotations. Whitaker studies medieval racism through metaphors of Blackness, which function as a "rhetorical mirage" that "funnels material reality through a set of material condi-tions...that produce illusions that engage the imagination" (Whitaker 5). Heng argues that in a mod-ern context it would be irresponsible to refrain from using the term "race": "the refusal of race destigmatizes the impacts and consequences of certain laws, acts, practices, and institutions in the medieval period, so that we cannot name them for what they are, and makes it impossible to bear adequate witness to the full meaning of the manifestations and phenomena they install" (Heng 23). See Cord J. Whitaker, *Black Metaphors: How Modern Racism Emerged from Medieval Race-Thinking* (Philadelphia, PA: University of Pennsylvania Press, 2019); Geraldine Heng, *The Invention of Race in the European Middle Ages* (Cambridge: Cambridge University Press, 2018).

dual human and environmental body, facilitated by the homophonic slippage between "hew" and "hue," Shakespeare's play reveals how early material constructions of African Moors both generated and reflected signs of environmental degradation.

In this chapter, I offer further insight into the link between the theatrical construction of early modern forms of racial difference and environmental degradation by showing how the stage's physical materials for representing African Moors relied upon the exploitation of European and colonial environments. Two plays in particular, *Titus Andronicus* and Thomas Dekker's *Lust's Dominion* (1600), each written during the height of the timber crisis in Elizabethan England, depend on physical and linguistic technologies to connect the materials used to represent the black skin of African Moors onstage with their ecological and social price tag.[10] By focusing on the imported wooden ingredients that constituted the black skin worn by the White actors who played Aaron and Eleazar—Moors who have been both reduced by critics to racist representations of dark-hearted villains and at the same time admired for their rhetoric and intelligence—I investigate how the materials of the stage may have mediated early modern representations and interpretations of emergent racial categories.[11] Through reorienting our understanding of Aaron and Eleazar around the wooden commodities that may have constituted their black skin in performance—namely, cork and galls—I hope to show how natural commodities dictate and influence an emergent racial discourse on the English stage.

The contemporary demand for foreign galls reframes our understanding of nature's role in representing Moors like Eleazar and Aaron on the English stage. Galls, as early modern playwrights would have known, were common ingredients in both ink and blackface cosmetic recipes of the period. Eleazar and Aaron are two of several Moors of the English stage whose black skin associates them with a discursive deception, such as forgery or the

---

[10] Thomas Dekker, *Lust's Dominion; or, The Lascivious Queen*, in *The Dramatic Works of Thomas Dekker*, vol. 4. Edited by Fredson Bowers (Cambridge: Cambridge University Press, 1961), 114–230.

[11] Emily Bartels suggests that *Titus Andronicus* "does not challenge the racial stereotype" associated with Blackness, though she later revises her argument to offer a more nuanced reading, where "interpretations of the Moor happen *inside*, not *outside*, the cultural moment." Ian Smith argues that Aaron is also "drawn from the exodus narrative, of Aaron the eloquent spokesman, the resistor in history's mimetic drama of ethnic and racial oppression." See Emily Bartels, "Making More of the Moor: Aaron, Othello, and Renaissance Refashionings of Race," *Shakespeare Quarterly*, Vol. 41, No. 4 (1990), 442; Emily Bartels, *Speaking of the Moor: From Alcazar to Othello* (Philadelphia, PA: University of Pennsylvania Press, 2008), 99; Ian Smith, *Race and Rhetoric in the Renaissance: Barbarian Errors* (New York: Palgrave Macmillan, 2009), 129.

dissemination of inauthentic publications.[12] Eleazar issues and distributes printed texts in order to gain leverage and power, and Aaron forges a letter to frame the Andronicii for a crime they did not commit. Eleazar even hints at the material technology responsible for his black skin when he refuses to "digest this Gall" (1.2.163) of banishment, and hopes that his revenge on Cardinal Mendoza for "this disgrace, / Shall dye [his] soule, as Inky as my face" (1.2.190–1). Punning on the material and humoral associations of "gall," Eleazar betrays an anxiety about how his audience will read or interpret his black body—his "inky" face. By calling attention to galls as a potential material ingredient in his own complexion, the actor playing Eleazar in blackface invites audiences to reflect on the metonymic association between the specific provenance of galls and the Moor he embodies on stage. Eleazar's pun also links his dark skin to the utilities and assumptions associated with imported galls in early modern England. But whereas imported Aleppo galls were valued for yielding a more permanent and endurable ink on paper, the potential use of galls in performance produces the opposite effect when signifying black skin on stage. When worn by an actor playing a Moor, galls mediate the meaning of black skin. Aaron and Eleazar may attempt to use ink to assert a single dominating narrative about themselves, but they also undermine those narratives, and open them to an expansive array of environmental, social, political, and humoral connotations.

Galls were not the only wooden commodities used in blackface cosmetics on the early modern stage. Cork wood, which did not grow in England, and which had been regularly imported to England from Portugal before the English trade embargo with the Iberian peninsula, was also likely used to represent Moors on stage, and similarly reinforces a metonymic association between populations of Moors and the materials used to represent them. If cork was used to represent Aaron's black skin on stage, then the play's discursive "hues" and "hews" might operate in a similar fashion to Eleazar's "gall" by linking black skin with a specific provenance of cork (Portugal) with a significant population of Moors. Aaron's pun ties his black "hue" not only to the violent hewing he orchestrates against the Romans but also to the material and environmental hewing that a White actor playing a Moor likely required for a cosmetic paint made of wooden ingredients. The theatricality of Aaron's false black skin showcases his control in managing his own representation at

---

[12] Other examples include Zanthia in John Fletcher, Nathan Field, and Philip Massinger's *The Knight of Malta* (1647), Beaupre (as the Moor Calista) in Philip Massinger's *The Parliament of Love* (1624), and Zisco in Samuel Harding's *Sicily and Naples, or The Fatal Union* (1618).

the same time that it operates as a racist justification for his villainy. As White actors in blackface, the characters Aaron and Eleazar each potentially exploit the materials that might compose their dark skin. Aaron's manipulation of the woods outside of Rome situates him in complicated relationship with the natural world, which is akin to Eleazar's relationship with galls and his manipulation of print.

A growing body of research emphasizes how the emergent status of "race" in the early modern period coalesced with the emergent status of the "human," which was ontologically indistinct from the natural world.[13] But in *Titus Andronicus*, Aaron embodies the fluid complexity of these emerging racial and ecological discourses. Aaron is aligned with the non-human natural world not only because he is a White actor in blackface who is defined by the hues (and hews) required to darken his complexion before a given performance; he also vows to live as a single father on what nature provides. On the other hand, Aaron is a true husbandman, a master at manipulating and exploiting his environments to gain his revenge. Aaron is also routinely positioned as an Other in Rome by the Andronicii, even though he is arguably the play's best father, and displays his most honest self before he is planted in the earth. Aaron's proximity to the natural world and his complex relationship with it showcases the degree to which a modern racial ideology relies upon environmental violence. The modern concept of racial difference cannot be apprehended within an ontological framework where humans and nature are indistinct. The material representation of Aaron and Eleazar both facilitates and exposes the environmental violence necessary to bring cork, galls, (and by extension) stage Moors to England. Aaron's ambiguous relationship to nature is comparable to Eleazar's ambiguous relationship with the written word because of how both Moors deliberately exploit the wooden commodities upon which their theatrical representation potentially depends. Their wordplay further catalyzes the discursive and environmental violence that (according to these plays) must accompany the formation of a racial discourse. A hierarchy of one group of humans over another cannot exist without the damage dealt by these puns, which conflate the hued skin of Moors with a tree's hewn limbs, humoral gall with imported galls, and Black characters of the stage with black characters of the page.

---

[13] Jean Feerick's work is most prominent in showing how early modern racial logic tied a discourse of "blood" and nobility to land and plant imagery. Much of the recent scholarly work on grafting in early modern England demonstrates how hierarchies in nature are appropriated for an emergent racial discourse to describe categorical differences between humans. See Chapter 1. Jean E. Feerick, *Strangers in Blood: Relocating Race in the Renaissance* (Toronto: University of Toronto Press, 2010).

Cork and Moors on the Early Modern Stage

Although "race" bore a different connotation in early modern England than it does today, markers of racialized difference were already emerging. Scholars have shown that early modern racial categories were rarely fully signified by skin color, and often conflated or intersected with gender, nationality, religion, class or nobility, and even political affiliation.[14] But whereas most scholars discuss race as a deliberate and discursive social construction which justifies patriarchal, colonial, or class oppression, I believe we have more to gain by asking not what race is for, but rather: what are the materials race uses?[15] Cork is one substance whose use in blackface cosmetics may have issued some important consequences for the fluid racial discourse of the late sixteenth century. For example, if cork was used by White actors to play Moors, it likely fashioned an associative link between the Moor character and the specific provenance from which cork derived. Furthermore, cork also may have created an association on the stage between Moor characters and the specific uses to which these materials were put in English culture, which included enterprises linked to expanding trade and the overconsumption of wooden commodities.

The White actor playing Aaron the Moor during any one of the several performances that *Titus Andronicus* enjoyed during Shakespeare's lifetime may have used any number of prosthetic devices to represent Aaron's black hue. Soot, which was used to blacken faces in village festivals during the mid-sixteenth century, was later abandoned for black velvet masks, gloves, and stockings.[16] Pleasance, "a fine, gauze-like material" used to represent Black Moors during a 1510 revels at Whitehall, was preferable at court to a substance like soot.[17] A 1598 inventory of Philip Henslowe's includes "Moores lymes," which was presumably some type of black cloth for representing Moors.[18] Robert Greene's *Orlando Furioso* (1591) includes a scene where

---

[14] See Bartels, *Speaking of the Moor*, 2008; Kim F. Hall, *Things of Darkness: Economies of Race and Gender in Early Modern England* (Ithaca, NY: Cornell University Press, 1995); Ayanna Thompson, *Performing Race and Torture on the Early Modern Stage* (New York: Routledge, 2008); Matthieu Chapman, *Anti-Black Racism in Early Modern English Drama: The Other "Other"* (New York: Routledge, 2017).

[15] I am indebted to Miles Grier for posing this question to his 2017 SAA Panel on Race and Materiality.

[16] Eldred Jones, *Othello's Countrymen: The African in English Renaissance Drama* (London: Oxford University Press, 1965), 120.

[17] Ian Smith, "Othello's Black Handkerchief," *Shakespeare Quarterly*, Vol. 64, No. 1 (Spring 2013), 12.

[18] Virginia Mason Vaughan, *Performing Blackness on English Stages, 1500–1800* (Cambridge: Cambridge University Press, 2005), 10.

Orlando disguises himself as a Moor using only a "scarfe before his face" (ll. 1350). But cosmetics were also an option, and playwrights often incorporated popular cosmetic recipes into their plays.[19] Several early modern English cosmetic recipes called for imported ingredients, which were associated with a specific provenance, and which may have informed how Aaron's black "hue" and Eleazar's "inky" face were understood in relation to the stage's participation in an expanding economy of wood.[20]

A number of scholars—including Dympna Callaghan, Farah Karim-Cooper, Virginia Mason Vaughan, Andrea Stevens, and Richard Blunt—have proposed that Elizabethan actors may have used burnt cork to darken their white skin in order to play African Moors.[21] If cork was used, the cork most likely came from Portugal, since cork oak did not grow in England, and since the fifteenth-century Anglo-Iberian cork trade is well documented.[22] Thus, Aaron and Eleazar may have embodied a material and commercial triangulation between England, the Iberian peninsula (from which the English had once imported cork), and parts of Africa, where the English were increasing trade.

The history of Anglo-Iberian trade relations provides an important context to critical speculations that cork was used as a cosmetic ingredient on the early modern stage to represent African Moors, who had occupied the Iberian peninsula for centuries. As a cosmetic agent on stage, cork may have cemented

---

[19] Kimberly Poitevin shows how Jonson very likely consulted Ruscelli's or Platt's cosmetic recipes in order to parrot them on stage in several plays, including *Cynthia's Revels* (1603), *Catiline* (1611), and *The Devil is an Ass* (1616). See Kimberly Poitevin, "Inventing Whiteness: Cosmetics, Race, and Women in Early Modern England," *Journal for Early Modern Cultural Studies*, Vol. 11, No. 1 (Spring/Summer 2011), 75.

[20] One recipe used "To make the Face Fresh and Ruddy" required "Brazeel-Wood." See Hannah Wooley, *The accomplish'd ladies delight in preserving, physick, beautifying and cookery* (London, 1683), F10r. One recipe for a "water that will make the face redde and glisteryng" calls for "an vnce of Brasill that is good, ten Cloues orientall, and ten graines of Nasturtium, otherwise called Cardamom." See Girolamo Ruscelli, *The seconde part of the Secretes of Master Alexis of Piemont*, 1560, B1v. Cloves were native and specific to the Moluccas, and cardamom was native to Southeast Asia.

[21] Dympna Callaghan, *Shakespeare Without Women: Representing Gender and Race on the Renaissance Stage* (London: Routledge, 2000), 78; Farah Karim-Cooper, "'This alters not thy beauty': Face-paint, Gender, and Race in Richard Brome's *The English Moor*," *Early Theater*, Vol. 10, No. 2 (2007), 147; Vaughan, *Performing Blackness on English Stages*, 11; Andrea Stevens, *Inventions of the Skin: The Painted Body in Early English Drama* (Edinburgh: Edinburgh University Press, 2013), 91; Richard Blunt, "The Evolution of Blackface Cosmetics on the Early Modern Stage," in *The Materiality of Color: The Production, Circulation, and Application of Dyes and Pigments, 1400–1800*, edited by Andrea Feeser, Maureen Daly Goggin, and Beth Fowkes Tobin (Burlington, VT: Ashgate, 2012), 222.

[22] For more on the fifteenth-century Anglo-Iberian cork trade, see Wendy R. Childs, "Anglo-Portuguese Trade in the Fifteenth Century," *Transactions of the Royal Historical Society*, Vol. 2 (1992), 204, 210; V. M. Shillington and A. B. Wallis Chapman, *The Commercial Relations of England and Portugal* (London: Routledge, 1907), 39; Jennifer C. Geouge, "Anglo-Portuguese Trade During the Reign of Joao I of Portugal, 1385–1433," in *The New Middle Ages: England and Iberia in the Middle Ages, 12th–15th Century: Cultural and Political Exchanges*, edited by Maria Bullon-Fernandez (New York: Palgrave Macmillan, 2007), 121.

a material link between African Moors and the Iberian peninsula in the English imagination, prompting Protestant audiences to associate Moors with Catholicism as well as Islam. The benevolence of fifteenth-century Anglo-Portuguese trade relations was owed in part, as Wendy Childs argues, to the close political ties that had solidified after English Crusaders helped drive Islamic Moors from Portugal during the Reconquest.[23] The geographical presence of Iberian cork forests may have even functioned as a symbolic religious border before the Moors were expelled; J. R. McNeill argues "the frontier between Christian and Muslim powers in medieval Spain was often a parklike expanse of cork oak woodland."[24] Cork was a monopolized trade under King John II of Portugal in the late fifteenth century, the profits of which financed the king's "imports of copper for his new naval ordnance."[25] Several seventeenth-century English sources identify cork as a main import, although they remain nebulous about demand, quantity, and the purposes to which cork was put in England.[26] But as the sixteenth century wore on, a desire for Portuguese merchandise became laced with appetites for new commodities, spawned by Portuguese colonial expansion.[27] Eventually, motivated in part by an embargo on trade with the Iberian peninsula, the English would follow the Portuguese example and bypass their former intermediary for direct access to commodities from Africa, Asia, and the Mediterranean. In the case of *Lust's Dominion*—a play that ends with the newly installed King Philip banishing "all the Moors" (5.3.183) from Spain in reaction to Eleazar's rule (a pronouncement that anticipated Philip III's actual banishment of Moors from Spain in 1609)—the use of cork to represent Moors potentially undermines King Philip's decree by suggesting that one can separate the Moors from Iberia, but one cannot separate Iberia from the Moors.[28]

[23] Childs, "Anglo-Portuguese Trade," 197. In addition to identifying the Portuguese exportation of cork to England (204, 210), Childs also notes the 1386 Treaty of Windsor and the marriage between Joao I and Lancaster's English daughter Philippa as important markers for improving trade relations.

[24] J. R. McNeill, "Woods and Warfare in World History," *Environmental History*, Vol. 9, No. 3 (July 2004), 405.

[25] Richard Barker, "Sources for Lusitanian Shipbuilding," *Proceedings of the International Symposium "Archaeology of Medieval and Modern Ships of Iberian-Atlantic Tradition,"* edited by F. Alvez (Lisbon, 1998), 223.

[26] Both Roberts and Malynes list cork as one of the many commodities offered by Spain and Portugal. See Lewes Roberts, *The Merchants Mappe of Commerce* (London, 1638), Aa2v; Gerard Malynes, *Consuetudo, vel lex mercatoria, or The ancient law-merchant* (London, 1622), H5r.

[27] As Robert Brenner points out, it was only through trade with the Iberian peninsula "that English merchants initially sought those highly valued products of the Far East and the Americas." See Robert Brenner, *Merchants and Revolution* (London: Verso, 2003), 46. By the end of the fifteenth century, along with providing the English with cork, wax, wine, figs, and raisins, Portugal also began to provide sugar and other semi-luxury goods for the English (Childs, "Anglo-Portuguese Trade in the Fifteenth Century," 211).

[28] Bartels, *Speaking of the Moor*, 118.

If cork was used as a stage cosmetic, Moors on the English stage also may have been materially tied to a host of English industries that relied on wood to generate capital, including trades that were essential for English exploration and colonial expansion. Cork was used in fishing (for nets and lures) and shoemaking; it was used to stop barrels and bottles; and it was believed to possess medicinal properties and meteorological value. It was also used in shipbuilding.[29] As a navigational tool, William Barlow considered cork "very requisite for many purposes that euery Traueller either by land or especially by sea should always haue," especially since cork and a common sewing needle could be used to manufacture an improvised compass.[30] It is not difficult to imagine actors appropriating cork from fishing or shoemaking trades to use on the stage. Although cork was available in London, an embargo on Anglo-Iberian trade in 1585 likely drove the English either to seek it elsewhere, or else to learn to do without it.

If cork was scarce in England because of an embargo on trade, other species of wood were scarce because of a general overconsumption of timber in England, and a lack of sustainable forest management practices. In turn, the scarcity of wood in England drove English endeavors of economic and colonial expansion abroad. According to Eoin Neeson, England's timber crisis had its roots in the new attention on building ships to strengthen the English Navy, which coincided with corruption within the forest administration. The

---

[29] Philemon Holland's 1601 translation of Pliny's *The Historie of the World* notes some of the ancient uses of cork—as buoys, as stops for bottles and barrels, and as shoe-soles—which lasted into the early modern period. See Pliny, *The historie of the vvorld Commonly called, the naturall historie of C. Plinius Secundus* (London, 1601), Rr3r. For cork as a shipbuilding material, see James J. Parsons, "The Cork Oak Forests and the Evolution of the Cork Industry in Southern Spain and Portugal," *Economic Geography*, Vol. 38, No. 3 (July 1962), 202; Barker, "Sources for Lusitanian Shipbuilding," 216. For cork as a fishing lure and net, see Juliana Berners, *The booke of hauking, hunting and fysshyng, with all the properties and medecynes that are necessary to be kept* (1556), L2v–L3r; Leonard Mascall, *A booke of fishing with hooke & line, and of all other instruments thereunto belonging* (London: 1590), F4v. Wendy Childs notes that cork that was used for floats and buoys by the English came primarily from Portugal and Seville. See Wendy R. Childs, *Anglo-Castilian Trade in the Later Middle Ages* (Manchester: Manchester University Press, 1978), 122. For cork as a bottle stopper, see Parsons, "Cork Oak Forests," 207; Americo M. S. Carvalho Mendes and Jose A. R. Graca, "Cork Bottle Stoppers and Other Cork Products," in *Cork Oak Woodlands on the Edge: Ecology, Adaptive Management, and Restoration*, edited by James Aaronson, Joao S Pereira, and Juli G. Pausas (Washington, DC: Island Press, 2009). Cork-soled shoes were incredibly popular among noblewomen in fourteenth- and fifteenth-century Spain, though the fashion clearly caught on in England by the sixteenth century (Parsons 206). Pliny also mentions medicinal uses for cork, including for the repression of bloody flux (Pliny Q5v). John Gerard notes a similar recipe, where cork can work "against the bloudy flix." Gerard also clarifies that cork was good insulation for shoes. See John Gerard, *The herball or Generall historie of plantes* (London, 1633), Vuuuu6r. Cork was also used to fashion an early crude barometric device meant to predict rainfall. See Anonymous, *A table plainly teaching ye making and use of a wetherglas* (London, 1631).

[30] William Barlow, *Magneticall aduertisements: or Diuers pertinent obseruations, and approued experiments, concerning the natures and properties of the load-stone* (London, 1618), F1r.

result shaped how the English regarded Ireland as a timber reserve ripe for exploitation, which in turn informed the frequency and quantity with which England began increasing trade with the African continent.[31] The environmental crisis in England provided a strong motivation for economic and colonial expansion, and helped to shape the racial discourse playing out in the theater. On stage, the link between an environmental and a racial justification for colonial enterprises is borne out in the representational conventions, which were already immersed in the consumer practices of London's expanding marketplace.

Aaron and Eleazar: Embodying the "Indistinct Human" on the Early Modern Stage

While cosmetics involving burnt cork or galls were likely used to darken the skin of White actors on the English stage, skin color was by no means a stable marker of difference or of "race" in the early modern period. (Nor was it the only marker.) In *Titus Andronicus*, Aaron's black "hue" may position him as an outsider in Rome, but the "hews" he orchestrates against the Andronicii and his environment also signal his *belonging* in a city that burns hewn bodies atop piles of hewn wood. Concentrating on these materials that discourses of race make use of in early modern England allows modern audiences to see the environmental violence that attends the formation of a racial hierarchy. *Titus Andronicus* suggests that the ontological categories of the human and the natural must be severed—and violently—before a modern ideology of "race" can develop. The racist logic that allows one group of humans to see themselves as superior to another group of humans is negotiated in *Titus* along with an ontological shift in which humans begin to see themselves as superior to the natural world. Shakespeare's play engages with this ontological shift through staging Aaron's dubious relationship with his environment. Aaron's investment in protecting his son induces a shift in his attitude toward nature; his difference in Rome becomes marked by the communion he holds with nature when he attempts to be its steward rather than its master. Violence in this play, which is almost always environmentally inflected, serves to racialize Aaron's difference. But Aaron's environmental affiliation only reinforces the fluidity of early modern racial markers.

---

[31] Eion Neeson, "Woodland in History and Culture," in *Nature in Ireland: A Scientific and Cultural History*, edited by John Wilson Foster (Dublin: The Lilliput Press, 1997), 139–40.

An unstable ontology of the "human" during this period only underscores the ephemerality of the play's racial categorization. As several scholars have pointed out, this period marked a transition for the category of the "human," which was more often seen as *a part of* the natural world, rather than *apart from* it.[32] Jean Feerick's reading of *Titus Andronicus*, which demonstrates how the play's racial logic is rooted in the overlapping discourses of horticulture and nobility, foregrounds an important ontological premise of early modern thought: during this period, the ontological category of the "human" was indistinct from the modern category of "nature." Shakespeare and Dekker were writing during a moment *before* "the differences structuring categories like human, animal, and plant would be emphasized and reinforced, and systems of discrimination would be set into place to perform the work of assigning each kind of body a discrete place within a vast and all-encompassing taxonomic order."[33] Nature, then, was both a human and a non-human conception at the same time that travel writers, scholars, and playwrights were calling into question the subjectivity (or humanity) of Black Africans.[34]

Within Rome's wooden body politic, before an English audience feeling the economic and ecological effects of a wood shortage, *Titus Andronicus* conflates human and environmental violence, and registers the depletion of wood as a loss of body parts. Lavinia's rape and mutilation, for example, is also emphasized as a loss of limbs from a healthy body politic. Lavinia's mangled form arrests the gaze of an audience for whom wood has become precious. When Marcus beholds her bereft "of her two branches" (2.4.18), when Chiron cruelly mocks her "stumps" (2.4.4), when Aaron boasts how she was "washed, and cut, and trimmed; and 'twas / Trim sport for them which had the doing of it" (5.1.95–6), and when Titus regards her mangled form and asks, "What fool hath added water to the sea / Or brought a faggot to bright-burning Troy?" (3.1.69–70), they invite audiences to read Lavinia as a representation of Rome's (and England's) disjointed and unnatural body politic.

---

[32] For examples of how early modern culture positioned itself within rather than outside of the natural world, see Jean Feerick and Vin Nardizzi, eds., *The Indistinct Human in Renaissance Literature* (New York: Palgrave Macmillan), 2012. More recently, Maisano and Campana's collection on *Renaissance Posthumanism* also offers examples of an "indistinct" human ontology. Renaissance humanists were invested in asserting an anthropocentric worldview of human exceptionalism, but not exclusively. See Kenneth Gouwens, "What Posthumanism Isn't: On Humanism and Human Exceptionalism in the Renaissance," in *Renaissance Posthumanism*, edited by Joseph Campana and Scott Maisano (New York: Fordham University Press, 2016), 50–1.

[33] Jean Feerick, "Botanical Shakespeare: The Racial Logic of Plant Life in *Titus Andronicus*," *South Central Review*, Vol. 26, No. 1 and 2 (Winter and Spring 2009), 82.

[34] Chapman, *Anti-Black Racism in Early Modern English Drama*, 3.

Although Aaron's skin color is neither a marker of his "race" in the play nor what determines his behavior, he nevertheless offers his "hue" as an explanation for his villainy. When Aaron tricks Titus into sacrificing his hand—one of his "withered herbs...meet for plucking up" (3.1.178–9)—in exchange for (the heads of) Quintus and Martius, Aaron points to his hue to justify his double hewing: "Let fools do good and fair men call for grace; / Aaron will have his soul black like his face" (3.1.205–6). Similar to Eleazar's reference to his "Inky face," Aaron's reference to his own hue seems to invoke an older theatrical tradition, and collapses a represented African Moor with devils and vice characters who blackened their faces in medieval theatrical performances to signify their moral aberration.[35] Through matching his outer and inner darkness, Aaron conflates his black hue with the hewing of Titus's hand. At the same time, the pun he visualizes for his audience between his successful "hew" and his black "hue" underscores his wit and intelligence, qualities that were also associated with black skin and the melancholic disposition resulting from black bile during the period.[36] The hewing he performs against the bodies of the Andronicii extends his exploitation of the wooded space outside of Rome back into and onto the body politic. Aaron's crude husbandry supplants the natural world and punishes the most loyal arm of the Roman military with a few simple strokes.

At the same time that the hewn and burnt cork (which might have supplied the material makeup of Aaron's physical hue on stage) seems to position him within the natural world, the hewings that he orchestrates in the play also situate him above nature. The play's scenes in the wooded space on the outskirts of Rome depict Aaron's preoccupation with manipulating and exploiting his environment in order to reap a hasty and profitable revenge against the Andronicus family. Aaron buries a bag of gold beneath a tree (2.3.2), which he hopes will yield a profitable revenge. Beneath the same tree, Aaron digs a "subtle hole," covers it "with rude-growing briers" (2.3.199–200), and transforms the earth into a symbol of transgressive female sexuality, which operates as the site of both Tamora's revenge and Lavinia's rape. Aaron reshapes this landscape, both physically and rhetorically, in order to profit in his revenge. As a "swallowing womb" (2.3.239) that entraps, condemns, and ingests (rather than births) the bodies of Bassianus, Martius, and Quintus, Aaron's pit—which is also called a "loathsome pit" (2.3.176), an "unhallowed and bloodstained

[35] Annette Drew-Bear, *Painted Faces on the Renaissance Stage: The Moral Significance of Face-Painting Conventions* (Lewisburg, PA: Bucknell University Press, 1994), 18; Stevens, *Inventions of the Skin*, 92.

[36] Floyd-Wilson, *English Ethnicity and Race in Early Modern Drama*, 69.

hole" (210), a "den...of blood and death" (215–16), a "detested, dark, blood-drinking pit" (224), a "fell devouring receptacle" (235), and a "gaping hollow of the earth" (249)—bears the mark of Aaron's environmental penetration. Aaron's complicity in Lavinia's rape manifests itself through his subtle terra-forming. He rehearses her rape through digging in the earth.

On stage, Aaron is both immersed within and situated above the natural world. The wooden ingredients responsible for Aaron's skin on stage fail to distinguish him from the play's violent economy of vengeful hewings. What *does* distinguish Aaron in Rome is his investment in being a father, a responsibility that also induces a change in Aaron's attitude toward the natural world. Once he learns he has a son, Aaron's black "hue" becomes unmoored from its associations with moral aberration and environmental exploitation, and instead becomes affiliated with honesty and environmental stewardship. In a play where Roman, Goth, and Moor each commit heinous acts of violence against human and nature, Aaron's revised attitude toward his environment becomes his most glaring trait of distinction. The nurse who brings the boy to Aaron reinforces the play's theatrical and racist associations between Blackness and evil. She exclaims the child is "A devil" (4.2.66), "A joyless, dismal, black, and sorrowful issue," and even implores Aaron to "christen it with [his] dagger's point" (4.2.68, 72) on Tamora's behalf.

The violent death of the infant, the play suggests, is required to prevent Saturninus's discovery of Tamora's infidelity, and to ensure that a Black Moor will not have a claim to the empire. The nurse also suggests that a violent death is required simply because it is a Black child. In response, Aaron interrogates the nurse's racist interpretation of color and asks, "Is black so base a hue?" (4.2.73). In one of the few moments of the play where Aaron prevents rather than instigates violence, he aims to christen Blackness with a different connotation, one predicated on its permanence rather than its fluidity. To prevent the dagger from validating the nurse's prejudicial judgment of the "black" and therefore "sorrowful issue," Aaron tells Chiron and Demetrius:

> What, what, you sanguine, shallow-hearted boys,
> You white-limed walls, you alehouse painted signs!
> Coal black is better than another hue
> In that it scorns to bear another hue;
> For all the water in the ocean
> Can never turn the swan's black legs to white,
> Although she lave them hourly in the flood.
>
> (4.2.99–105)

For Aaron, black is superior to white because it cannot be inscribed upon with any other color. His color, he believes, affords him the privilege of a private and inner self.[37] He is proud that he will never blush, as Chiron does when he reflects upon his mother's newborn. For Aaron, white is a "treacherous hue, that will betray with blushing / The close enacts and counsels of thy heart" (4.2.119–20). The irony, of course, is that the actor's hue is not permanent, and *will* wash off at the end of the performance. Thus, even his explicit attempt to rhetorically position black above white is undermined by the theatricality of his hue and the material that makes him appear black.

Aaron's paternalism over his environment is reinforced when his child's life is threatened. When Aaron and the baby are discovered by the Goths, Lucius calls for "A halter, soldiers, hang him on this tree, / And by his side his fruit of bastardy" (5.1.47–8). In yet another instance of metaphorical violence, Lucius entertains the ontological position that conflates humans and plants when he proposes they literally graft Aaron's "base fruit" (5.1.43) to a tree. It is one more collision between woody plants and human bodies; but it is also a proposal that the play will not allow. Aaron's protection of his son, according to Jean Feerick, demonstrates how he is similar to Titus in his aspirations for his offspring; Titus has "spent his life promoting the advancement of a family of warriors up the botanical ranks, hoping to one day graft them onto the royal cedar."[38] But Aaron, who is either fed up with figurative language or simply knows that the graft has already borne fruit, resists the grafting metaphor that Lucius imposes: "Touch not the boy, he is of royal blood" (5.1.49). The confession Aaron delivers will spare them both from the tree; he is fated to be planted in the earth and starve. With a royal son, Aaron feels justified in sacrificing himself so that his son may live. Aaron also seems to know that Lucius subscribes to the same ideology about bloodlines. Even though Lucius has no reason to trust Aaron—who "believest no god" (5.1.71)—Aaron knows that the distinction his son's "royal blood" affords him means something to Lucius. If the child's royal blood is meant to have some legitimacy over the charge of "bastardy," if the child is meant to pose a threat to the future of Rome, and if the child is meant to hold dominion over humans and nature, then he must, the play suggests, be distinguished from the natural world. Convincing the Goths to spare his son's life also spares one more tree from being grossly misappropriated by the unsustainable ecological rhetoric of Rome.

---

[37] Stevens, *Inventions of the Skin*, 97. [38] Feerick, "Botanical Shakespeares," 97.

To preserve his son's life, Aaron eventually reveals the counsels of his own heart in an honest confession at the end of the play. Aaron's earlier soliloquies train his audience to read a correlation between his inner "soul" and his outward "face," a correlation he makes public when he spills his insides outward in order to save his child. In addition to naming several other atrocities not staged in the play, Aaron also confesses that he "begot" the child (5.1.87), "wrote the letter," "hid the gold" (5.1.106–7), and "played the cheater for [Titus's] hand" (5.1.111). Aaron's honesty is important because it underscores how his son has caused a rupture of his principles. Aaron's black "hue" may scorn "to bear another hue," but Blackness is not a fixed signifier of deception and evil. His honesty underscores his new concern for the preservation of his child, as well as a new regard for nature as something to be dependent upon rather than something to exploit and manipulate. The infant's "hue bewray[s] whose brat" (5.1.28) he is, and the perceived insolubility of his black skin creates a problem in the play that cannot be solved with a disguise.[39] Aaron thus prepares the child for a pilferer-scavenger's diet:

> I'll make you feed on berries and on roots,
> And feed on curds and whey, and suck the goat,
> And cabin in a cave, and bring you up
> To be a warrior and command a camp.
>
> (4.2.179–82)

Aaron's determination to preserve his child makes him a better parent than both Titus, who slays first his son Mutius (1.1.295), then his daughter Lavinia (5.3.46), and Tamora, who demands her newborn's death, and who naively walks Chiron and Demetrius into Titus's kitchen. Aaron's brand of fatherhood also encompasses a unique pact with nature. He decides to live in secret, without agriculture, and to survive on what nature provides, or what he can steal from livestock. Imagining his life as a single father, Aaron supposes that the full potential of his child's military and political threat to Rome might be

---

[39] A consideration of the potential woodenness of some of the play's props only emphasizes the environmental hue of Aaron's stewardship over his son and the environment. If the infant was staged using a wooden doll, for example, then the child could even be read as the direct result of Aaron's hewing, the product of his illicit husbandry in the woods. Similarly, if the pie containing the flesh of Chiron and Demetrius that Titus serves to Tamora in the final act is also made of wood, it could accentuate Rome's (and London's) excessive consumption of wood by conflating the ingestion of wood with the taboo of cannibalism. Richard Brome's *The Antipodes* (1638) includes a scene where Peregrine stumbles into a playing company's tiring house and discovers "wooden pies" among the inventory (3.1.294). See Richard Brome, *The Antipodes* (1636), in *Three Renaissance Travel Plays*, edited by Anthony Parr (Manchester: Manchester University Press, 1995).

realized with little more than the pastoral fantasy of a cave to live in, a goat to suck, and a few berries and roots to sustain them both. As a father, Aaron shifts from perceiving himself as a black villain, who sets traps in the woods as a way of killing or framing his enemies in Rome, to perceiving himself instead as a resourceful thief, who must either live off of his own stewardship or else the stewardship of others. Once he becomes a father, his perception of nature as an abundant and exploitable resource shifts into something that is far more precious and scarce, since it must sustain him and his son.

Eleazar, Inkface, and the Manipulation of the Written Word

As I have shown above, Aaron's manipulation of his environments—from the woods where he ensnares the Andronicus family in his vengeful plot to the remote cave where he hopes to raise his son—works to destabilize the meaning of his black skin in the play. Although Eleazar never ventures into any kind of green space beyond the civic center in *Lust's Dominion*, he nevertheless relies on the manipulation of woody commodities to maintain power and to exact revenge. Like Aaron's dominion over his forested surroundings, Eleazar's control over gall, ink, and public texts might be read as an attempt to control the meaning of his black skin through controlling the material that constitutes it.

English playwrights likely contributed to the demand for galls—another material that race "uses" on the English stage—because of their importance as an ink ingredient.[40] Galls are bulbous growths on plants caused by parasitic insects. Like cork, galls also had a specific provenance, and may have been useful in creating blackface cosmetics on stage. Also like cork, galls on stage had the potential to link a Moor's black skin to various English industries, such as writing and husbandry. Although various kinds of galls were available

---

[40] One recipe for "black Ynk very good" calls for "three vnces of the waighttest Galles you can finde…two vnces of Romaine vitriolle…an vnce of Gomme Arabicke…and an vnce of the pill of Pomegranades" (Ruscelli, A1v). Galls and gum Arabic were common ink ingredients, and both were imported commodities. Botti et al. note that gum Arabic was found in "several species of African acacia trees, particularly the Senegal acacia." See Lorean Botti, Orietta Mantovani, and Daniele Ruggiero, "Calcium Phytate in the Treatment of Corrosion Caused by Iron Gall Inks: Effects on Paper," *Restaurator*, Vol. 26, No. 1 (January 2005), 45. Early modern English ink recipes would have contained several ingredients from Africa. See also Blunt 224; and Mitchell M. Harris, "The Expense of Ink and Wastes of Shame: Poetic Generation, Black Ink, and Material Waste in Shakespeare's Sonnets," in *The Materiality of Color: The Production, Circulation, and Application of Dyes and Pigments, 1400–1800*, edited by Andrea Feeser, Maureen Daly Goggin, and Beth Fowkes Tobin (Burlington, VT: Ashgate, 2012), 69. Blunt cites Johann Jacob Wecker's *Cosmeticks or, the Beautifying Part of Physick* (1660); Harris cites Wecker's *Eighteen Books of the Secrets of Art & Nature* (1660) translation.

in England, the best galls for ink-making, dyeing, and tanning were imported by the Levant Company, primarily from Aleppo, Tripoli, and Iskenderun.[41] In a play like *Lust's Dominion*, where the Moor Eleazar connects his bitter "Gall" (1.2.163) to his "inky" (1.2.191) face, the pun on the ink ingredient and the bodily humor links artificial blackness, anger, and ink.[42] Ink recipes proliferated in early modern England, and were common in books of housewifery, household chemistry, and magic.[43]

One recipe, dubbed "The best way to make Ink," from Johann Jacob Wecker's *Eighteen Books of the Secrets of Art & Nature* (1660), calls for "the best Galls," "Gum Arabick poudred half a pound, [and] Vitriol bruised eight ounces."[44] "The best galls" were presumably Aleppo Galls, thought to have the highest concentration of tannic acid.[45] Aleppo galls are the result of an extremely specific ecological relationship between a cynipid gall wasp— *Andricus Infectorius* or *Andricus tinctoriusnostris*—which induces a gall on the Aleppo Oak, *Quercus Infectoria* or *Quercus Lusitanica*.[46] This insect–plant ecology helped to make English trade with Aleppo viable and profitable for the Levant Company, because it yielded gall nuts that contained 70 percent tannins, compared to galls of Istria (40 percent) or Morea (30 percent) or even Bassora (25–30 percent), which were vastly inferior.[47] Playwrights likely made their own ink, and likely knew the foreign provenance of the imported ingredients.[48] This hierarchy of galls, which is only significant in an economic context, provided an ecological arena for early modern notions of botanical difference to take shape around constructions of economic value. The hierarchical thinking yielded from such economic-botanical logic is one way the materials of the stage might influence an early modern discourse of race. Some gall-inducing and host-plant relationships, the reasoning suggests, are simply better than others at supplying tannins for human use.

The strongest evidence we have that galls may have been used as a blackface cosmetic on the stage comes from a different recipe for "Waters that black

---

[41]   Alfred C. Wood, *A History of the Levant Company* (London: Frank Cass & Co., 1964), 76.

[42]   As Mitchell Harris points out, Shakespeare makes use of the gall pun more than once to emphasize a material link between an ingredient in ink and a bitter secretion of the body (Harris, "Expense of Ink," 70).

[43]   Harris, "Expense of Ink," 69.

[44]   Johann Jacob Wecker, *Eighteen Books of the Secrets of Art & Nature*, 1660, Tt1v.

[45]   Jonathan D. Briggs, "Historical Uses of Plant Galls," *Cecidology*, Vol. 1, No. 1 (Spring, 1986), 7.

[46]   Marcello Malpighi, *De Gallis: On Galls*, ed. and trans. Margaret Redfern, Alexander J. Cameron, and Kevin Down (London: Ray Society, 2008), 1.

[47]   Franco Brunello, *The Art of Dyeing in the History of Mankind*, trans. Bernard Hickey (Vicenza: N. Pozza, 1973), 355.

[48]   Mitchell Harris speculates that Shakespeare likely produced his own ink because Henslowe's diary does not include ink or paper as an expense (Harris, "The Expense of Ink," 69).

the Face," from Wecker's *Cosmeticks* (1660). The recipe instructs readers to extract "a most clear water, from green Walnut-shells and Gaules; with which if you wet the face or hands, they grow black by degrees, like to an Aethiopian; which if afterwards you would restore to their former whiteness, you must distil Vinegar, Juice of Lemmons, and Colophonia, and washing with that will take off the blackness."[49] Galls, along with walnuts and colophonia (a resin distilled from turpentine), were all natural commodities available in England.[50] But the English clearly preferred imported galls for their higher concentration of tannic acid. Thus, the foreign provenance of galls was widely known, and the use of galls by theater companies to portray black skin may have influenced how authors represented (or how audiences interpreted) Moors in performance.

Like cork, galls had a number of uses in early modern culture, which also may have influenced how black bodies were read on the English stage. In addition to their commercial use in inks, dyes, and tanning, galls were used to treat common afflictions like toothaches, and were even sources of food for livestock and humans.[51] Their chief utility was as an ingredient in recipes for iron gall inks, which were part of a material effort to create a more enduring, unified, and authoritative text. Iron gall inks were a relatively recent innovation in the early modern period. Developed during the Middle Ages, iron gall inks quickly superseded the use of carbon inks, which were "susceptible to spreading in the presence of humidity" and which "did not penetrate the support deeply and thus could be removed by washing, or even by simple abrasion."[52] Eventually, ink-makers discovered that "ferrous sulphate would react with tannic acid" found in gallnuts "to produce black particles"; this

---

[49] Johann Jacob Wecker, *Cosmeticks or, the beautifying part of physic*, 1660, D2r.

[50] While we now know that galls are growths on trees caused by parasitic insects, the early modern English were less certain. In his *Herbal*, John Gerard dedicates an entire chapter to the "Gall tree." Though he admits that "Of trees that bring forth Galls there be diuers sorts," and even notes that within galls, "there is also found a certaine excrescence of a light green colour, spongie and waterie, in the middle whereof now and then is found a little flie or worme," he nevertheless discusses the tree as if it were its own species, and galls as if they were the fruit of a tree, rather than the result of an insect–plant ecology (Gerard, Vuuuu6v). He also notes the popular early modern uses for galls; they are "fit for medicine, and to thicken skins with" (i.e. useful in tanning) and also notes "Galls are vsed in dying and colouring of sundry things, and in making of inke" (Gerard, Xxxxx1r). Marcello Malpighi was the first to determine the origin of insect-inducing galls in the seventeenth century. See Malpighi, *De Gallis*, 1.

The OED defines "colophony" as "the dark or amber-coloured resin obtained by distilling turpentine with water" ("colophony," n. *Oxford English Dictionary*).

[51] For toothaches, see Margaret M. Fagan, "The Uses of Insect Galls," *The American Naturalist*, Vol. 52, No. 614 (February–March 1918), 159; for galls as a food source for humans, see Rosalind Blanche, *Life in a Gall: The Biology and Ecology of Insects that Live in Plant Galls* (Collingwood, Vic.: Csiro Publishing, 2012), 8.

[52] Botti et al., "Calcium Phytate in the Treatment of Corrosion," 45.

would prevent carbon ink from browning over time, and improved the bond between the ink and the fibrous structure to which it adhered.[53] When texts were written using an inferior carbon ink (and when paper was difficult to acquire), old texts could be wiped away and simply written over, sometimes leaving traces of the original text behind. Palimpsests, which reveal the two conflated texts simultaneously, can yield an effect of "supersession" or of "untimely irruption."[54] But palimpsests became obsolete with the iron gall innovation. The popularity of iron gall inks can be seen as an attempt to produce a more stable and permanent authoritative text. This is perhaps why iron gall inks became normalized for legal documents in the eleventh century, and for bank notes in the twentieth century.[55] But if galls created a more authoritative written text, their potential role in representing Moors may have actually multiplied the valences attached to black skin on the English stage.

When Eleazar refuses to digest the "Gall" (1.2.163) of banishment, for example, he is likely referring to the common humoral definition of gall, which identified the bitterness associated with black bile, and which was believed to produce a melancholic disposition within the body. Eleazar's pun depends on the color black as the associative connection between the ink that required galls to manufacture and the internal bile that generates ire. As Robert Burton notes in *The Anatomy of Melancholy* (1621), gall was also associated with anger or choler: "Choler is hot and dry, bitter, begotten of the hotter parts of the chylus, and gathered to the gall: it helps the natural heat and senses, and serves to the expelling of excrements."[56] But to understand Eleazar solely as an angry Moor reduces his material complexity to a stereotype that bore little weight during the period. As Mary Floyd-Wilson has shown, English colonial and economic expansion promoted an increasingly unstable understanding of Blackness as a racial and ethnic signifier, especially as it related to the body's humors. A shifting geohumoral discourse sought to invert dominant notions of "northern 'whiteness' and English identity as barbaric, marginalized, and mutable" with notions of Blackness as a symbol of "wisdom, spirituality, and resolution."[57] *Lust's Dominion* likely registers a

[53] Botti et al., "Calcium Phytate in the Treatment of Corrosion," 45.

[54] Harris, *Untimely Matter*, 15.

[55] On legal documents in the eleventh century, see Botti et al., "Calcuim Phytate in the Treatment of Corrosion," 45. Fagan also notes: "In some places the law required that records be made with ink compounded of gall-nuts" (160). On bank notes in the twentieth century, see Briggs, "Historical Uses of Plant Galls," 6.

[56] Robert Burton, *The Anatomy of Melancholy* (1621), edited by Holbrook Jackson (1621; repr. New York: New York Review Books, 2001), 148.

[57] Floyd-Wilson, *English Ethnicity and Race in Early Modern Drama*, 11.

material cause of this shift; as colonial expansion prompted the English to recast Blackness in the terms of their own barbaric history, the blackness of "gall" materially associated the dark humoral condition with the increasing traffic of the imported natural commodity.

Lust's Dominion routinely exploits the associations between ink, black skin, and internal bodily humors. Eleazar's acquisition of the Spanish crown, for example, is only possible through his manipulation of writing and ink—the best, longest lasting, most durable, and most authoritative of which required Aleppo galls. Eleazar becomes king of Spain through disseminating and regulating publications in order to erode the legitimacy of Prince Philip's claim. Eleazar's "inkface"—a term coined by Miles P. Grier to denote the "shared field of blackface performance, tattooing, writing, and printing" that "enables a rich account of performances of literacy as rituals that invented an elastic racial category of illiterate, legible blacks"—represents his Blackness as a transferrable material.[58] Eleazar himself is obviously literate as a skilled rhetorician, but he is fooled nevertheless by the blackface disguises worn by Philip and Hortenzo. The conflation of his black skin with ink paired with his paranoid regulation of publications underscores his concern with how his black skin will be read and interpreted by an audience predisposed either to condemn or to celebrate him as a usurper. Meanwhile, Philip and Hortenzo infiltrate Eleazar's court and regain the Spanish throne by racially cross-dressing as Moors. Philip and Hortenzo's blackface performance calls attention to the theatricality of Eleazar's own black skin, while reinforcing black skin as a legible, textual, and interpretable surface.

If ink is one medium through which the English are attempting to revise their own colonial history as colonial subjects to Rome, as Grier suggests—if ink is one avenue through which human subjects become inhuman objects—then it is also worth considering the role that galls have in this process as well.[59] As Grier shows, the hegemony of exclusively *black* ink on exclusively *white* paper did not emerge until the early modern period. This new black and white binary not only facilitated an ongoing racial discourse, but was largely negotiated by the materials that were available for publication: "Producing texts that were for something other than luxury consumption

---

[58] Miles P. Grier, "Inkface: The Slave Stigma in England's Early Imperial Imagination," in *Scripturalizing the Human: The Written as the Political*, edited by Vincent L. Wimbush (New York: Routledge, 2015), 195.

[59] Grier, "Inkface," 195. Grier shows how inkface services the imperial invention of a racial hierarchy by associating ink with property and slavery. He argues, "producing and interpreting inkface helped Britons struggling with memories of their own past as tattooed slaves in ancient Rome by transferring the ink mark of servility to other ethnicities as a property of their character."

required the use of materials that were more abundant and less expensive. Black ink and bleached linen-rag paper served this industry better than more expensive parchment and colored inks made from rarer ingredients."[60] The Levant Company made quality galls readily (and cheaply) available for English consumption. Grier invokes a number of Black characters from the early modern stage—including Aaron and Eleazar—who were staged "before audiences who did not, themselves, need print literacy to understand the illiterate and gullible blackamoors they watched."[61] But if even the most illiterate audiences could see how Aaron and Eleazar's words come back to bite them in the end of their respective plays, audiences would also be able to see these Moors as closely associated with the material act of writing.

Eleazar's concern about how his audience will read him is not baseless. Before Eleazar is banished from Spain, Cardinal Mendoza points to the Moor's black body as evidence for his offenses: "His treasons," the Cardinal argues, "need no tryal, they're too plain" (1.2.157). Eleazar perceives himself as the victim of a prejudiced gaze that regards his Blackness as evidence of his prodigality and his promiscuity. He is not seen in public but

> ... every hissing tongue cries, There's the Moor,
> That's he that makes a Cuckold of our King,
> There go's the Minion of the Spanish Queen;
> That's the black Prince of Divels, there go's hee
> That on smooth boies, on Masks and Revellings
> Spends the Revenues of the King of Spain.
>
> (1.1.87–92)

During the play's original performance, Eleazar's affair with the queen may have been "too plain" due to the black and white cosmetic materials (one transforming a male actor into a Moor and the other into a woman) that perhaps accumulated on their faces after they privately kiss several times. A smudged cosmetic may even be the intention behind noting the queen's "ashy cheeks" (1.1.119). But the Cardinal's justification also demonstrates a haphazard racist logic. Like the invisible ontology of "racecraft"—a term coined by Karen and Barbara Fields to describe the tendency of racist folk logic to obstruct or intrude upon scientific reasoning that would otherwise disprove the biological "fact" of race—the play presents evidence from a

---

[60] Grier, "Inkface," 200.   [61] Grier, "Inkface," 210.

variety of outlets to justify the banishment of the Moors.[62] For the Cardinal, Eleazar's Blackness is necessarily evidence of his offense—that, and his penchant for theater, "Masks and Revellings." Eleazar's affinity for performance underscores his own ability to dissemble, which may solicit an English audience into sharing Mendoza's gaze. Once Eleazar's banishment is pronounced, he refuses to "digest this Gall" (1.2.163), and vows revenge upon Cardinal Mendoza, noting "this disgrace, / Shall dye thy soule, as Inky as my face" (1.2.190–1). Drawing attention to his humoral gall, Eleazar's inner anger seems to show on his skin, which is itself only a theatrical veneer masking an actor's white skin. Promising to "dye" the Cardinal's "soul," Eleazar himself seems to uphold his outward Blackness as a sign of an inherent, inward, and contagious moral darkness. But at the same time that Eleazar is reduced to a mundane association between black ink and black skin, he also uses ink to win back control over the court and the state.

If galls were used to stage the Moors in *Lust's Dominion*, then galls created a complex material network between Eleazar's presentation as a Black character, his choice of the written word as a political weapon, and his inability to distinguish authentic black skin from theatrical stage paint. The contest over the state between Philip and Eleazar turns out to be a battle over galls, and who can put them to the more effective political use. Although he recognizes the power of the black characters on the page to win him political favor, Eleazar is nevertheless beguiled by Black characters on the stage when Philip and Hortenzo use a cosmetic paint to disguise themselves as Moors. Eleazar's "gall" or anger facilitates the construction of a racist and scrutinizing gaze by linking his black skin to an imported commodity that can, on the one hand, pass off fake news as the truth, but that can also disguise Philip as a Moor on the other.

Eleazar's role as a manipulator of texts earns him a dubious position. Eleazar stands as a skilled rhetorician who is able to sway a contending public to trust him. As Emily Bartels argues, Eleazar positions himself "next to Philip as a Spanish insider and not a Moorish outsider" by giving "political action precedence over genealogy."[63] Eleazar's request that readers view him not by

---

[62] Karen E. and Barbara J. Fields, *Racecraft: The Soul of Inequality in American Life* (London: Verso, 2012). As the Fields sisters describe invisible ontology, "You never see it, yet you can always see it. Real-world evidence is ever at hand. By its nature, though, such evidence is miscellaneous" (203). According to the authors, racecraft refers to the "mental terrain" that justifies the existence of race, which "originates not in nature, but in human action and imagination" (18). Although the book situates racecraft in a twentieth-century American context, the book usefully compares the logic of early modern witchcraft to modern iterations of racecraft (210).

[63] Bartels, *Speaking of the Moor*, 131.

his birth, but by his "losse of blood, / Which I have sacrificed in Spains defence" (3.2.2078) displays a convincing rhetorical appeal, which "not only takes charge of the Spanish bloodline but also undermines its stability and significance."[64] So at the same time that Eleazar characterizes himself metonymically with ink, he also attempts to redirect how the Spanish population reads his "inky" face, especially in contrast to Philip.[65]

As the actor playing Eleazar might use galls to darken his white skin, the character himself uses galls in the form of the written word in order to direct his audience's attention away from his black body, and toward the false narrative about his political enemy's illegitimate birth. Eleazar seeks to regulate his own representation through publication. He plans to have Prince Philip's own mother proclaim her son a bastard; in the absence of verifiable proof, Eleazar supplies readers with texts. He instructs the queen to hire the friars "to *write books*, preach and proclaim abroad, / That your son Philip is a bastard" (2.2.49–50, emphasis added). Eleazar invokes the gall trade once more in explaining his plan to the queen:

> By this means shall you thrust him [Philip] from all hopes
> Of wearing Castiles diadem, and that spur
> *Galling* his sides, he will flye out, and fling,
> And grind the Cardinals heart to a new edg
> Of discontent.
>
> (2.2.53–7, emphasis added)

Both Eleazar and the written texts he disseminates function as the "galling" spur responsible for the prince's evacuation from Spain. Through disseminating these publications, Eleazar issues a vengeful banishment for Philip, and seeks control over the narrative.

Much like Eleazar, Aaron also manipulates ink in order to deceive his enemies. Aaron arranges for the vengeful hewing (or decapitation) of the Andronicus brothers partly through forging a false letter. Aaron later admits that he "wrote the letter" (5.1.106), the "fatal-plotted scroll" (2.2.47) that frames Quintus and Martius for the murder of Bassianus. His confession

---

[64] Bartels, *Speaking of the Moor*, 131.

[65] Eleazar's association with ink and galls seem to position him as a poor interpreter of Black characters. As Miles Grier argues, "to link a person to ink was to designate [him or] her as one who could never be an insightful reader because [he or] she was meant *to be read* by a white expert" (Grier, 195, italics original). Eleazar may be a strong manipulator of gall and print, but his outward gall also *characterizes* him—that is, makes him into a printed character, emphasizing his ability to be read over his ability to read.

solidifies his association with dissembling and galls, and opens his "hue" to the audience's scrutiny about the meaning of his black skin. But Eleazar's regulation of the written word as a means of gaining power and revenge is more public than Aaron's. He cannot ascend the Spanish throne without first influencing public opinion through the manipulation of written and oral media. His pawns, Friar Crab and Friar Cole—or *coal*, as the audience might hear it—demonstrate their loyalty to Eleazar in the dissemination of his message: "For you, our lives wee'l sacrifice…Cole will be burnt, and Crab be prest" (2.2.134, 139). Eleazar's task is not merely to produce a rumor but to manage the material dissemination of that rumor through publication by using two credible (though corruptible) friars. Eleazar punctuates his message by having the Moors Zarack and Baltazar murder the friars during their oration in the middle of the Seville marketplace. After Cole pronounces Eleazar "a fair black gentleman" (3.3.72) who cannot be compared to "that bastard" (3.3.83) Philip, the friar is murdered, which convinces the lookers-on that "This is Philips treason" (3.3.89–90).

Philip's riposte, however, also involves exploiting galls and friars, though he prefers disguise to public oratory and the dissemination of the written word. Prince Philip dresses up as both friar and Moor during the play—a friar to escape, and a Moor to infiltrate Eleazar's court. It is of course troubling that Eleazar should be fooled by Philip's cosmetic disguise involving "the oil of hell" (5.2.171), not only because it reduces Baltazar and Zarack to racial types whose personalities are effaced by their skin color but also because Eleazar's figurative language and dissembling character seem to establish his skill in recognizing disguise.

Philip and Hortenzo's use of galls via blackface gives them the privilege of reading and imitating Eleazar's body in order to capture it. After the queen, Cardinal Mendoza, and Prince Philip have all been arrested, Eleazar turns his attention to Hortenzo and Alvero, noting,

> They have supple knees, sleack'd brows, but hearts of gall:
> Their bitterness shall be wash'd off with blood,
> Tyrants swim safest in a crimson flood.
>
> (5.1.226–8)

Eleazar's metaphor for bitterness as some type of cosmetic material that might be "wash'd off" registers how the body's humors might become legible externally on the body, and identifies gall as both an internal humor and an external cosmetic ingredient. Hortenzo and Philip, through making their

Whiteness illegible to Eleazar, gain access to Eleazar's "library," and glimpse into his paranoid regulation of the written word. Hortenzo and Philip do not outsmart Eleazar beyond their disguises; rather, he sets his own trap. His explicit association with fetishized publications reaches its zenith when he characterizes himself as the hero of his own revenge tragedy—which of course he is:

> O! Saint revenge: to thee
> I consecrate my Murders, all my stabs
> My bloody labours, tortures, stratagems:
> The volume of all wounds, that wound from me;
> Mine is the stage, thine is the tragedy.
>
> (5.3.56–60)

Ecstatic to share his plan for how he will murder Philip and Mendoza, Eleazar transforms the "prison" (5.3.61) that houses the "*volume* of all wounds that wound from me" into both a theater—with "volume" enough to "stage" his consecrated murders, as well as his own "tragedy"—and a library, which houses the "volume[s]" of his "bloody labours." Eleazar invites Zarack and Baltazar—Philip and Hortenzo in disguise—to "survey my Library" of "villainy" (5.3.62–3). And though he is eager to share a "good book" (5.3.65) with Zarack and a "better book" (5.3.67) with Baltazar, he saves one volume for himself: "The best of all: / And therefore do I chain it every day, / For fear the Readers steal the art away" (5.3.68–70). Eleazar's "best" book is simply a metaphor for his plan to murder Philip and Mendoza. But the metaphor also exposes Eleazar's secrecy and paranoia, his fear that his audience might "steal the art away" or misinterpret him somehow.

In the same way that Aleppo galls were the "best" for making ink, *Lust's Dominion* reinforces the idea that some uses of galls are more effective than others. Eleazar's "best book" shrouds his plan to outsmart and kill Philip and Mendoza in a metaphor of print. But Philip and Hortenzo's *material use* of a blackface disguise (that may have required galls) ultimately outsmarts and outdoes Eleazar. If Philip and Hortenzo used galls on stage in a blackface disguise, they not only regain control of the narrative that Eleazar's dissemination of print seeks to upset; they also link galls to an early modern racial discourse that reinforces black skin as more duplicitous than white. Eleazar enlists Philip and Hortenzo in staging his proposed murder of Philip and Cardinal Mendoza; he asks that they help him to "play the Cardinall" (5.3.96) by handcuffing "his hands as thou dost mine" (5.3.99). Through ensnaring himself in his own performance, Eleazar stages the danger of sharing his inner self with his "readers." His revelation seems to justify a scrutinizing gaze by reinforcing the legibility of his black skin. As Grier suggests, Eleazar's "inky" face condemns him to be read without variation: "By suggesting that some persons were actually *comprised* of the very medium used to represent them, inkface held that such persons could not exceed the capacity of that medium to represent them."[66] The cosmetic used to represent Eleazar—likely composed of the same galls required to author a play, and no different from the one used by Philip and Hortenzo to trick him—suggests that he is hiding something beneath his skin, which cannot be apprehended without a closer reading. He unchains his secret text only to find himself in chains. Furthermore, Eleazar's suspicion that readers might "steal the art away" also proves prophetic, since his theatrical staging must come to a halt when Philip reveals himself, "ransom'd from that prison / In which the Moor had cloistered him" (5.3.134–5). Philip views his racial disguise as a kind of prison, which keeps his external Whiteness hidden; his liberation is only possible once Eleazar makes his inner text visible. Philip takes advantage of Eleazar's bondage, and slays "the Moor, the actor of these evils" (5.3.146). Thus, Eleazar's anxiety about reader response is in the end a material concern about how to read and interpret his inky face.

Lust's Dominion and *Titus Andronicus* both stage the perceived political and environmental consequences of integrating Moors into European social structures. The violent spectacles produced by Aaron and Eleazar reflect potential English anxieties about increasing trade with Moors of northern Africa. At the same time, each play draws attention to how English consumption of wooden commodities and published texts was driving English expansion into more global economies of wood. While attending to the materials that physically composed Moors on the English stage might seem to privilege non-human objects over human subjects, it actually accentuates the agency that Moor characters possessed on the English stage. Both *Titus Andronicus* and *Lust's Dominion* represent Moors who are capable colonizers, effective rulers, and brilliant rhetoricians. To reduce Aaron to a "black ill-favoured fly" (3.2.67), as Marcus does, is to fatally underestimate what Aaron is capable of accomplishing with little more than the woody product of a wasp's life cycle. Furthermore, through exploiting ink and galls to gain or facilitate power, Aaron and Eleazar demonstrate and celebrate the agency of wooden

---

[66] Grier, "Inkface," 196–7.

commodities on the stage, and perhaps even test their limits. The invisible logic of a racial ideology is one of its most dangerous qualities, but even in its iteration on the early modern stage, the invisibility of racial logic "turns out to have properties that can be explored empirically."[67] The emergent production of race on the English stage was far from immaterial; it was shaped by the ecology and economy—the wooden *oikos*—of the theater itself.

[67] Fields and Fields, *Racecraft*, 202.

3

Hemp, Tobacco, and Hot Commodities on the English Stage

In 2015, Matt Ridley—libertarian, member of the House of Lords, science writer, and regular contributor to *The London Times*—justified his self-described "lukewarm" skepticism of climate change by calling the alleged promises of "ecological apocalypse" nothing more than a bunch of "damp squibs":

> Another thing that gave me pause was that I went back and looked at the history of past predictions of ecological apocalypse from my youth—population explosion, oil exhaustion, elephant extinction, rainforest loss, acid rain, the ozone layer, desertification, nuclear winter, the running out of resources, pandemics, falling sperm counts, cancerous pesticide pollution and so forth. There was a consistent pattern of exaggeration, followed by damp squibs: in not a single case was the problem as bad as had been widely predicted by leading scientists.[1]

His observation on the one hand illustrates why what Rob Nixon terms the "slow violence" of climate change is sometimes difficult to see and experience: for those of us who consume violence in the media with our breakfast cereal, "cataclysmic violence [is] something explosive and instantaneous, a recognizably cinematic, immediately sensational, pyrotechnic event."[2] The problem is not, in Nixon's view, that ecological apocalypse is a damp squib, it's that we are thinking of it as a squib (a thing that ought to explode if used correctly) in the first place. (Ridley's metaphor of a "damp squib" also showcases a willful

---

[1] Matt Ridley, "Matt Ridley: My Life as a Climate Change Lukewarmer," *The London Times*, 19 January 2015. Accessed 1 July 2021. https://www.thetimes.co.uk/article/matt-ridley-my-life-as-a-climate-change-lukewarmer-8jwbd8xz6dj; Dana Nuccitelli, "Matt Ridley Wants to Gamble the Earth's Future Because He Won't Learn from the Past," *The Guardian*, 21 January 2015. Accessed 1 July 2021. https://www.theguardian.com/environment/climate-consensus-97-per-cent/2015/jan/21/matt-ridley-wants-to-gamble-earths-future-because-wont-learn-from-past.
[2] Rob Nixon, *Slow Violence and the Environmentalism of the Poor* (Cambridge, MA: Harvard University Press, 2011), 13.

Anthropocene Theater and the Shakespearean Stage. William H. Steffen, Oxford University Press.
© William H. Steffen 2023. DOI: 10.1093/oso/9780192871862.003.0004

ignorance of legislative actions that have since mitigated things like "cancerous pesticide pollution," "nuclear winter," and "the ozone layer" since the time of his "youth.") Nonetheless, Ridley's skepticism of apocalyptic rhetoric might seem more than valid to scholars of the early modern period. Sixteenth-century ministers and pamphleteers were convinced they were inhabiting the final "age of Man," and now climate scientists are humming a similar tune more than four centuries later. Such a historical lens might, on the one hand, justify accusations that climate scientists are simply crying wolf. On the other hand, just because the world hasn't ended yet is no reason to deny that there is in fact a problem or to ignore the evidence of human behaviors being the source of that problem. What Ridley characterizes as "damp squibs" are really anything but. On the early modern stage, squibs, or small fireworks, were routinely used to generate the spectacle of cannon fire or lightning, the sounds of ordnance or thunder, the smells of sulfur and gunpowder. *Damp* squibs would produce no such spectacle, and leave the gunplay of a sea fight or the smells of the battlefield to the audience's limp imagination. On the early modern stage, as in Ridley's misconception of the Anthropocene as an apocalyptic wasteland straight out of *Mad Max* or *The Matrix*, the hazards of a "damp squib" can be quite dire; they can signal that something has gone terribly wrong quite by accident.

But squibs that did explode brought consequences too. It was a spark from an exploded squib, after all, that burned Shakespeare's Globe to the ground. Pyrotechnics used in early modern theatrical performances may have enhanced an otherwise ordinary spectacle, but they also carried grave risks for London's wooden theaters. The Globe's ashes only added fuel to the flames of condemnation fanned by Puritanical anti-theatricalists, who saw theaters as houses of sin, lighthouses for the four horsemen, so to speak, and who saw God's hand in every mislaid spark. And while such fire-and-brimstone rhetoric proved a damp squib against deterring playwrights and playing companies from producing ever-bloodier plays and more sensational stage spectacles, there may have been an exception or two. Robert Daborne's *A Christian Turn'd Turk* (1610) calls for a stage property—a ladder of ropes—to be set ablaze on stage. If the play was ever successfully performed (and the entry in the stationers' register from 1 February 1612 insists that it "hath bene publiquely acted," though there is no other extant record of a performance),[3] the ladder scene must have delivered quite a spectacle. Though Daborne's play

---

[3] Database of Early English Playbooks. "A Christian Turn'd Turk (The Two Famous Pirates)," 1612. http://deep.sas.upenn.edu/viewrecord.php?deep_id=576.

is the only one to put fire to a ladder of ropes on stage, other scenes involving ladders of rope are linguistically entwined with fire imagery. Two of Shakespeare's plays, for example, *The Two Gentlemen of Verona* (c. 1589–91) and *Romeo and Juliet* (c. 1595), invoke the fire of Phaeton—the "fiery-footed steeds" of "Phoebus" (*Romeo and Juliet*, 3.2.1–2) and "Merops' son," the Ethiopian king who "with [his] daring folly burn[ed] the world" (*Two Gentlemen*, 1.3.153–5)—in close proximity to a ladder of ropes on stage.[4] All three plays employ the ladder in a similar way—as a means for a male suitor to climb to the bedroom of a female lover in order to escape detection from the woman's father or husband. In *A Christian Turn'd Turk*, the pirate Gallop climbs a ladder to Agar's window, where he plans to sleep with her and to make her husband Benwash a cuckold. In *The Two Gentlemen of Verona*, Valentine plans to use the ladder to steal Sylvia away from her father so they can be married in secret. Romeo instructs Juliet's nurse to obtain a ladder of cords so that he can more easily visit his new wife, so that they may consummate their secret marriage.

In this chapter, I want to suggest that these ladder plays stage the risks and rewards of investing in and consuming commodities of foreign provenance. I suggest that the ladders of rope, which were more than likely made of hemp, position hemp in a discourse that on the one hand resists globalization, but that ultimately contributes to the production of an early racial logic on the other. In *The Two Gentlemen of Verona*, the geographical anomalies of the play paired with the changing of Julia's "weeds" (2.7.42) reveal that Proteus may have investments tied up in hemp abroad, which could potentially pose a threat to his patriarchal security in Milan. In *Romeo and Juliet*, if the "tattered weeds" (5.1.42) of the apothecary from whom Romeo purchases poison do not explain his poverty, then perhaps the eccentric foreign commodities in his shop do. Romeo prefers to obtain "cords made like a tackled stair" (2.4.192) from his "man" (2.4.191) to make "adventure for such merchandise" (2.2.84) as Juliet. Romeo's ladder will allow him to consummate his marriage without detection, but the payoff of his "adventure" shall be brief, much like Gallop's in *A Christian Turn'd Turk*. Daborne's play stages the risk and reward of adventuring for commodified female bodies, which must be sought either through religious conversion or by climbing a ladder. But the spectacle of fire that accompanies this adventuring serves a dual purpose of turning

[4] William Shakespeare, *Romeo and Juliet*. Edited by Barbara A. Mowat and Paul Werstine (New York: Washington Square Press, 1992); William Shakespeare, *The Two Gentlemen of Verona*. Edited by Bertrand Evans (New York: Signet, 1964).

anti-theatrical fire-and-brimstone Puritanical rhetoric into a commercial spectacle while also invoking the perceived cultural risks of burning hemp. Anti-tobacco discourse, which fashioned tobacco as threatening to White English masculinity in part because of smoke's ability to turn Whiteness into something Black and Other, often conflated the smoking of tobacco with other combustible inhalants, such as hemp's cousin, cannabis. In short, the burning of the ladder in Daborne's play might help to shed some light—or at the very least, some smoke—on Shakespeare's motif, where ladders of rope facilitate the changing of White women into "Ethiopes" (*Two Gentlemen*, 2.6.26).

Commercial Hemp in Shakespeare's Ladder Plays

The ladders of rope used in these plays may have been appropriated from a naval context and would have been read as a hot commodity by audiences. Both Elizabeth and James invested in the expansion of the English Navy, a project that was heavily dependent on two important commodities: wood and hemp. Coincidentally, theater was heavily dependent on these two commodities as well. As Gary Taylor reminds us, "the two great joint stock companies of early modern England, the King's Men and the East India Company, both did their business in large, multistory, rope-worked, hollow, resonating wooden structures designed and built by London carpenters."[5] Much like the expansion of London's theatrical enterprises, a need for a greater quantity of larger ships made an already dire wood shortage in England worse. The demand for ship timber encouraged the expansion of the eco-military colonization of Ireland, expanding English plantations through mass deforestation.[6] The need for hemp similarly drove English commercial interests abroad. Although hemp was available in England, a product of stronger quality grew in Russia.

It is difficult to overstate the importance of hemp to English sailing vessels in the early seventeenth century. Because hemp provided material for both the sails and the rigging on a ship, one historian estimates that it took ninety tons of hemp, or 450 acres of the crop, to rig a single vessel.[7] Hemp was used

---

[5] Gary Taylor, "Hamlet in Africa 1607," in *Travel Knowledge* (New York: Palgrave Macmillan, 2001), 234.

[6] Neeson, "Woodland in History and Culture," 156.

[7] John Charles Chasteen, *Getting High: Marijuana Through the Ages* (Lanham, MD: Rowman & Littlefield, 2016), 46.

to make the three types of naval cordage: strands, ropes, and cables. It was first spun into yarns or threads, which were then twisted into threads of either twine, which could be used to sew flags and sails, or marlin, which prevented fraying at the ends of ropes.[8] Three or more strands could be twisted together to form rope, which were ubiquitous and necessary on any sailing vessel: bolt ropes prevented the tearing of a sail; head ropes led from the masthead and served as a stay; latchet lines served as fasteners; cringles formed apertures on sails through which other ropes could pass; shrouds descended from the masts; and rattling helped create the steps for climbing the shrouds. Ropes were needed for sounding and depth lines, for nettings, and for lashing lines, which kept heavy equipment (such as guns) in place. Hawsers were of considerable thickness and were used as anchor cables on smaller vessels, as well as for hauling ships over sandbars.[9] (In *A Christian Turn'd Turk*, Gismund and Gallop conspire to cut Ward's hawsers when he is grappled to Francisco's ship (4.72).) Cables were attached to anchors and required a significant amount of hemp: "A twenty-two inch cable 103 fathoms long weighed almost 9,000 pounds and contained more than 2500 threads."[10] Cordage could also be repurposed as oakum, which was used for caulking on ships.[11] It is no wonder that hemp played a role in England's commercial and colonial expansion. Demand for hemp drove ships to new shores, but hemp itself held those barks together, and even formed the sails that caught each driving wind.

Both Elizabeth and James went to great lengths to increase the cultivation of and access to quality hemp. In 1563, Elizabeth decreed that landowners with more than sixty acres were required to grow hemp. Its cultivation was required at the early English settlements in Virginia and Massachusetts as well.[12] Colonists were even allowed to pay some of their taxes in hemp fiber.[13] The English had a few domestic sources of cordage production, the most enduring of which began in thirteenth-century Bridport.[14] But the English had several reasons to seek cordage outside of England as well. The Muscovy (or Russian) Company was commissioned in 1555, largely to acquire quality cordage from Russia. The English learned that it would be expensive to import raw materials to England, so the Muscovy Company established a factory at Vologda and began to manufacture rope in Russia.[15] The English also learned

---

[8] Morris, "Naval Cordage Procurement," 82.   [9] Morris, "Naval Cordage Procurement," 82–3.
[10] Morris, "Naval Cordage Procurement," 83.   [11] Morris, "Naval Cordage Procurement," 89.
[12] Barney Warf, "High Points: An Historical Geography of Cannabis," *The Geographical Review*, Vol. 104, No. 4 (2014), 426; Chasteen, *Getting High*, 46–7.
[13] Chasteen, *Getting High*, 47.   [14] Morris, "Naval Cordage Procurement," 85.
[15] Morris, "Naval Cordage Procurement," 87–8.

that Russians were more skilled than domestic laborers in manufacturing quality cordage, and domestic production could not meet the demand for an expanding fleet of military and commercial ships.[16]

The fact that hemp was in such high demand when Shakespeare was writing his plays might help to explain some of the geographical anomalies in *The Two Gentlemen of Verona*. The confusing geography of Shakespeare's northern Italy in this play suggests that traveling by boat between two places might not always be possible, but traveling anywhere by boat—for the English, anyway—would likely not have been possible at all without some investment in hemp. Proteus exploits hemp in this play to win Valentine's banishment, but the comic resolution of the play is also made possible by Julia's handling of her hemp "weeds." Because "ladders of rope" were common fixtures on ships, the prop makes sense in Daborne's play about Mediterranean pirates. But when the Duke of Milan wants Valentine to tell him where he might "have such a ladder" (3.1.122), Valentine dodges the question. The geographical anomaly of *The Two Gentlemen of Verona* (one of many in a play where outlaws are all too eager to elect a stranger as their leader, and where the only Crab is in fact a dog) is that sailing between Verona and Milan is a physical impossibility. And yet the play repeatedly suggests that ships are ferrying passengers the 160-odd kilometers over land. Valentine's first lines in the play are dedicated to enticing Proteus to join him in seeing "the wonders of the world abroad" (1.1.6). Panthio similarly imagines that travel for a young man is meant for "Some to discover *islands* far away" (1.3.9, emphasis added). But Valentine's travels do not exceed the confines of northern Italy. When Speed is late to attend Valentine, he supposes he has "shipped already" to Milan (1.1.72); Proteus tells Speed to hurry and "be gone, save your ship from wrack, / which cannot perish, having thee aboard, / being destined to a drier death on shore" (1.1.148–50). Later, when Proteus learns from his father that he will be accompanying Valentine in Milan, he is ashamed that he was unable to confess to his father his love for Julia: "Thus have I shunned the fire for fear of burning, / And drenched me in the sea, where I am drowned" (1.3.78–9). His metaphor suggests he anticipates encountering water on his journey. Then, when Proteus bids Julia farewell, he claims that the real ocean is beckoning him to leave, not the metaphorical one: "The tide is now:—nay, not the tide of tears; / That tide will stay me longer than I should" (2.2.14–15).

Adding to the confusion is the fact that when Launce arrives in Milan, Speed greets him by saying, "welcome to Padua" (2.5.1). But it is also the

---

[16] Morris, "Naval Cordage Procurement," 88, 91.

clowns who make sense of these geographical inconsistencies. Panthio tells Launce that his "master is shipped, and thou art to post after with the oars…You'll lose the tide if you tarry any longer" (2.3.35–9). Launce's reply reminds his audience that they should be thinking about "the tied" in Verona differently: "It is no matter if the tied were lost; for it is the unkindest tied that ever any man tied" (2.3.39–40). Launce is of course referring to his dog Crab, "he that's tied here" (2.3.42). Launce shifts the audience's gaze from crabs on the shore to his dog in Verona, from the tide at sea to the tied knot around Crab's neck. Thus, the play calls attention to ships and to the sea not to represent travel accurately but rather to signal the distance that "the tied"—the ladder of cords, the rope around Crab's neck—have had to travel to appear on stage. Furthermore, in another exchange between the clowns, Speed asks Launce, "What news with your mastership?," to which Launce replies, "With my master's ship? Why, it is at sea" (3.1.280–1). Launce could be making another reference to how Proteus is still abroad, sailing (however impossibly) between Verona and Milan. But he could also mean simply that Proteus has investments abroad, like Antonio in *The Merchant of Venice*, that have not yet come in to port.

Proteus's plan to win Sylvia from his best friend, Valentine, depends on Valentine's exile. Proteus gets Valentine banished by tipping off Sylvia's father to Valentine's plan of stealing Sylvia away, using a ladder of ropes. But if Proteus exploits hemp to get what he wants, he is also undone by the mobility that hemp affords his betrothed, Julia. She associates herself with the hemp market when she tells Lucetta her plan to change her clothes in order to make the journey from Verona to Milan:

> Not like a woman, for I would prevent
> The loose encounters of lascivious men.
> Gentle Lucetta, fit me with such weeds
> As may beseem some well-reputed page.

> (2.7.40–3)

While "weeds" may be a simple metonym for clothing here, it is likely that Julia is specifically identifying clothing made of hemp or other plant fibers.[17]

---

[17] Joshua Calhoun provides a strong suggestion in his reading of Shakespeare's sonnets that Shakespearean "weeds" refer to plant-based clothing because of how they are recycled into paper after they have been reduced to rags, and thus preserve the author's sonnets: "Wearing clothes, one impresses his or her body onto plant matter. In Renaissance society, this inhabiting process also served the purpose of breaking down stiff fibers and preparing clothing for paper." Joshua Calhoun,

Much like the hemp of a sail or the "cords made like a tackled stair" that serve as Romeo's "convoy" to the "high topgallant of my joy" (2.4.192–4), Julia's hemp "weeds" make her passage possible from one part of Italy to the next.

"Weeds" are also used to describe the clothing of a character in *Romeo and Juliet*, though they offer a very different connotation where the global market-place is concerned. Instead of making travel, trade, and profit possible, the "tattered weeds" (5.1.42) of the apothecary signal instead the risk of poverty that investing too heavily in foreign commodities can bring. When Romeo receives word that Juliet is dead, he immediately begins planning his suicide by seeking poison from a shop he remembers in Mantua:

> I do remember an apothecary,
> (And hereabouts he dwells) which late I noted
> In tattered weeds, with overwhelming brows,
> Culling of simples. Meager were his looks,
> Sharp misery had worn him to the bones.
> And in his needy shop a tortoise hung,
> An alligator stuffed, and other skins
> Of ill-shaped fishes; and about his shelves
> A beggarly account of empty boxes,
> Green earthen pots, bladders, and musty seeds,
> Remnants of packthread, and old cakes of roses
> Were thinly scattered, to make up a show.
>
> (5.1.40–51)

Many of the details Romeo recalls about the apothecary's shop illustrate the poverty of the merchant, but the "alligator stuffed" suggests he might be poor because he is trying to sell things that are simply unmarketable in Mantua. His tortoise and his alligator sit in his "needy shop," unsold.

Although Romeo doesn't see his purchase from the apothecary as an investment, his use of the hemp ladder to obtain what he wants from Juliet is a venture that carries a significant risk. Romeo establishes himself as a climber

---

"Ecosystemic Shakespeare: Vegetable Memorabilia in the Sonnets," *Shakespeare Studies*, Vol. 39, No. 1 (2011), 67. For more about early modern clothing, see Timothy McCall, "Materials for Renaissance Fashion," *Renaissance Quarterly*, Vol. 70, No. 4 (2017), 1449–64. As McCall points out, clothing made of hemp was often worn by people of lower social status: "Most men, women, and children wore coarse, drab clothing made of scratchy wools and vegetable fibres such as linen and hemp, often tattered, and if not shapeless, then certainly less tightly fitting than the array of the Renaissance 1 percent" (1455).

when he vaults the walls of the Capulet orchard to visit Juliet for the first time. She speaks to him from her balcony:

> How camest thou hither, tell me, and wherefore?
> The orchard walls are high and hard to climb,
> And the place death, considering who thou art,
> If any of my kinsmen find thee here.
>
> (2.2.62–5)

The risk Romeo runs is substantial, but it is one he is willing to take: "wert thou as far / As that vast shore washed with the farthest sea, / I should adventure for such merchandise" (2.2.82–4). A ladder of ropes, or the "tackled stair" that will bring him to his "topgallant" (2.4.195–6), seems a fitting prop for such an "adventure" and situates Juliet as a commercial prize that must be sought at sea, by ship and sail. Romeo's venture cannot be accomplished without help, of course. Juliet's nurse obtains the ladder for Juliet, "by the which your love / Must climb a bird's nest soon when it is dark" (2.5.74–5). And Friar Laurence, who marries the two lovers, urges Romeo to "Ascend her chamber, hence and comfort her" (3.3.147). Unlike the ladder of ropes in *The Two Gentlemen of Verona*, which is discovered beneath Valentine's overcoat but never actually used, the ladder in Romeo's play must bear Romeo's weight in the scene where he leaves for Mantua from Juliet's bedroom: "One kiss, and I'll descend" (3.5.42). Like the ladder in *A Christian Turn'd Turk*, it is used to stage a man seeking a female prize in a context of commercial expansion and venturing at sea.

The "Ropery" of Gallop's Ladder
in *A Christian Turn'd Turk*

While the ladder of ropes in *Romeo and Juliet* positions the forbidden romance of these "star-crossed lovers" (Prologue, 6) in a commercial and global setting, the ladder in *A Christian Turn'd Turk*, a play about pirates in the Mediterranean, is already firmly rooted in an environment of tackling and topgallants. But the ladder in *A Christian Turn'd Turk* has a much more metaphysical role in staging the ups and downs, the hazards and rewards, the virtues and vices attending a life of sea venturing. Juliet's nurse does complain of the "saucy merchant" Mercutio's "ropery" (2.4.152–3)—his wickedness or debauchery—but the "ropery" tied to the ladder of ropes is much more apparent in the latter play than the former.[18]

The ladder scene in *A Christian Turn'd Turk*—a play revived in 2014 by the "Read Not Dead" project at the Sam Wanamaker Theater simply because it was the "worst play they possibly could" have chosen—delivers a heavy-handed message about the spiritual cost of pursuing riches on the high seas, a temptation that gets conflated with sexual gratification, apostasy, and conversion to Islam.[19] The play offers a cautionary tale by tracing the fates of two pirates: Ward commits suicide after he converts to Islam to win the hand of the unrequiting Voada, and Dansiker, who seeks redemption for his piracy by setting Tunis on fire, also commits suicide to avoid incarceration in Tunis. The play's subplot offers a similar moral, and features another pirate, Gallop, who climbs a ladder of ropes to sleep with Agar, the wife of Benwash, a Jewish convert to Islam in Tunis. Gallop climbs the ladder intending both to sleep with Agar and to rob Benwash. After he climbs the ladder, two sailors follow him, also intending to rob Benwash, but they decide to rob Gallop instead while he is preoccupied with Agar.

A Christian Turn'd Turk is unique for the way in which it appeals to Puritanical anti-theatricalist audiences. The play's rhetoric of fire and damnation seems to embrace rather than resist the discourse of Puritans and the moral framework of those Londoners who would not be caught dead in a playhouse. The play emphasizes the temptation and consequences of piracy and of "turning Turk" in a straightforward way. Monsieur Davy casts pirates as a kind of national regurgitant: they are

> A race of thieves, bankrupts that have lain
> Upon their country's stomach like a surfeit,
> Whence, being vomited, they strive with poisonous breath
> To infect the general air.
>
> (2.44–7)[20]

The play's pirates seem to forecast their ends in providential terms each time they commit an unlawful act. When Gallop and Gismund betray their captain

---

[18] *Oxford English Dictionary* online. "ropery," *n.* 2.

[19] Peter Kirwan, "*A Christian Turn'd Turk* (Read Not Dead) @ the Sam Wanamaker Playhouse." 6 October 2014. Accessed 13 June 2019. http://blogs.nottingham.ac.uk/bardathon/2014/10/06/a-christian-turnd-turk-read-not-dead-the-sam-wanamaker-playhouse.

[20] Robert Daborne, *A Christian Turn'd Turk*, in *Three Turk Plays from Early Modern England*. Edited by Daniel J. Vitkus (New York: Columbia University Press, 2000), 149–240.

Ward and abscond with his wealth and fleet, Gallop casts his advantage in an ominous light: "So that I rise, let the world sink, heaven fall" (4.81). Gallop will "rise" in more than one way as the play continues, but he always seems conscious that a punishment is coming.

The play's anti-theatricalist leanings are perhaps most explicit when Rabshake attempts to betray Benwash. After Agar and Gallop are murdered for their illicit tryst, Benwash asks Rabshake to bind him, and to "stab me an inch into the breast and arm" (16.111) to make him appear like a victim. But once Benwash is bound, Rabshake attempts to rob his master, claiming that, "I have seen the play of Pedringano, sir—of Pedringano, sir" (16.128–9). By suggesting that he learned to rob not from Benwash himself but from a play—from Kyd's *Spanish Tragedy* in particular—Rabshake seems to confirm the fears of Puritans like William Prynne, who promoted the idea that stage plays not only represented but actively taught illicit behavior. Quoting Saint Cyprian, Prynne writes, "Why is he [the play-goer] delighted with these Images of lusts; that so having deposited his modesty in them, he may be made more bold to commit the crimes themselves? He learnes to commit, who accustometh himselfe to behold the Theatricall representations of uncleaness."[21] The play seems to appease these moralizing sentiments as well, especially when the two pirates give remorseful speeches before committing suicide at the end. Dansiker, having been denied an expected pardon in France, tries to redeem himself by killing Benwash on behalf of France. While he succeeds in his mission, he commits suicide to escape punishment in Tunis, and teaches his audience how they should interpret his death: "Let my example move all pirates, robbers, / To think how heavy thy revenging hand / Will sit upon them. I feel thy justice now" (16.233–5). Ward's dying speech ultimately accomplishes the same goal:

> All you that live by theft and piracies,
> That sell your lives and souls to purchase graves,
> That die to hell, and live far worse than slaves,
> Let dying Ward tell you that heaven is just,
> And that despair attends on blood and lust.
>
> (16.317–21)

---

[21] William Prynne, *Histrio-mastix, The players scourge, or, actors tragaedie, divided into two parts* (London, 1633), VV2r/331.

The play's moralizing themes may be a bit heavy-handed, but they may also have been necessary to avoid over-valorizing criminal apostates like Ward in a Jacobean theater.

The ladder scene in Daborne's play stages the consequences involved with living a life of self-interest on the high seas. The consequence of Gallop's sexual misadventure and his pursuit of money through robbery is not metaphorical fire, but real fire. Gallop's attempted robbery coincides with the moment Dansiker unleashes "a pot of wildfire" (5.40) upon Benwash's house. Gallop's ascension to Agar's window quickly inverts into a hellish descent toward a burning venereal nightmare: "Flames and brimstone, I am in hell!...A plague on venery, a hot end comes on't still!...Those sheets have brought me low enough already" (10.78–86). In the same way that the pirates Dansiker and Ward emphasize a moral in their deaths, Gallop reinforces the didactic meaning of his leap from Agar's window: "A plague on whores, I say, whose vast desires, / Begins in watery tears and ends in fires" (10.91–2). Benwash rehearses an apocalyptic cry when he discovers his house on fire and evidence of his wife's adultery: "A ladder of ropes! Gallop's breeches! Burn on, burn on! Singe all the world! Consume it with thy flames, thou best of elements! Burn on, I say!" (11.6–8). Benwash also appeals to a higher power to inflict punishment on his enemies in another Puritanical refrain: "Be just, you powers of heaven, and throw thy wildfire down upon the heads of these adulterers!" (11.13–15). Thus, a ladder of rope provides Gallop access to a commodified female body, though it also seems to bring an instantaneous and providential punishment, manifested in the physical burning of—and the venereal burning in—his breeches.

Gallop's ascension into "hell" rehearses Ward's temptation to marry Voada, which requires his conversion to Islam. Ward's temptation and conversion visually summons hemp to the stage in the form of the bound slaves who serve as the voices of Virtue as Ward contemplates renouncing his religion. When Ward proclaims himself Voada's "captive, by heaven, by my religion" (7.111), she argues that his vow, even to "Mahomet," is "too weak a bond to tie a Christian in" (7.114–5). Her ultimatum—that he convert to Islam if he wishes to "enjoy" her (7.125)—functions as a ceremonial bond, since he must renounce Christianity, profess his faith to Islam, and presumably undergo circumcision in order to prove his fidelity to Voada. In turn, she promises to "raise" (7.167) him—sexually and financially—through his conversion and marriage. Ward is prompted on by the heat he feels for her, which echoes the apocalyptic connotations of Agar's lust for Gallop, and Voada's lust for Fidelio: "Away, the flame doth burn / Which sets the world on fire and makes me turn"

(7.172–3). Alizia warns him about the potential for that same flame to scorch him: "You cast your eyes too much upon the flame / Proves your destruction" (7.240–1). The "bond" Ward enters into through his conversion and the access to Voada's body that his conversion allows him are challenged by the Christian slaves on stage, who enter bound (presumably with hemp rope), and who urge Ward to reconsider his apostasy. There is no ladder here to represent the transition between a heaven above or a hell below, but the high/low binary is reinforced in the language used by Ferdinand, who can forgive Ward for selling him into slavery, and who will endure his life as a galley slave "with patience" (7.260), but who warns him that Ward's conversion will be unforgivable: "no hell I see's so low / Which lust and woman cannot lead us to" (7.281–2). Raymond's second son also offers his forgiveness to Ward, who killed their father and sold them into slavery: "Our blood, our father's blood— all is forgiven, / The bond of all thy sins is cancelled. / Keep but thyself from this" (7.266–8). These bound captives on stage function as the voices of Virtue in Ward's rehearsal of a scene of temptation by Vice from the medieval mystery play cycles. Although they do not succeed in preventing Ward's conversion, they present their bondage as a happy alternative to the physical and metaphysical consequences of renouncing Christianity and "turning Turk."

Bondage in hemp and metaphors of fire in *A Christian Turn'd Turk* drive home a moral to audiences about the everlasting consequences of sailing for oneself rather than for one's country or one's religion. Fire promises to burn eternally in the next world if one spends too much time pursuing pleasures and riches in this world, the play suggests. But metaphors of fire serve an economic function on the stage as well, insofar as they help to promote the play's spectacles of real fire, which would have posed a spectacle (if not an outright threat) to audience members packed into a wooden theater. As Ellen MacKay argues, fire on the early modern stage "is the most self-evident expression of an antitheatricalism intrinsic to performance," but it is also "the discourse via which opponents of the stage condemn the problem of the theater's palpable experience with unprecedented ingenuity."[22] Fire on stage may have been a symbol of a theater's propensity to burn, but it was also likely one of the things that made a play worth seeing. One stage direction in Daborne's play reads, "*Sound of cannonfire is heard*" (SD 2.53), which suggests that squibs may have been used. Dansiker's plan to "redeem our honor" through setting "afire / Some houses in the town" (5.13.31–2) promises arson to its audience, which is delivered in the scene with Gallop's ladder. Furthermore, Dansiker's

[22] MacKay, *Persecution, Plague, and Fire*, 147.

promise of fire suggests that it is not only destructive; it can be redemptive if used to promote one's national or religious ideology. On the other hand, Dansiker's use of fire in Tunis fails to redeem him in the eyes of France, which suggests that fire has some agency of its own. Though fire may burn hot in the mouths of anti-theatricalists and Puritanical moralists, the play shows that fire does not adhere to a single political or religious ideology. The use of fire on stage also signals a much larger blaze burning offstage in the harbor, as Rabshake notes: "The house is saved, but all the ships in the harbor / Unquenchable do burn" (11.19–20). A burning ship is tantamount to burning not only acres of wood but also acres of hemp. While the spectacle of fire or smoke on stage helps to signal that an entire fleet of ships is burning offstage, the cost of such a fire would have resonated with English audiences, who were not only experiencing a wood shortage as a partial consequence of English efforts to expand the Navy but who were also experimenting with new ways of accessing and consuming hemp.

What Were the English Smoking?

The amount of smoke that is called for to stage the arson scenes of *A Christian Turn'd Turk* might seem less gratuitous if we consider what English anxieties about smoking had in common with English anxieties about conversion to Islam. Anti-tobacconist rhetoric had a different audience of subscribers but a similar set of rhetorical devices to anti-theatricalist Puritans, and often conflated everything the English were smoking out of pipes with "tobacco." At the turn of the seventeenth century, tobacco was dubiously characterized; it was both a noxious threat to one's health and a powerful medicine, a recreational stimulant and a moral corrosive. Scholars of the tobacco debate in early modern England have signaled how the material cloudiness of tobacco smoke made it a powerful metaphor for the transgressions of gender, race, and nation that the foreign substance seemed to catalyze. Craig Rustici shows how tobacco smoke was associated with a transgressive female sexuality, and Kristen Brookes has shown how African bodies were implicated in tobacco sales as a way of emphasizing the threat of consuming this foreign substance: that it would turn a familiar, White English body into something alien, Black, and Other.[23] As Tanya Pollard points out, "the capacity of smoke to infiltrate

[23] Craig Rustici, "The Smoking Girl: Tobacco and the Representation of Mary Frith," *Studies in Philology*, Vol. 96, No. 2 (1999), 164; Kristen G. Brookes, "Inhaling the Alien: Race and Tobacco in

the body seems to have been reflected in an ability to erase borders between people."[24] But the perceived threat of tobacco smoke to infiltrate and penetrate human boundaries might be further complicated by the smoky semantic discourse of "tobacco" itself. There is physical and discursive evidence to suggest that the word "tobacco" might have signified a number of different substances that were consumed through English pipes during this period. A 2001 chemical analysis of several seventeenth-century clay pipes recovered from the site of Shakespeare's home in Stratford-upon-Avon found traces of nicotine but also of myristic acid (a hallucinogenic), cocaine, and cannabidiol (though the traces of cannabis were not unequivocal).[25] The researchers do not conclude that the pipes examined belonged to Shakespeare himself, but they do suggest that seventeenth-century English pipes were "not entirely for the smoking of tobacco."[26] Francis Thackeray argues elsewhere that "there were several kinds of 'tobacco' in those days."[27]

Furthermore, the assumption made by Rustici and Brookes that anti-tobacconist rhetoric promoted an association between Black bodies and smokers of *tobacco* exclusively overlooks the access that certain African populations had to other non-tobacco inhalants, such as cannabis.[28] Anti-tobacconists in London, like Samuel Rowlands, represented smoking tobacco as a threat to English bodies and boundaries by associating tobacco smoke with Africans as well as indigenous Americans:

> So by that error they Tobacco got,
> And fell to smoke it very burning hot,
> As common and frequent with euery Moore,
> As with th'infernall furies t'was before.[29]

For Rowlands, smoke is evidence of an association between Moors and "th'infernall furies" of hell. While trans-Atlantic trade routes made it possible

Early Modern England," in *Global Traffic: Discourses of Trade in English Literature and Culture from 1550–1700*, edited by Barbara Sebek and Stephen Deng (New York: Palgrave Macmillan, 2008), 163.

[24] Tanya Pollard, "The Pleasures and Perils of Smoking in Early Modern England," in *Smoke: A Global History of Smoking*, edited by Sander L. Gilman and Zhou Xun (London: Reaktion Books, 2004), 43.

[25] Francis Thackeray, N. J. van der Merwe, and T. A. van der Merwe, "Chemical Analysis of Residues from Seventeenth-Century Clay Pipes from Stratford-upon-Avon and Environs," *South African Journal of Science* Vol. 97, No. 1 (2001), 19–20.

[26] Thackeray, van der Merwe, and van der Merwe, "Chemical Analysis of Residues," 21.

[27] Francis Thackeray, "Shakespeare, Plants, and Chemical Analysis of Early 17th Century Clay 'Tobacco' Pipes from Europe," *South African Journal of Science*, Vol. 111, No. 7–8 (2015), 1.

[28] Rustici, "The Smoking Girl," 167; Brookes, "Inhaling the Alien," 163.

[29] Samuel Rowlands, *More Knaves Yet* (London, 1613), D1v.

for tobacco to reach African shores at the beginning of the seventeenth century, it is more likely that Rowlands is conflating New World tobacco with another plant that African populations had been smoking for centuries. Pipes were plentiful in Africa before Europeans learned to smoke New World tobacco from Americans. The psychoactive strain of cannabis originated in central Asia and traveled throughout ancient China and Southeast Asia.[30] It even reached England by the fifth century.[31] Moors carried it into Spain during the eighth-century invasion.[32] Moroccans had been growing, smoking, or making hashish from psychoactive cannabis for centuries.[33] One historian of cannabis speculates that psychoactive cannabis arrived in the New World accidentally as Europeans attempted to cultivate hemp for industrial purposes in the colonies. It may have arrived by way of an African slave who knew what it was, or perhaps an errant hempseed of *Cannabis indica* had mixed somehow with the less psychoactive strain of the plant.[34] The dubious and potentially subversive emergence of psychoactive cannabis in the Americas may have contributed to its conflation with tobacco.

On the other hand, anti-tobacconist rhetoric might also highlight an unexpected distinction that European consumers were aware of between tobacco and cannabis. In *Tobacco Battered & the Pipes Shattered* (1616), Joshua Sylvester seeks to admonish smokers of tobacco by suggesting it is as deadly and as noxious as a hangman's noose:

> Of All the Plants that Tellus bosome yeelds,
> In Groues, Glades, Gardens, Marshes, Mountains, Fields,
> None so pernitious to Mans Life is Knowne,
> As is TOBACCO, sauing HEMP alone.[35]

While Sylvester's suggestion that tobacco poses the same threat to human life as an executioner's noose might further conflate cannabis and tobacco, his comparison also calls attention to the difference between the two commodities. Sylvester's verse goes on to identify the various populations across the globe who "howrely drowne / In this black Sea of Smoak."[36] Sylvester gives the impression that *tobacco* is spreading like wildfire throughout Europe and Asia:

[30] Warf, "High Points," 420.   [31] Warf, "High Points," 422.
[32] Warf, "High Points," 424; Chasteen, *Getting High*, 54.
[33] Chasteen, *Getting High*, 54.   [34] Chasteen, *Getting High*, 54.
[35] Joshua Sylvester, *Tobacco Battered & the Pipes Shattered* (London, 1616), 86.
[36] Sylvester, *Tobacco Battered*, 91.

> But out it rushes, ouer-runns the Whole,
> And reaches, wel nigh round, from Pole to Pole;
> Among the Moores, Turks, Tartars, Persians,
> And other Ethnicks.[37]

However, because tobacco was still largely an American crop, it is likely that Sylvester is conflating the practice of smoking *something* in parts of Africa, the Middle East, and Asia with the practice of smoking tobacco specifically. "Moores, Turks, Tartars, [and] Persians" knew about psychoactive cannabis long before they knew about tobacco.

While it might be enticing to think that Daborne wanted to set a ladder of ropes on fire to give the audience a more sensational spectacle after inhaling a bit of the smoke, the smoke would have generated no such stimulation. But the burning ladder in *A Christian Turn'd Turk* does beg the question: how much did the English know about different varieties of hemp? And what were they smoking out of their pipes, in addition to tobacco? Of the two common subspecies of the Cannabis plant—*Cannabis sativa L.* (non-psychoactive hemp) and *Cannabis sativa* (psychoactive cannabis)—is the former better than the latter for producing cordage? The answer to this question seems to be no; because the industrial utility in hemp products derives from the stalk of the plant rather than the leaf, both species of cannabis might be used to manufacture cordage of the same quality. (This is also the reason why Gallop's burning ladder would not have produced any psychoactive effect on the audience in the playhouse; delta-9-tetrahydrocannabinol (THC) is housed in the leaves of the female plant of *Cannabis sativa*, not the stalk.) And yet, the supposed poorer quality of English hemp raises questions about what the English valued hemp for, and why they had been cultivating it. The English had been making cordage at Bridport since 1211, but *Cannabis sativa* had been growing in England since the Anglo-Saxon invasion of the fifth century.[38] The English did not smoke anything before learning about pipes from native Americans, but does that mean that they did not know how to extract THC from the plant in other ways?[39] Were the English cultivating hemp for its psychoactive properties at the same time that they were putting the plant to more industrial uses? Does cultivating *Cannabis sativa* for its leaves diminish the quality of its stalk over time, and could that lead to a less industrious plant?

---

[37] Sylvester, *Tobacco Battered*, 91.   [38] Morris, "Naval Cordage Procurement," 85.
[39] Warf, "High Points," 417.

Adding to the confusion about just what exactly the English were smoking out of their pipes was the fact that they made little or no distinction between psychoactive and industrial hemp. John Gerard's description of three kinds of hemp in his *Herbal* (1597) offers little distinction between them, which is symptomatic of the cultural confusion and conflation between these two strains of cannabis. His entry on "Hempe" includes an illustration of the different male and female plants, and a list of ailments that consuming the seed might help to alleviate—such as jaundice and ear pain.[40] The key difference in the application between hemp and "Wilde hemp" is that the latter "are not vsed in physicke where the other may be had."[41] This may be an indication that cultivated or non-wild hemp was grown primarily for human consumption, though Gerard's sources for the plant's application are mostly ancient and don't provide a clear sense of contemporary uses. "Water hemp," the third kind of hemp he describes, also has some healing properties against fever, poisoning, and skin ailments, and indicates the "herbe" should be "boyled in wine or water," a process that may release the psychoactive plant's THC content.[42]

As a result of English economic expansion, there were many different kinds of smoke swirling around early modern London, and likely even in London theaters. And while it remains difficult to say who was smoking what, even when smokers were sure they were smoking "tobacco," the slippage between tobacco and "hemp" might help to explain why the material ladders of rope are tied to an emerging discourse about race on the early modern stage.

"With thy daring folly burn the world": Hemp and Race in Shakespeare

In *The Two Gentlemen of Verona*, when he discovers Valentine's plot to steal away his daughter with a clandestine ladder of cords, the Duke of Milan protests, "Why, Phaeton—for thou art Merops' son— / Wilt thou aspire to guide the heavenly car, / And with thy daring folly burn the world?" (1.3.153–5). The duke quotes Phoebus from book 2 of Ovid's *Metamorphoses*, who has promised his son Phaeton anything he desires, and who immediately regrets making his promise when Phaeton asks to drive his chariot. In Ovid's version, Phoebus suggests the risk Phaeton is taking on—trying to drive the chariot that even Jupiter cannot control—far outweighs the reward of proving that

---

[40] Gerard, *The herbal*, NNN5r.   [41] Gerard, *The herbal*, NNN5v.
[42] Gerard, *The herbal*, NNN6v.

Phoebus is his real father: "you're asking for a penalty / and not a gift" (II.144–5).[43] But if the Duke of Milan points out Valentine's misguided aspirations in trying to use his ladder to climb closer to Silvia, who is herself "a celestial sun" (2.6.10), his quotation also harbors the ancient Greek explanation (that was still popular among contemporary humanists) for the dark skin pigmentation of Africans. Phaeton of course loses control of the chariot, which brings the sun so low that it scorches the earth, so that "on every side / he is surrounded by hot smoke" (II.335–6). Furthermore, "the Ethiopians / Had their blood drawn to the body surface / And turned black" (II.340–2). The duke perceives Valentine's ascension to his daughter's bedroom as a threat to her sexuality, imagined here in the racial imagery of an unscorched earth, or a White feminine body.

Proteus also associates the ladder with an African body, though he imagines Julia turning Black, rather than Silvia. In the same speech where Proteus decides that he must betray his closest friend and tell the duke of his plan "to climb celestial Silvia's chamber window" "with a corded ladder" (2.6.33–4), Proteus reasons that Silvia "witness Heaven that made her fair!— / Shows Julia but a swarthy Ethiope" (2.6.25–6). After Julia changes her clothes—her "weeds" (2.7.42), as she calls them—and her gender, she also begins to see herself as "black." When Silvia asks Sebastian (Julia in disguise) whether Julia was "passing fair," Julia replies that

> She hath been fairer, madam, than she is…
> …since she did neglect her looking glass
> And threw her sun-expelling mask away,
> The air hath starved the roses in her cheeks
> And pinched the lily-tincture of her face,
> That now she is become as black as I.
>
> (4.4.148–56)

Julia's "black" complexion is seemingly the result of being over-exposed to the sun, not unlike the Africans who were scorched by the son (and the sun) of Merops.

Julia is not the only Shakespearean heroine who runs the risk of turning black because of a man's "daring folly" with a ladder of ropes. When he first

---

[43] Ovid. *The Metamorphoses*. Translated by Ian Johnston. Accessed 18 December 2019. http://johnstoniatexts.x10host.com/ovid/ovid2html.html.

lays eyes on Juliet, Romeo introduces the motif of Juliet being a source of light or whiteness in a room full of "crows":

> O, she doth teach the torches to burn bright!
> It seems she hangs upon the cheek of night
> As a rich jewel in an Ethiope's ear—
> Beauty too rich for use, the earth too dear!
> She shows a snowy dove trooping with crows
> As yonder lady o'er her fellows shows.
>
> (1.5.46–51)

His description of the other women as "crows" seems fitting, given that Benvolio has promised Romeo that if he comes to the party and sees some of the other "admired beauties of Verona" who are not Rosaline, he will "think thy swan a crow" (1.2.87–90). Juliet's father also describes her to his preferred suitor, Paris, as a source of light in a place of darkness: "look to behold this night / Earth-treading stars, that make dark heaven light" (1.2.24–5). However, once they are wed, and Juliet anticipates Romeo's coming, "whiter than new snow upon a raven's back" (3.2.19), then Juliet is at the mercy of the darkness. While the Duke of Milan chastises Valentine with his ladder of ropes for acting like some rookie wagoner driving the car of heaven across the sky without a permit, Juliet instead laments that the novice Phaeton is *not* driving the sun as she impatiently awaits its setting:

> Gallop apace, you fiery-footed steeds,
> Towards Phoebus' lodging! Such a wagoner
> As Phaeton would whip you to the west
> And bring in cloudy night immediately.
>
> (3.2.1–4)

Juliet's impatience for night is not simply a desire for it to be dark so that her love can "come" (3.2.17) to her. Rather, she seems to echo Julia's desire to turn black, if only until Romeo arrives:

> Come, civil night,
> Thou sober-suited matron all in black,
> And learn me how to lose a winning match,
> Played for a pair of stainless maidenhoods.
> Hood my unmanned blood, bating in my cheeks,

> With thy black mantle till strange love grow bold,
> Think true love acted simple modesty.

> (3.2.10–16)

Juliet wants not just her face but her "unmanned blood" to be draped, "hooded," with night's "black mantle." Though Phaeton is not the one turning her black in this metaphor, making her into "a swarthy Ethiope" (*Two Gentlemen*, 2.6.26), she wishes to be absorbed by the night for once instead of providing a brilliant or shining relief against it. Juliet's speech may summon night, but it also summons her nurse to the stage, who bears "the cords, / That Romeo bid thee fetch" (3.2.34–5). Just as the Duke of Milan imagines Phaeton burning the world when he beholds Valentine's ladder of ropes, so Juliet conjures the tackled stair to the stage by romanticizing Phaeton's infamous ride.

The metaphysical connotations attached to ladders of rope, which are best showcased in *A Christian Turn'd Turk*, position hemp as a material that can at once win sexual gratification and financial reward on the high seas, or bring destruction and damnation. In Shakespeare's plays, hemp is exploited for personal gain or access to feminized treasure that is fraught with risk. But its physical appearance on stage in these plays is also routinely saturated in imagery of fire, smoke, and classical theories explaining racial difference. *The Two Gentlemen of Verona* uses hemp props to demonstrate the risks that commodities of foreign provenance pose to patriarchal security, European selfhood, and White femininity. And while hemp is regarded with suspicion in the play, it was also a commodity that made access to other foreign commodities possible. Without hemp, the English would have no direct access to tobacco. In Shakespeare's play, the fear about what foreign commodities can turn a person into also anticipates how abjection itself could be commodified—as it would be later on when the English ramped up their participation in the slave trade. Launce's dog, after all, is the intended signifier of his "tied"—a thing bound, neither entirely dog nor entirely crab, definitely not human, which Launce thinks "unkind"; he cares not if his "tied" gets "lost." Crab is the non-subject that a little knot of hemp threatens to turn one into. Its ability to bind might be what makes hemp just as noxious to the English as any tobacco plant.

PART II

ECO-GLOBAL PERFORMANCE

Part I of this book attempted to provincialize the Anthropocene by emphasizing the agency of non-human actants in the global assemblage of the early modern English stage. The stage properties evaluated in the previous chapters have rich lives in the natural world before they enter the ecology, or *oikeios*, of the global marketplace. The geologic agency of the entire human species becomes difficult to sponsor in a theatrical arena where natural materials facilitate the transformation of human subjects into objects, and where the outcome of human-to-human struggles for power are determined by ecological factors, rough-hew them how we will. On the early modern English stage, these properties intersect with, shape, and are shaped by human actors performing before an audience. But our evaluation of the relationship between the empire of nature, the circulation of capital, and the acquisition of geologic agency during this early phase of globalization would be incomplete if we did not attend to the ways in which the circulation of Shakespearean performance itself also helped to shape and reshape the *oikeios*.

Chapters 4 and 5 of this book will provincialize the Anthropocene further by attending to the circulation of Shakespearean performance as a commodity within the British Empire. In addition to addressing Jason Moore's question, "How does nature work for capitalism?," I turn to the ecological sites of performance to address two additional questions: "How does nature work for Shakespeare?" and "How does Shakespeare work for nature?"[1] The turn to ecocriticism in Shakespeare studies has produced some important studies of how Shakespearean performances make use of ecological space to enhance the generative possibilities of a play. Rebecca Salazar's study of the 2014 Bard in the Barracks outdoor production of *Hamlet* in Fredericton, New Brunswick, for example, has shown how a performance space can be manipulated to "expose the performativity of nature and naturalness," which can in turn

---

[1] Moore, *Web of Life*, 12.

"challenge hegemonic ideas about nature and ecological space, and thus participate in active environmentalism."[2] Similarly, Gretchen E. Minton traces the tour of *Macbeth* that spanned sixty-one locations in and around Montana during the summer of 2017. The tour provided a conscious and deliberate "engagement with *oikos*: the dwelling place of habitat and species relations."[3] This tour emphasized that "we are all implicated in a violent culture that has been and continues to be destructive to the ecosystem" by demonstrating that "Macbeth's actions transcend the boundaries of a clan or even a nation, for tyranny has global implications (just as carbon emissions do)."[4] And while these site-specific studies of Shakespearean performances can and should continue to help audiences understand their individual role in the narrative of the Anthropocene, we must not ignore the rich archive of performance history that have the potential to help us see that narrative in a new light.

One key difference between attending an outdoor performance of *Hamlet* in Fredericton, New Brunswick in 2014 and attending an outdoor performance of *Hamlet* in South Africa at the turn of the twentieth century is that there is a different intention behind how each performance interacts with the ecological elements of the performance space. The Bard in the Barracks Company is thoughtful and deliberate in how they choose to embrace the environmental conditions in which they perform; the performance asked audience members to move themselves to different scenes of action throughout the park and woods, resulting in some unfortunate mishaps, but which also produced "opportunities for meaning-making that certainly reward and sometimes justify the risk."[5] On the other hand, the evidence from the travel journals and memoirs of Shakespearean performers reviewed in Chapter 4 makes it clear that any ecological disruption during a live performance that was unaccounted for in the play's rehearsal was a nuisance to the performer and a disservice to the Bard. These ecological mishaps in the colonial history of Shakespearean performance constitute an important yet understudied

---

[2] Rebecca Salazar, "A Rogue and Pleasant Stage: Performing Ecology in Outdoor Shakespeares," *Shakespeare Bulletin*, Vol. 36, No. 3 (2018), 451.

[3] Gretchen E. Minton, "'The season of all natures': Montana Shakespeare in the Parks' Global Warming *Macbeth*," *Shakespeare Bulletin*, Vol. 36, No. 3 (2018), 440.

[4] Minton, "The season of all natures," 443.

[5] Salazar, "A Rogue and Pleasant Stage," 455. Some mishaps included actors being "swarmed and bitten by mosquitos" while trying to play dead, and audience members stumbling "over rocks or roots, or [stepping] in puddles" (454). On the other hand, Salazar reports that the divided action of the performance gave one group of audience members a chance to see Ophelia as a kind of protagonist of the play (458). Elsewhere the ghost of Hamlet's father appearing in the woods "added an appropriate aura of mystery to the appearance of the ghost's figure among the trees" (452).

archive where we can begin to address the complex relationship between the Shakespearean commodity and nature's agency.

Storms and weather events offer another entry-point into a reevaluation of the Anthropocene narrative from the perspective of Shakespearean performance. Books have been written about weather events in Shakespeare, but they have not necessarily attended to the ways in which weather events are increasingly viewed as the result—if only partially—of human behaviors or as a reflection of human geologic agency in the Anthropocene. The intersection between outdoor Shakespearean performances and unplanned weather events requires some theorization, especially in the context of the British Empire. The modern view of weather as (partially) human-generated has much in common with the early modern view of weather, which was often interpreted as a providential punishment or reward. Chapter 5 explores what happens when the intention behind a colonial production of a Shakespeare play—which on some level is always to promote British culture and empire— becomes subordinate to the agency of an unplanned weather event. Can the ecological conditions of a performance generate a postcolonial production *by accident*?

The first known performance of a Shakespeare play given outside of England was actually a 1607 performance of *Hamlet*, played aboard an East India Company vessel docked at Sierra Leone.[6] Shakespearean theater would not be confined to London, and became explicitly tied to England's overseas joint-stock enterprises even during Shakespeare's lifetime. But in order to see the far-reaching effect of Shakespearean performance within the history of British imperialism, globalization, and the Anthropocene, we need to look beyond the early modern period, and beyond England. Expanding our time-frame for analyzing Shakespearean performance history sheds light on a mutually reinforcing relationship fostered between Shakespearean performance and British imperial ideology. Furthermore, addressing Shakespearean performance on a more global stage allows us to align the history of British imperialism with the narrative of the Anthropocene and the global consequence that humans are facing today. Turning from the commercial properties of the sixteenth-century stage that were indelibly linked to ecological imperialism and the globalization of nature, the chapters in this part focus on Shakespearean performance itself as a global commodity whose commercial value may have been more tied to the natural world than previously thought.

---

[6] Richmond Barbour, *The Third Voyage Journals: Writing and Performance in the London East India Company, 1607–10* (New York: Palgrave Macmillan, 2009); Taylor, "Hamlet in Africa 1607."

But in addressing Shakespearean performance as a commercial agent in a global marketplace, we should also keep in mind the ways in which Shakespeare has changed the natural world as well. We can no more easily measure the carbon emissions that have been emitted in the name of the Bard than we can identify the amount of ink that has been generated and spilled in his name. But while Shakespeare's cultural capital might be dependent upon the non-human, accidental, and unforeseeable ecological factors influencing performance conditions, his works have nonetheless legibly impacted environmental change. The most famous example of Shakespeare's complicity in altering an environment is Eugene Schieffelin's acclimatization of the European starling to Central Park in 1890. A member of the American Acclimatization Society, Schieffelin was motivated "in part because he allegedly wished to introduce all the birds mentioned in the works of Shakespeare to Central Park."[7] Of the hundred pairs of starlings that Schieffelin released, only one pair made it through the harsh New York winter, successfully nesting under the eaves of the Natural History Museum. And as is usually the case with successfully acclimatized species, starlings were able to thrive in North America because of a lack of natural predators, and because of their ability to displace other populations. Kim Todd reminds us that Shakespeare's one reference to starlings from *Henry IV, Part One*, which presumably inspired Schieffelin's project, is in fact "a curse."[8] The line is Hotspur's, and it issues a diatribe against the king, who has commanded Hotspur never to speak of the captive Mortimer or plea for his release again. Hotspur replies, "I'll have a starling shall be taught to speak / Nothing but 'Mortimer,' and give it him / To keep his anger still in motion" (1.3.230–2). Hotspur's characterization of the starling registers the bird's ability to "mimic" noises, and seems appropriate considering its legacy as a nuisance to native bird populations and North American farmers: "They decimate fruit crops and outcompete other birds that nest in holes, including eastern blue-birds, northern flickers, great crested flycatchers, and red-bellied woodpeckers. A single flock of starlings, called a murmuration, can grow up to a million or more birds, blanketing the sky with darkness and the ground with excrement."[9] Of course, Shakespeare is only complicit if we look backward, and take Schieffelin's apocryphal motive for truth. But I think Shakespeare's role

---

[7] Edward Tenner, *Why Things Bite Back: Technology and the Revenge of Unintended Consequences* (New York: Vintage, 1997), 153.

[8] Kim Todd, *Tinkering with Eden: A Natural History of Exotics in America* (New York: W.W. Norton & Co., 2001), 140.

[9] Todd, *Tinkering with Eden*, 142.

in the acclimatization of the starling points to the concrete, material impact that Shakespeare, or perhaps theater or literature more generally, can have on the world. The starling may have brought only trouble to the American farmer or to the other species of birds that it managed to outcompete. However, its dominance in North America today depends on a network of factors (whose agency may be distributive)—ecological, biological, cultural, historical, climatological, and literary. That Shakespeare might have played a role at all is astounding; it means that literature and ecology are not as distinct as we might assume. If a study of early modern drama is to be of any significance to the predicament faced by humans living in the Anthropocene, we would do well to find more ways in which literature exists in ecological relationships with life, trash, and climate.

4

Monkeys, Floods, and the "Immortal William"

Enduring Nature and Playing Shakespeare in the British Empire

On April 23, 2014—Shakespeare's 450th birthday—a group of actors from the Globe Theater in London set out on a tour of the globe with a single play in their repertoire: *Hamlet*. The tour was a success, as the subtitle to Dominic Dromgoole's memoir indicates: *Two Years, 190,000 Miles, 197 Countries, One Play*. And while the company may have delivered on its geographical coverage and its quantity of individual performances, a tour of such magnitude also raises questions about the company's goals. Why just one play? Why *Hamlet*? And why every country in the world? Dromgoole confesses in the introduction to his book that the project began as a drunken proposition in a hotel bar: "Somewhere in that merry drinkathon, within a bleary mayhem of flirt and wind-up and raucous laughter, someone said, 'We need another big idea, something like the [Globe to Globe] festival.' With barely a pause for thought, I said, 'Let's take *Hamlet* to every country in the world.'"[1] Dromgoole's answer to the question, "Why?" seems to be a rather loaded "Why not?": "Why not use the potential of the world to transport not terror or commodities, but sixteen human souls, armed with hope, technique and strong shoes, their set packed into their luggage, the play wired into their memories, and present to every corner of the world, with a playful truth, the strangest and most beautiful play ever written[?] Why not?"[2]

Although conscious of the purchase that Shakespeare's name and works have in a global marketplace, Dromgoole seems at the same time oblivious to the more particular ideological purposes involved when drunken actors have proposed similar projects in the past. Furthermore, his answer to the question,

---

[1] Dominic Dromgoole, *Hamlet: Globe to Globe* (New York: Grove Press, 2017), 8, 2–3. Dromgoole explains that they were celebrating the end of their 2012 Globe to Globe festival, which aimed "to present within a six-week festival every one of Shakespeare's thirty-seven plays" (1).

[2] Dromgoole, *Hamlet: Globe to Globe*, 8.

Anthropocene Theater and the Shakespearean Stage. William H. Steffen, Oxford University Press.
© William H. Steffen 2023. DOI: 10.1093/oso/9780192871862.003.0005

"Why *Hamlet?*," that it is "the strangest and most beautiful play ever written," fails to question the ideology embedded in such a claim, and overlooks an important colonial and pedagogical history that makes it possible for a general, English-speaking audience to take such a hyperbolic claim for granted.

Dromgoole is hardly the first Shakespearean actor to propose a global tour of Shakespeare; he is only one of the most recent. And not unlike the Shakespeareans who have preceded him, Dromgoole exposes the process by which Bardolotry takes place. It begins with an idea: that Shakespeare is the best writer, the national poet of England, and all of the world should be able to enjoy—and learn from—his work. The idea, of course, is tied to an ideology—that English is the best and most civilized language, that it should be understood if not spoken everywhere, and anyone who does not speak English is either less than, worse off, uncivilized, or Other. Shakespeare, after all, is for all time, and "*Hamlet* is one of those rare documents that can be said to have brought the world closer together."[3] In this chapter, I trace the lineage of this type of Bardolotry from its origin—not from sixteenth-century England, but from the burgeoning British colonies of the eighteenth and nineteenth centuries. I show how Shakespeare's cultural status developed as the result of actors touring Shakespeare through the British colonies. Although a Shakespearean performance may have represented to some colonial audiences an attempt by the British state to control, teach, or even "civilize" them, the difficulty and labor it required on the part of the actor often allowed actors to see themselves as martyrs for Shakespeare. Most of the performances involved in the Globe to Globe project, much like the performances offered by British playing companies touring in the colonies of the nineteenth century, were performed in English, and provided no translation for non-English-speaking audiences.[4] I want to explore how Shakespeare's imposition onto other cultures and the ecological assemblages that resulted helped to produce his greatness, his universalism, and his "genius."

Shakespeare's role in legitimizing British colonial authority throughout the Empire has been well documented. Although Shakespeare was upheld as an idol of British cultural superiority, it is important to recognize, as Michael Dobson does, that Shakespeare did not produce the British Empire so much

---

[3] Dromgoole, *Hamlet: Globe to Globe*, 6.

[4] Dromgoole describes an incident during a Mexico City performance where he offered to narrate scenes in which the actor playing Horatio, who had fallen ill with food poisoning, was meant to appear. When the audience complained that he was not narrating in Spanish, he grabbed one of the nearby Mexican production managers, who "look[ed] terrified, never having been on stage before" (84). He then describes the trouble that occurred when she could not translate the word for "battlements" into Spanish, all while the company were running back and forth to the bathroom (86–7).

as the British Empire produced Shakespeare, and turned him into the cultural icon he is today. Before the Enlightenment, Shakespeare was just another early modern playwright; he only became the "national poet of England" as the Empire gained strength and systematically employed his works in a pedagogical and civilizing mission, which also worked to disseminate the English language as the imperial vernacular.[5] In India, for example, Thomas Babington Macaulay was likely thinking of Shakespeare in his infamous "Minute of 2 Feb. 1835" when he wrote of "the intrinsic value of our literature," which he claimed was essential for the production of "a class of persons Indian in blood and colour, but English in tastes, in opinions, in morals and in intellect."[6] That same year, the Indian Educational Act made English the official language of education in India, and Shakespeare was incorporated into the curriculum at schools and colleges, where his plays were taught as well as performed.

Shakespeare's popularity in India cannot be denied. There were a few different modes and venues for performing Shakespeare in India, and each had different political implications. Attendance at early British dramatic productions in Calcutta was initially reserved exclusively for English sahibs and memsahibs, though it was not long before elite Indians were allowed to access the number of European theaters in Calcutta.[7] The initial exclusivity of the theaters reinforced the cultural superiority of European art and culture over Indian forms of theater and performance, and attempted to cultivate an English taste among elite Indian populations. Indian actors were eventually allowed to perform Shakespeare, which was policed by British surveillance in some cases, but which also brought Shakespeare to a largely non-elite and illiterate population.[8] Indian vernacular translations and appropriations of

[5] Michael Dobson, *The Making of a National Poet: Shakespeare, Adaptation, and Authorship, 1660–1769* (Oxford: Clarendon Press, 1992), 5. Dobson traces how seventeenth- and eighteenth-century revisions of Shakespeare's plays contributed to his canonization. He argues that "adaptation and canonization, so far from being contradictory processes, were often mutually reinforcing ones."

[6] Thomas Babington Macaulay, "Minute of 2 Feb. 1835," in *Archives of Empire, Volume I: From the East India Company to the Suez Canal*, edited by Mia Carter and Barbara Harlow (Durham, NC: Duke University Press, 2003), 235.

[7] Nandi Bhatia, *Acts of Authority, Acts of Resistance: Theater and Politics in Colonial and Postcolonial India* (Ann Arbor, MI: University of Michigan Press, 2004), 12–13. Though British theater in India can be traced back to 1757, when the East India Company came to power in Bengal, the prominent theaters of Calcutta were not built until the late eighteenth and early nineteenth centuries. By 1817, Calcutta had three prominent theaters and five smaller ones (12).

[8] In 1848, the Bengali actor Baishnava Charan Adhya—also known as "Addy"—was invited to play the lead in *Othello* at the private residence of Mr. Berry. Bhatia reads this performance, which aroused anxieties about "the cultural contamination of the English stage," as part of the English project to create Macaulay's buffer class, who would possess English culture, and who would spread it to the rest of India (Bhatia 13). Addy's performance was subject to intense scrutiny by an anxious European audience; the anxiety his performance aroused was illustrated before he even had the chance to perform. As noted in the *Bengal Hurkaru and India Gazette* following what was supposed to be the opening

Shakespeare, which proliferated in Bengal after the 1870s, provided an outlet for political protests that were subversive but at the same time "relatively safe from the rigors of censorship."[9]

Touring companies, which carried popular comedies and musicals of London's West End to colonial audiences, also brought Shakespeare to the Empire. Touring companies made it possible for colonial audiences to indulge in the same cultural consumption as audiences of the metropole, and thus they provided an important unifying function within the Empire.[10] However, the environmental conditions under which this cultural imperialism and dissemination of Shakespeare took place have yet to be sufficiently explored.

In spite of performing the same play night after night in a different country, the Globe to Globe project went far from smoothly; the company encountered several severe risks. During a performance in a Syrian refugee camp in Zaarati in the north of Jordan, an unexpected sandstorm forced the company to stop the show: "Here we were, with the walls shaking, the sky filled with a thick haze, and the sun well and truly shut out."[11] The history of Shakespearean performance in the British colonies is full of similar accounts of all kinds of storms and natural disasters and phenomena. But far from dooming these theatrical tours to certain failure, the copious risks, hazards, losses, accidents, and misfortunes encountered by British actors throughout the Empire turned the global stage into a haven for Shakespearean performance. Before introducing the non-human characters populating this arena of the *oikeios*, it is necessary to introduce the human players who endured the dubious privilege of playing Shakespeare in the colonies. I suggest that actors and actresses were motivated to perform Shakespeare not in spite of but *because of* the ecological and environmental hazards they were bound to encounter. In the modern

---

night, "the parties who were severally to have played Iago, Brabantio, and Emilia, were prohibited from doing so by the preemptory military order of the Brigadier of Dum Dum" (quoted in Frost 97). Bhatia also shows how early Parsi theater companies that performed Shakespeare sought to entertain more than advance a political ideology, and even had names like the "Imperial Company" and the "Victorian Theatre Troupe" to highlight their fidelity to British colonial culture. These companies performed for non-elite audiences who had no access to education (Bhatia 54–5). See Christine Mangala Frost, "30 Rupees for Shakespeare: A Consideration of Imperial Theatre in India," *Modern Drama*, Vol. 35, No. 1 (1992), 90–100.

[9] Bhatia cites the example of Bharatendu Harishchandra, whose nationalistic and political dramas were often stifled under the Censorship Act. After the Vernacular Press Act was passed in 1879, however, Harishchandra wrote *Durlabh Bandhu* (1880), a Hindi adaptation of *The Merchant of Venice*, which reframes the play's conflict between Antonio and Shylock as a conflict between the Britain and India. The play casts Shylock as the intrusive foreign (British) foe and offers a "parable for a strategy for independence from the growing encroachment of British authority" (Bhatia 63–4).

[10] Tobias Becker, "Entertaining the Empire: Theatrical Touring Companies and Amateur Dramatics in Colonial India," *The Historical Journal*, Vol. 57, No. 3 (2014), 702.

[11] Dromgoole, *Hamlet: Globe to Globe*, 331.

example provided by Dromgoole, the actor is all too keenly aware of the potential for the sand to bury "us all and all our silly gestures." And yet, *because* of the risk involved, Dromgoole, like the wandering players that came before him, is encouraged to defend Shakespeare's work from nature's wrath: "Shakespeare asserts the power of his words to survive, to endure beyond any destruction. There is a perversity in his faith in the indestructibility of words."[12] Dromgoole's reflection participates in a long tradition of defending Shakespeare from the elements.

These Our Actors: "Endeavours to Keep the Shakespeare Flag Flying"

While it may be safe to assume that the actors who played Shakespeare (in English) to colonial audiences were by default promoting British cultural hegemony, not all colonial-era attempts to valorize Shakespeare were necessarily imperialist. Sir Israel Gollancz's 1916 *Book of Homage to Shakespeare*, while neither a theater nor a statue, was the result of a heated debate among fastidious Shakespeareans about how best to celebrate the Tercentenary of Shakespeare's death in 1916—a debate that roiled in spite of the First World War. As Gordon McMullan notes, the edited collection walks a fine line in praising Shakespeare in a global, but not necessarily imperialist, way. The book contains 166 tributes to Shakespeare from authors around the world, written in twenty-three languages.[13] The collection includes entries from prominent imperialists like Rudyard Kipling, and an English professor who sees "Shakespeare as the Central Point in World Literature." But it also includes a lay about Stratford as a site of peace written in Gaelic by Douglas Hyde, the future president of the Irish Republic. It includes an entry from a Burmese scholar at Rangoon College, who praises Shakespeare for his Buddhist ethics, and another written by an anonymous South African (later identified as Solomon Tshekisho Plaatje) who praises Shakespeare's representation of Black Africans for the way they "show that nobility and valour, like depravity and cowardice, are not the monopoly of any colour."[14]

---

[12] Dromgoole, *Hamlet: Globe to Globe*, 332.

[13] Gordon McMullan, "Goblin's Market: Commemoration, Anti-Semitism, and the Invention of 'Global Shakespeare' in 1916," in *Celebrating Shakespeare: Commemoration and Cultural Memory*, edited by Clara Calvo and Coppelia Kahn (Cambridge: Cambridge University Press, 2015), 186–7.

[14] Israel Gollancz, ed., *A Book of Homage to Shakespeare*, 1916 (Oxford: Oxford University Press), Internet Archive, 15 October 2009. R. G. Moulton was a professor of literary theory and interpretation at the University of Chicago and includes an entry on "Shakespeare as the Central Point in World

The book is notable for its subtle, often overlooked, but no less admirable attempt to situate Shakespeare in a framework that is cosmopolitan without being outright jingoistic. McMullan comments on the collection by noting Gollancz's "degree of playfulness paired with an emerging ideology of globalization that recognizes the beginnings of the end of empire (for Britain, at least) and the possibility of an international story on a broader stage."[15] The anecdotes, essays, and poems included in the *Homage* are also a useful vantage from which to hear praise of Shakespeare coming from the subjects of British colonialism in their own words. In many of the reports given by traveling thespians below, it is difficult to determine the sincerity of the gratitude and praise granted to the actors by the colonial audiences, especially given the bias of the authors.

For some actors and actresses on the colonial circuit, the chore of bringing Shakespeare to colonial audiences was its own reward, and more appealing than financial success or even fame. From 1879 to 1882, Daniel E. Bandmann toured all over Australia, New Zealand, India, and China. Bandmann, who was actually German, became one of the most famous crusaders of Shakespeare in the English-speaking world. Bandmann estimates that over three and a half years he traveled 70,000 miles and gave 700 performances, two thirds of which were Shakespearean.[16] In India, Bandmann observed, Shakespeare was not so much desired as demanded: "the love of Shakespeare is inherent in the Hindu mind, or rather, it is an inevitable blossoming of inherent qualities and dispositions beneath the influence of European education, which all the higher classes in India now enjoy." Observing the effects of the English Education Act, Bandmann perceived that Shakespeare formed the foundation of Indian "taste." A true Bardolotrist, Bandmann even argued that Shakespeare had a kind of religious presence in India, since India's population was divided by religion but united under Shakespeare.[17] When Bandmann

---

Literature" (228–30). The final lines of Hyde's lay, "An Rud Tharla Do Ghaedheal Ag Stratford Ar An Abhainn (How It Fared with a Gael at Stratford-on-Avon)" (275–9), drive home Stratford as a locus of peace against Gaelic strife: "On me that Druid has worked a druidism / Which I now set down here in my verse: / He has won pardon from me for his land: / I at Stratford on the Avon" (279). Maung Tin finds correlation between Shakespeare's works and the teachings of the Buddha: "Shakespearean literature manages to teach the same high standard of ethics as the Buddhist, without a distinct ethical tendency. In spite of his vigorous appreciation of the world, Shakespeare shakes hands with the Buddha, in his utter renunciation of the world" (329). McMullan identifies the South African author as Solomon Tshekisho Plaatje (McMullan, "Goblin's Market," 187).

[15] McMullan, "Goblin's Market," 198.

[16] Daniel E. Bandmann, *An Actor's Tour, or Seventy Thousand Miles with Shakespeare* (New York: Brentano Brothers, 1886), 302. Bandmann notes that he primarily played *Hamlet, The Merchant of Venice, Macbeth, Othello, Richard III,* and *Romeo and Juliet.*

[17] Bandmann, *An Actor's Tour,* 134.

played *The Merchant of Venice* and *Othello* for an audience in Calcutta, he found performing was its own reward: "It is a pleasure beyond description to see the natives of India enjoying a Shakespearean performance...I have never been so well understood as Shylock as I was that evening by those three thousand Hindus and Moslems."[18] Bandmann's performance seemed to produce his own imperial justification as well. When Bandmann was persuaded to let a "Eurasian" man play the part of Dogberry, the man was "delighted at the concession, but when he came into the wardrobe he nearly swooned, and complained of the heat to such an extent that I had to send a servant to get him a pankha boy. Now, this man was born in India, and had lived all his life beneath its skies, and yet he was not able to stand as much as we were, although he had only to wear a light domino, while we were dressed in silks, velvets, and furs."[19] At the same time that Bandmann refuses to acknowledge the legitimacy of non-Western art forms, he also suggests that only a European with his constitution for the heat of the Indian stage is equipped to perform Shakespeare in such conditions.[20]

Allan Wilkie was another martyr of Shakespearean performance. Wilkie and his wife, Frediswyde Hunter-Watts, lugged eighty tons of scenery across Asia from 1911 to 1913 and produced more than thirty plays.[21] Wilkie, who was apparently mistaken for Shakespeare himself by some of his less educated Australian audiences,[22] claimed that he performed "Shakespeare in many places for the first time and frequently to alien races whose enthusiastic appreciation testified once more that not only is Shakespeare for all time but for all peoples."[23] In Bangalore, Wilkie's travels and efforts found validation in a group of students who had traveled sixty miles by foot through the jungle and 300 more by train in order to see him perform *Hamlet*: "When it is

---

[18] Bandmann, *An Actor's Tour*, 141–2.   [19] Bandmann, *An Actor's Tour*, 145.

[20] Bandmann, *An Actor's Tour*, 189. Bandmann finds "nothing charming" in Chinese theater, where "all true dramatic art is conspicuously absent."

[21] Richard Foulkes, *Performing Shakespeare in the Age of Empire* (Cambridge: Cambridge University Press, 2002), 151; Allan Wilkie, *All the World My Stage: The Reminiscences of a Shakespearean Actor-Manager in Five Continents.* Unpublished autobiography, MSS 92 W6825, University of Adelaide Special Collections, 114, 135.

[22] Wilkie, *All the World My Stage*, 286–7. "Frequently after seeing me upon the stage," Wilkie recalls, "people complained that I was not at all like a greatly enlarged portrait of Shakespeare displayed upon my posters on the hoardings and thought to represent me!" Wilkie perhaps relishes this association a bit too much when he recalls how he overheard one fellow tell some friends that Wilkie was not only the "original" Shylock, but that he actually authored the play. "Thus," Wilkie comments, "did he for ever dispose of the Baconian, and all other theories regarding the authorship of Shakespeare's plays."

[23] Wilkie, *All the World My Stage*, 197; Foulkes, *Performing Shakespeare*, 151. Foulkes seems to echo Wilkie's imperialist homogenizing sentiment: "Shakespeare's direct emotional force and thrilling story line transcended barriers of time, culture, race and language."

realized that they were all men in very humble circumstances and that the expense of such a trip would probably demand rigid economy of their finances for a year afterwards, one cannot but lament that such extreme devotion to our national poet is rarely, if ever, to be found amongst his fellow countrymen."[24] From 1920 to 1930, Wilkie, with his Australian Shakespeare Company, embarked on an ambitious venture to produce all thirty-seven of Shakespeare's plays on a prolonged tour of Australia and New Zealand. He only succeeded in producing twenty-seven, but he gave 1,239 consecutive performances of Shakespeare over the course of the decade.[25] On one occasion, when Wilkie's finances were particularly dear, he turned down an enticing offer—"the like of which I have never had before or since"—to star in *Chu Chin Chow* at £100 per week—in order to keep on with his Shakespeare project.[26] When he experienced difficulty booking theaters for Shakespeare's less popular plays, like *Coriolanus* and *The Two Gentlemen of Verona*, Wilkie admits, "I was playing a lone hand in my endeavours to keep the Shakespearean flag flying."[27] The prime minister of Australia commended Wilkie for "carrying on his self-appointed task," especially since "the production of Shakespearean plays cannot be regarded as the most lucrative of theatrical enterprises." The prime minister recognized that Wilkie was "really performing a duty of national character" for Australia.[28] Even after the theater in Geelong caught fire—a disaster that was not uncommon for touring players— and destroyed all of his (uninsured) property, Wilkie did not abandon his Shakespearean crusade. He managed to raise over £4,000 through the press and through benefit performances, which he saw as "a most welcome proof that our labours were considered of national importance, and that its termination would be a distinct loss to the community."[29]

Geoffrey Kendal's particular strain of Bardolotry emulated Bandmann's and Wilkie's, though it also carried nostalgia for an Empire united under Shakespeare as it routinely confronted an India transitioning toward independence. In 1945–6, Geoffrey Kendal's English Repertory Company toured India with *Macbeth*, *Julius Caesar*, *Othello*, and *Romeo and Juliet*. His company consisted of his wife Laura, their daughter Jennifer, their infant Felicity, and others. They also picked up players along the way, including Utpal Dutt, who was known for his political theater. After the Partition, Kendal embarked on a second tour with his new Shakespeareana Company, whose repertoire

---

[24] Wilkie, *All the World My Stage*, 155.   [25] Wilkie, *All the World My Stage*, 276.

[26] Wilkie, *All the World My Stage*, 257.   [27] Wilkie, *All the World My Stage*, 266.

[28] Quoted in Wilkie, *All the World My Stage*, 277.   [29] Wilkie, *All the World My Stage*, 280–2.

consisted exclusively of Shakespeare and Shaw. From 1953 to 1956, Kendal's troupe gave 879 performances of Shakespeare at schools, colleges, and theaters all over India, China, and Malaysia. Their tour became the subject of the Merchant and Ivory film, *Shakespeare Wallah* (1965), which stars Geoffrey, Laura, and Felicity Kendal, as well as Shashi Kapoor, who became part of the company (and then part of the family when he married Jennifer). Kendal initially objected to the film's premise: "The actors were seen as the last of the British Raj, hanging on to a dying culture in an out-of-date medium, while the cinema, representing modern India, took over with its new and vital power." Though Kendal asserts that his company "had been a great success and had brought Shakespeare to the furthest places of India," his own account of his tour *does* betray a degree of desperate clutching for a "dying culture"—though it is not the culture of theater or even of Shakespeare.[30] Rather, it is the cultural imperialism that Shakespeare once represented in India, which was changing in the wake of Indian independence.

In the spring of 1947, after performing *Julius Caesar* and *Othello* at Trivandrum, the company received a letter from a local amateur group, who commended their performance, and who ended the letter by saying, "Let Shakespeare keep India and Britain united!"[31] Kendal's nostalgia for empire shows in other ways as well. Kendal imagines Shakespeare as a weapon of protection against a potentially dangerous political climate: "Armed with Shakespeare, whose plays were so much appreciated in India, we felt we could ignore the warnings about the nationalist movement and possible troubles."[32] His mission seems all the more important after experiencing Independence Day in Shillong: "People were walking idly along the roads, with an aimless, helpless look. There was no rejoicing, no singing or dancing. No one seemed to know what would happen next."[33] He cites one Calcutta reviewer, who felt that their performance of *Othello*, and their very presence, had "raised the cultural level of the city, and could they be persuaded to make it their home, at least during every winter, Calcutta would be less cut off from the rest of the world."[34]

But not all audiences were as receptive to Kendal parading Shakespeare through India during the country's transition to independence. When the

---

[30] Geoffrey Kendal and Clare Colvin, *The Shakespeare Wallah: The Autobiography of Geoffrey Kendal* (London: Sidgwick & Jackson, 1986), 145.
[31] Kendal and Colvin, *The Shakespeare Wallah*, 89.
[32] Kendal and Colvin, *The Shakespeare Wallah*, 85.
[33] Kendal and Colvin, *The Shakespeare Wallah*, 95.
[34] Kendal and Colvin, *The Shakespeare Wallah*, 100.

company played *The Merchant of Venice* in Mysore before the Maharaja, he "did not smile or laugh, so none of his officials would be caught doing so" either. In fact, Kendal remembers playing "to dead silence throughout" the entire evening, which was unusual for this Shakespearean comedy, since it "happened to be one of the favourite plays of the repertoire in India."[35] Kendal is quick to blame himself for the laughless evening, but perhaps misses the political significance of the audience's performance of silence. Like Tamora, dressed as Revenge for an audience who can all too easily see through her disguise, Kendal clings to an illusion that his performance was desired, necessary, and effective. In reality, the Maharaja may have wrested control of the audience away from Kendal and away from Shakespeare, and in an important political gesture did not laugh at the playwright who had long been a symbol of British colonial occupation in India.

In China, Kendal experienced another uphill battle from an audience with whom he was eager to share Shakespeare. Chinese audiences, he comments, "always laughed or smiled, and the more you put on your dramatics in a play, the more they would see the funny side of your efforts and kill themselves laughing, which could be frustrating for those who saw themselves as serious actors portraying the classics and tragedies of this world."[36] Again, rather than accept that his audiences were laughing *at* him, Kendal dismisses this as a "strange sense of humor."[37]

Other British actors were equally fixated on staging Shakespeare in the British Empire. George Crichton Miln toured India, China, and Japan from 1890 to 1891 with an all-Shakespearean repertoire. Miln's company was the first to perform several Shakespeare plays in their entirety in Japan. During their two-week stay in Yokohama in May 1891, Miln's company performed *Hamlet, The Merchant of Venice, Romeo and Juliet, Macbeth, Othello, Julius Caesar,* and *Richard III.*[38] Miln had also toured the US in 1882, performing

---

[35] Kendal and Colvin, *The Shakespeare Wallah*, 114.

[36] Kendal and Colvin, *The Shakespeare Wallah*, 135. Frank Gerald makes a similar observation when playing to a segregated audience on Thursday Island: "What an audience! The coloured people laughed, generally in the wrong place, and applauded everything and everybody, heroes and villains indiscriminately" (60). While Gerald's comment seems intended to highlight an inability for this audience potentially consisting of "Chinese, Japanese, Cingalese, Kanakas, Malays, and Aboriginals" (58) to appreciate Western theater, he also underscores the subversive potential for an audience to wrest power away from the performers merely by laughing or applauding in the "wrong" places. See Frank Gerald, *A Millionaire in Memories* (London: Routledge, 1936).

[37] Kendal and Colvin, *The Shakespeare Wallah*, 135. "This sense of humor," he continues, "extended to their own dramas. I remember seeing a Chinese standing by the side of the road where his car had been wrecked in an accident, laughing his head off."

[38] Kaori Kobayashi, "Touring in Asia: The Miln Company's Shakespearean Productions in Japan," in *Shakespeare and His Contemporaries in Performance*, edited by Edward J. Esche (Aldershot: Ashgate, 2000), 58.

Hamlet, Macbeth, and *Othello* seventy times in forty different cities over the course of two months.[39] Miln was criticized in the states for his antiquated acting style with Shakespeare, though it won him praise in Australia and Japan.[40]

Genevieve Ward performed *Macbeth, Othello, Hamlet, The Merry Wives of Windsor, The Merchant of Venice,* and *Much Ado About Nothing,* along with twenty other plays during her nine-month tour of South Africa in 1891–2.[41]

Matheson Lang toured various parts of the Empire with different companies. He toured with his wife, Hutin Britton, and W. E. Holloway in South Africa, India, China, and Malaysia, performing *The Merchant of Venice, Romeo and Juliet, Hamlet,* and *The Taming of the Shrew.*[42] With Frank Benson's company, Lang visited Jamaica, Trinidad, Barbados, and British Guyana, playing *The Merry Wives of Windsor, The Merchant of Venice, Hamlet, Much Ado About Nothing, Twelfth Night, Richard III,* and *The Taming of the Shrew.*[43]

Frank Benson, who one actor described as "an actor-manager with a mission...to present the classics, notably Shakespeare, in the provinces and the farther corners of the British Empire, wherever there was promise of an audience," organized a tour of South Africa in 1913.[44] His North Company performed *As You Like It, The Merry Wives of Windsor, Hamlet,* and *The Merchant of Venice* all over South Africa. When the tour ended, a few members of the company decided to stay on and "play Shakespeare on the veldt," traveling by train and ox wagon, performing in schools, town halls, bars, and hotel dining rooms.[45] Cedric Hardwicke characterized the tour by its hardships, which were always somehow successes: "No matter what the conditions, Shakespeare triumphed."[46]

Leonard Rayne, who was part of the Holloway Company that visited Johannesburg in 1895, and who eventually leased the Opera House and the Standard Theatre in Johannesburg, organized a Grand Shakespeare Festival in

---

[39] Kobayashi, "Touring in Asia," 58.   [40] Kobayashi, "Touring in Asia," 58–61.

[41] Genevieve Ward and Richard Whiteing, *Both Sides of the Curtain* (London: Cassell and Co., 1918), 182.

[42] Matheson Lang, *Mr. Wu Looks Back: Thoughts and Memories* (London: Stanley Paul & Co., 1941), 106. Lang describes how he was also persuaded to perform *Macbeth* by the Scottish Society in Shanghai, even though it wasn't part of his repertoire.

[43] Lang, *Mr. Wu Looks Back,* 65.

[44] Cedric Hardwicke, *A Victorian in Orbit: The Irreverent Memoirs of Sir Cedric Hardwicke* (Westport, CT: Greenwood Press, 1961), 81.

[45] Hardwicke, *A Victorian in Orbit,* 90–1.

[46] Hardwicke, *A Victorian in Orbit,* 91. Hardwicke's own triskaidekaphobia colors his recollection of their ill fortune on the tour: "There were thirteen men in the company, with a repertoire of thirteen plays. We left on September 13, 1913, and we opened at Capetown on October 13, with our next stop due on November 13 in Johannesburg" (85).

1907.[47] Over the course of only one week, Rayne produced and starred in *Macbeth, Hamlet, The Merchant of Venice*, and *Richard III*.[48]

Memoirs and written accounts of actors who toured the Empire playing Shakespeare raise questions about what motivated these excursions. Although touring provided occasional opportunities for stars to enjoy potentially more successful careers than they might have had in London and the English provinces, touring the Empire was usually not lucrative.[49] After a tour of South Africa with Frank Benson's North Company, for example, Cedric Hardwicke had fourpence in his pocket "as the net cash gain" from his Shakespearean circuit.[50] Traveling made sense for actors who were not well paid, but travel costs often ate up profits.[51] On the other hand, touring did provide some opportunities for fame, especially for performers who could not cut it on the London stage.

Perhaps more than acting ability or discipline, touring the empire required "adventurousness, perseverance and adaptability."[52] At the same time, it may have also required the gullibility to be swindled into a bad contract by a desperate company manager. The anonymous author of a brief article published in 1917 called "Theatrical Touring in the Far East by One Who Has Tried It" offers more of a warning than an endorsement of touring to potential traveling actors and actresses: "My purpose is to let my fellow-actors know exactly what they may expect when they sign their contracts for an Eastern tour."[53] Providing advice on health, money, playing conditions, and sightseeing, the author primes performers to "be prepared for a certain amount of disillusionment wherever you go."[54] Serious professionals, the author advises, should

---

[47] Jill Fletcher, *The Story of Theatre in South Africa: A Guide to Its History from 1780–1930* (Cape Town: Vlaeberg, 1994), 120.

[48] Fletcher, *The Story of Theatre in South Africa*, 123.

[49] Booth and Heckenberg note that Barry Sullivan, Frank Benson, and Genevieve Ward each fashioned a greater reputation abroad than they ever had in London. See Michael R. Booth and Pamela Heckenberg, "Touring the Empire," *Essays in Theatre*, Vol. 6 (1987), 51. They also note that touring the states was often lucrative, since it was a short voyage and guaranteed full houses at large urban centers, which were relatively easy to access via railways (50). Becker also mentions that Marie Tempest and Ada Reeve were two London stars who visited the colonies, but most colonial audiences rarely saw London stars (Becker, "Entertaining the Empire," 708).

[50] Hardwicke, *A Victorian in Orbit*, 97.

[51] Becker, "Entertaining the Empire," 703. Becker notes, "For stars, a long, winding tour through the empire was simply not profitable." Becker also notes that voyages from one place to another could be lengthy and drain profits (705). Because touring was an alternative to the London stage, it meant that touring companies were often composed of amateurs, and companies often allowed amateur actors from the communities they visited to join them on stage (Becker 709).

[52] Booth and Heckenberg, "Touring the Empire," 52.

[53] "Theatrical Touring in the Far East: By One Who Has Tried It," in *The Stage Year Book 1917*, 48.

[54] "Theatrical Touring in the Far East," 48. Though this author's description of colonial life is extremely subjective, the description of "an extraordinary lack of vitality, of enthusiasm in it" is insightful, if only because it describes a discontent that is borne by colonial subjects and British colonists alike.

just stay home: "every month spent in foreign countries is a month wasted so far as the building up of a London reputation is concerned."[55] Money could be made while touring, but only if it was saved and spent wisely.[56] Colonial audiences could also be harsh critics and impossible to predict, despite the fact that British colonial audiences, according to the author, endured droughts of entertainment: "In many places the theatres are empty for weeks at a stretch. The exiled European positively gasps to be entertained."[57]

Nevertheless, plays and genres that were successful in London were not guaranteed to succeed in the colonies.[58] Another author, writing from the perspective of a colonial audience member in Bombay, argues that it is too expensive to import good companies, and that the amateur companies that entertain between visits from touring companies "fail signally to amuse, and...to fill their own pockets."[59] One patron of Allan Wilkie's company in Quetta complained that it was more expensive to see Wilkie in the colonies than it was to see a lavish spectacle by Beerbohm Tree in London.[60] With little prospect of fame or fortune, and promising only disappointment, touring the British Empire seemed to some a road better left untraveled.

Rain, Wind, Thunder, Fire: Shakespeare Against the Elements

For those actors who decided that the Empire needed Shakespeare more than they needed fame, fortune, or even their health, their cause was more often than not justified by the environments they endured. The natural environments through which traveling companies passed on their circumnavigational tours of the British Empire shaped the playing conditions in which Shakespeare's plays were performed—for the first time, in some cases—in colonial settings. I suggest that this allows us to see an overlooked ecological aspect to the imperial production of Bardolotry. In other words, Shakespeare's cultural

---

[55] "Theatrical Touring in the Far East," 43.

[56] "Theatrical Touring in the Far East," 45. The author accounts for travel and boarding costs, and how long journeys between playing venues can get expensive: "If we are not earning money we are losing it. In addition to that, there are certain expenses entailed in boat or train journeys which can scarcely be avoided. Boats have stewards, and stewards expect tips. We must still smoke or have an occasional drink, or pass the time in some way. On railways there are porters to be reckoned with."

[57] "Theatrical Touring in the Far East," 47.

[58] The same was true of acting styles. Kobayashi shows how Miln's acting style was largely panned as antiquated by critics in Britain and in the US, but was celebrated in Australia (Kobayashi, "Touring in Asia," 59).

[59] H. A. D. Simpson, "Art in Afghanistan," *The Theatre*, Vol. 4 (1881), 141.

[60] Wilkie, *All the World My Stage*, 138. Wilkie explains that the expensive price of a ticket in the colonies pays for the labor of bringing a spectacle to the Empire.

capital owes itself in part to the floods, typhoons, hurricanes, dust storms, heat waves, droughts, earthquakes, and thunderstorms that actors endured to parade—or to drag, as the case may have been—Shakespeare's name and plays through the Empire.

For example, the animals and insects encountered by Shakespearean actors in the colonies often proved dangerous, deadly, or disturbing. Deadly snakes in Rangoon and man-eating tigers in Nainital posed a threat to Allan Wilkie and his wife.[61] Genevieve Ward complained of vermin in Johannesburg hotels, as well as in Sydney and Brisbane: "One night I felt a great rumbling under my pillow—rats!"[62] Another author forewarned prospective actors traveling through Asia: "If you are afraid of insects, be prepared for shocks. Insects abound. There are huge cockroaches (with wings), vast spiders, long-bodied winged ants, smaller-bodied wingless ants in myriads, white ants that eat your books and clothes, red ants that eat your food, black ants that eat you."[63] Russell Craufurd loathed the mosquitoes of Brisbane and claimed the mosquitoes of Calcutta were venomous from feeding on garbage in the streets.[64] He also describes battling a cloud of locusts on the veldt of South Africa.[65] Some locations were preferred among performers for their *lack* of insects—like New Zealand, Tasmania, and Barbados.[66] In Trinidad, while dressing for the part of Petruchio, Matheson Lang was fortunate enough to discover a tarantula in his boot before slipping his foot into it.[67] Geoffrey Kendal, who performed a Shakespeare repertoire with his family all over India before and after the Partition, remembers insects being a nuisance

---

[61] Wilkie, *All the World My Stage*, 130, 147. Wilkie describes being nonchalantly warned about kraits—"a particularly venomous little snake whose bite is almost certain death in about twenty minutes" (130)—under their dinner table by one hostess in Rangoon. The nonchalant attitude of this woman incurred a reflection on "the phlegm and sangfroid of the Anglo-Saxon race," which have "played no small part in their process of Empire building, and demonstrate how they can adapt themselves and indeed become almost oblivious of conditions that are happily unknown in their own 'precious isle'" (129). In Nain-i-Tal, Wilkie and his wife were abandoned by their dandy-carriers in the middle of the jungle on their way between the theater and the hotel; they arrived at the hotel to reports that they had already been devoured by a tiger (147–8).

[62] Ward and Whiteing, *Both Sides of the Curtain*, 115, 173.

[63] "Theatrical Touring," 48. The author continues: "There are scorpions, centipedes, lizards, hornets, mosquitoes, sandflies, flying beetles, dragon-flies, snakes, huge rats, and every description of crawling and creeping thing that it is possible to conceive, save—by a merciful dispensation of Providence—the common or garden English flea and bug of commerce!"

[64] Russell Craufurd, *Ramblings of an Old Mummer* (London: Greening, 1909), 123, 157.

[65] Craufurd, *Ramblings of an Old Mummer*, 151.

[66] Craufurd, *Ramblings of an Old Mummer*, 143; Bandmann, *An Actor's Tour*, 77; Lang, *Mr. Wu Looks Back*, 65. Craufurd praised New Zealand for having no mosquitoes or reptiles and a good climate. Daniel Bandmann noted Tasmania was "like New Zealand in having no disagreeable bugs, mosquitoes, snakes, or wild animals of any kind, except the black opossum, which abounds in considerable numbers." Matheson Lang praised Barbados for having "No malaria, no poisonous insects, and the most perfect sea-bathing in the world."

[67] Lang, *Mr. Wu Looks Back*, 67.

during performances as well: "If you played out of doors, tiny insects would creep under your wig, and mosquitoes would nibble at your ankles. We would make our exits calmly; then once out of sight of the audience, fall into a frenzy of scratching. At an alfresco evening, all the moths and mosquitoes of the area converged on our stage-lights and then turned their attention to us."[68] During one performance, Kendal, playing Othello, inhaled a bluebottle fly during his line to Desdemona. The fly likely made her next line that much more meaningful and effective: "Why do you speak so faintly? / Are you not well?" Kendal also recalls how the insects made playing dead on stage extremely difficult, since they would gnaw on any exposed skin.[69]

The heat was another common complaint among actors. Summer temperatures in Colombo, Allahabad, Napier, Adelaide, Brisbane, Johannesburg, and Pietermaritzburg caused considerable strain for performers: "Only madmen and actors could endure it."[70] In Calcutta, the heat made late-night performances common and practical; performances regularly went on after nine and ended well after midnight, simply because the temperatures were less extreme.[71] In Pietermaritzburg, Henry Herbert refused to play Falstaff in *The Merry Wives of Windsor* because he found the fat knight's padding too intolerable.[72] The heat drenched players' costumes and melted face paint.[73]

---

[68] Kendal and Colvin, *The Shakespeare Wallah*, 124–5.

[69] Kendal and Colvin, *The Shakespeare Wallah*, 124–5.

[70] Hardwicke, *A Victorian in Orbit*, 89. Ward says, "I think Colombo was the hottest place I was ever in," which owed, according to Ward, more to the fact that "the rays of the sun are vertical and you have no shadow" than to the actual temperature. She also notes the heat in Napier is "sweltering." Bandmann recounts, "Six months in the year Adelaide is unbearable on account of its dreadful dry heat, three months it rains, and the rest are the only endurable portion of the year." Craufurd, who got sunstroke in Port Lincoln, reported an outlandish temperature of 180 degrees Farenheit on Christmas Day in Brisbane, and noted that the only cool place was beneath the stage. Ward and Whiteing, *Both Sides of the Curtain*, 105–6, 113; Bandmann, *An Actor's Tour*, 103; Craufurd, *Ramblings of an Old Mummer*, 128, 127; Wilkie, *All the World My Stage*, 149.

[71] Wilkie, *All the World My Stage*, 119. Wilkie also reports playing only open-air performances in the middle of the night in Allahabad, when the temperature was a mere 98 degrees Farenheit; Allahabad was 125 degrees Farenheit during the day (149).

[72] Hardwicke, *A Victorian in Orbit*, 89. Hardwicke recounts how Herbert "rapidly substituted *Comus* on the bill, in which he wore nothing but a tiger skin. The rest of us paid for his air-conditioning. In addition to our massive costumes, which were no lighter than before, we had to wear masks to represent the various animals which appear in Milton's allegory. The temperature inside the masks was searing, and vision through the narrow eye slits was reduced close to zero." Hardwicke also includes an anecdote about the heat that seems intended to show the virility and backbone of the Shakespearean troupe. After noting that the temperature sometimes reached 115 degrees Farenheit, and that they performed during "the hottest summer in living memory," he explains how the company "recruited members of the Natal Mounted Police" to fill out the crowd scenes. These were "lean, robust, outdoor men, who frequently reeled offstage half-fainting from the feverish climate behind the footlights. Yet not a single member of the Benson company failed to complete the night's performance" (89).

[73] Craufurd remarks on having his costumes dried of the sweat after each performance in Calcutta. Kendal's description of performing in Indian heat is more intimate: "Often the stage clothes ended a performance wringing wet with perspiration. It was inevitable if you played in a temperature of 110F

For Lieutenant H. A. D. Simpson, India's climate, and its heat in particular, was the very thing that prevented the performing arts from thriving in the colonies: "In no part of the world is the theatre a more acceptable form of amusement, and no part of the world is, from its climate, more thoroughly unsuited for it than India." According to Simpson, India is simply too hot for an elite Indian to "appreciate what he sees" on stage, and "the enervating effect of the climate produces its evil results on the Englishman" as well, since "a play which the same man would watch with interest at home he turns from in disgust in India... 'We don't want the legitimate drama out here,' he says, 'with a thermometer at a century. Give us a light comedy, or better still a burlesque, or comic opera, but not too long.'"[74] By contrast, others saw the heat as the true test of a cultivated English taste. One author argues, "I know from many years' experience of the East that temperatures have no effect upon the ardent playgoer, and if the performers do not mind the heat in India and the Straits Settlements, or the cold in North China, the public will turn out to welcome them at any time."[75]

Storms, floods, and droughts also made living conditions difficult for Shakespearean players at the same time that they worked to justify their Shakespearean crusade in the colonies. Daniel Bandmann was prepared to depart Adelaide for a tour of India when four members of his company refused to go with him, simply because they were afraid of the climate they would encounter there.[76] Bandmann experienced a "slight typhoon" in Hong Kong, which claimed sixteen lives; the Shakespearean was surprised to learn that several thousand had perished in the previous one.[77] While driving in a car on the road between Manipur and Panitola, Kendal and his family were caught in a flash flood and had to abandon their vehicle. Most of their costumes were ruined beyond repair, and when they finally salvaged their car, they discovered it had been looted by divers.[78] Dust storms were frequent and

---

in costume, wig, make-up, false beard. Your tights would be drooping in wet folds, your beard on the verge of dropping off, and beads of perspiration would trickle down your nose to be passed on to your partner in an embrace." Hardwicke recounts the heat of Pietermaritzburg: "Grease paint would not stay on our slippery faces." Similarly, Lang remembers playing a Benjamin-Button Shylock in the tropical heat of Kingston, Jamaica: "I would commence a scene looking, according to the demands of the character, like an old Jew, but by the time that the scene was over all the make-up would have washed off and my ordinary young face would have taken its place." Craufurd, *Ramblings of an Old Mummer*, 162; Kendal and Colvin, *The Shakespeare Wallah*, 124; Hardwicke, *A Victorian in Orbit*, 89; Lang, *Mr. Wu Looks Back*, 64.

[74] Simpson, "Art in Afghanistan," 140.

[75] Campbell Henderson, "Touring in the Orient," *The Stage Year Book 1920*, 87.

[76] Bandmann, *An Actor's Tour*, 105.

[77] Bandmann, *An Actor's Tour*, 226–8. Craufurd also notes how unpleasant monsoons can be (Craufurd, *Ramblings of an Old Mummer*, 137).

[78] Kendal and Colvin, *The Shakespeare Wallah*, 97–9.

unpleasant in Johannesburg, and lightning strikes and thunderstorms were common on the veldt.[79] The Holloway Theater Company visited Johannesburg in 1895 during a drought. The water shortage prompted W. J. and John Holloway to pilfer water rations from the other guests at the Victoria Hotel for bathing. The drought also inspired some residents to send charges of dynamite skyward, tied to balloons, in the hope of exploding the rain out of passing clouds. President Kruger, however, put a stop to this dynamite idea by invoking another: "The Lord is angry with the cities of Sodom and Gomorrah. When He has punished them, He will send the rain."[80] Actors experienced earthquakes in New Zealand, Japan, and India.[81] Kendal offers an example of the earth-moving force of Shakespeare's language during a performance of *Othello* at a school outside of Delhi: "I had just declaimed, 'There should be now a huge eclipse of sun and moon and the affrighted globe should yawn in alteration,' when the whole building was rocked by an earthquake."[82]

Perhaps the most common cause of death among Shakespearean actors touring the Empire was disease. After the Scottish actor John Moody made a name for himself as a Shakespearean performer in Jamaica in the mid-eighteenth century, he imported his own company to the colony from England, most of whom were wiped out by "Jamaican Fever."[83] Typhoid, dengue fever, and other tropical ailments affected the cast size of Allan Wilkie's company in India; his ailing company inspired Wilkie to perform an "unprecedented feat" of trebling the parts of Friar Laurence, Mercutio, and Prince Escalus in a performance of *Romeo and Juliet*.[84] Wilkie became ill himself with influenza in Osaka, Japan, but still managed to play "Shlyock, Hamlet, and Othello on

---

[79] Craufurd mentions dust storms. Ward recounts watching a storm on the veldt. Craufurd, *Ramblings of an Old Mummer*, 150; Ward and Whiteing, *Both Sides of the Curtain*, 177.

[80] Quoted in Holloway. See David Holloway, *Playing the Empire: The Acts of the Holloway Touring Theatre Company* (London: Harrap, 1979), 68–9.

[81] Bandmann records a twenty-second earthquake at 5 a.m. on 26 June 1881, in the town of Howera, New Zealand. Craufurd experienced an earthquake in Wellington, New Zealand and in Yokohama, Japan. Wilkie recalls experiencing the great New Zealand earthquake of 1929 in the Hawkes Bay area of the North Island. Wilkie's account is somewhat humorous: "On the morning of our arrival in this town, as my wife and I were walking down the centre of the main street, we were both astonished and flattered to see all the inhabitants rushing from their houses and shops to gaze at their famous visitors. Or so we imagined for the moment, but were soon disillusioned when we realized they were merely collecting in the roadway for safety, as their buildings were swaying from the effect of the slight earth waves extending from the great 'quake then taking place in the South Island." Bandmann, *An Actor's Tour*, 145; Craufurd, *Ramblings of an Old Mummer*, 145, 176; Wilkie, *All the World My Stage*, 292–3.

[82] Kendal and Colvin, *The Shakespeare Wallah*, 125.

[83] Errol Hill, *The Jamaican Stage, 1655–1900: Profile of a Colonial Theatre* (Amherst, MA: University of Massachusetts Press, 1992), 76; Richardson Wright, *Revels in Jamaica, 1682–1838* (New York: Dodd, Mead & Co., 1937), 27.

[84] Wilkie, *All the World My Stage*, 154.

three consecutive nights with a temperature hovering between 103 and 104"
degrees.[85] The dust of Johannesburg caused a disease of the lungs and proved
fatal to both the juvenile lead of Ward's South African tour and to the tour
itself in 1892.[86] Ward herself contracted influenza in Johannesburg, but
refused to see a doctor. Her dismissive attitude toward medical treatment,
and her miraculous recovery three days later, made her illness much ado
about nothing, which also happens to be the play she was performing when
she got sick: "I wore two fur coats in the wings, while everyone else was melt-
ing with the heat, yet I shivered during the whole performance."[87] The great
influenza epidemic closed theaters in Sydney in 1919.[88] Daniel Bandmann
declined an invitation to perform in Manila after learning of a cholera out-
break that killed an entire opera company there.[89] While on their way to
Shanghai in 1893, the Kyrle Bellew and Mrs. Brown-Potter Company became
trapped by a quarantine when the plague broke out in Hong Kong. One member of that company, Sally Booth, survived the plague in Hong Kong, but suc-
cumbed to another plague years later in Sydney.[90]

Disease was one hazard that touring players were willing to brave in order
to fly the flag of Shakespeare in the British colonies, but traveling itself was
not without its obstacles. Travel for actors and actresses touring the Empire
sometimes provided opportunities for additional performances and revenue,
but travel conditions could also be extremely dangerous. The innovations of
the steam-powered ship and railroads made travel across the globe more feasible, and enhanced the popularity of traveling theater companies in the
Empire.[91] Theater companies often made time to rehearse on their voyages,
and even performed for audiences on deck at sea.[92] In 1953, Geoffrey Kendal's
Shakespeareana Company began their tour of India (with an all-Shakespeare

---

[85] Wilkie, *All the World My Stage*, 182.

[86] Ward and Whiteing, *Both Sides of the Curtain*, 180–1. After Mr. Eyre's death, Ward's company did not wish to continue their season. John Holloway identifies a poisonous agent in Johannesburg dust, which was a costly environmental side-effect of mining practices: "In dry weather, clouds of dust from the mine dumps, charged with cyanide of potassium, swept along, bringing discomfort to all, and death to the unfortunate with weak lungs and throats" (quoted in Holloway, *Playing the Empire*, 68).

[87] Ward and Whiteing, *Both Sides of the Curtain*, 174–5.

[88] Wilkie, *All the World My Stage*, 243. [89] Bandmann, *An Actor's Tour*, 229.

[90] Craufurd, *Ramblings of an Old Mummer*, 172–4. Craufurd describes how he and Ted Smart managed to escape the quarantine in Hong Kong and make their way to Yokohama.

[91] Booth and Heckenberg, "Touring the Empire," 49.

[92] The history of performing Shakespeare aboard ships dates all the way back to 1607, when the crew of two ships belonging to the East India Company staged performances of *Hamlet* and *Richard II*. *Hamlet* was staged for a Portuguese audience while moored in Sierra Leone. These are the first known productions of Shakespeare performed outside of England, and this was only the third voyage of the East India Company. The ships were on their way to open factories in Cambaya, Sumatra, Bantam, and the Moluccas. Richmond Barbour speculates that theater was used on these voyages as a

and Shaw repertoire), traveling from England to Bombay through the Red Sea. At the captain's request, the company performed (in the sweltering heat of the Arabian Sea) *Arms and the Man*, and selections from *Twelfth Night* and *Macbeth*. During his soliloquy in the latter play—"Is this a dagger which I see before me"—which was delivered on the choppy and swelling waters, Kendal had a "disconcerting moment as Macbeth when [he] was addressing the lounge floor with grim solemnity—'The sure and firm-set earth...'—and it gave a sudden lurch."[93]

While performances of Shakespeare at sea present their own set of challenges and ecological implications, sea-travel also involved risks, both real and imagined.[94] The eminent tragedian G. V. Brooke perished in a shipwreck in January 1866 when his vessel, the *London*, en route from Plymouth to Australia, was caught in a storm.[95] The Holloway Theater Company lost its sets and costumes when the ship carrying them sank in the Green Cape Reef.[96] In 1911, during a voyage from Zanzibar to Bombay on the *Palamcotta*, the Holloway Company encountered a cyclone. The European company members were trapped in the ship's saloon for three days of violent and

---

disciplinary measure for discouraging idleness, though the performance also served a diplomatic function before the Portuguese.

During a voyage on a Pacific Mail Steamer between Auckland and Honolulu, Daniel Bandmann's company gave a profitable performance for the Seaman's Shipwreck and Orphan Society of Sydney. In 1893, the Bellew and Brown-Potter Company rehearsed their twenty-play repertoire (which included *Romeo and Juliet* and *Hamlet*) on the voyage through the Suez Canal on the way to Calcutta. Russell Craufurd, a member of that company, also played for first class passengers on a voyage from Japan to Vancouver in the following year. He also recalls performances given by John Hare and G. W. Anson on his voyage from Sydney back to England. Ward's company rehearsed several of their plays on the voyage between England and Cape Town in 1891. Her repertoire included twenty-six plays, including *Macbeth, Hamlet, Othello, The Merry Wives of Windsor, The Merchant of Venice*, and *Much Ado About Nothing*. Kendal's company also rehearsed *The Merchant of Venice* and selections from *Macbeth* on board the *Strathmore*, which carried them from Southampton to Bombay through the Suez Canal in 1947. See *The Third Voyage Journals: Writing and Performance in the London East India Company, 1607–10* (New York: Palgrave Macmillan, 2009), 7; Bandmann, *An Actor's Tour*, 276; Craufurd, *Ramblings of an Old Mummer*, 156, 176, 147; Ward and Whiteing, *Both Sides of the Curtain*, 170; Kendal and Colvin, *The Shakespeare Wallah*, 85.

[93] Kendal and Colvin, *The Shakespeare Wallah*, 106.

[94] By considering "imagined risks," I am trying to think of these memoirs of touring the Empire as participating in the tropes of the travel literature genre. As such, authors perceive some threats that cannot be substantiated. For example, Daniel Bandmann records visiting a "cannibal village" outside of Port Darwin. Bandmann notes, "It is not seldom that a child, or stray Chinaman falls a victim to their ferocity and brutal tastes," and imagines that the women of his party "were considered as so many desirable sweet morsels." Bandmann also recalls how, when his vessel collided with the coral reef as it passed through the Torres Straits, an engineer seemed very anxious about landing on the coast of Queensland, "where the natives are all cannibals, and dine off any poor, unfortunate, ship-wrecked crews that are cast among them" (Bandmann, *An Actor's Tour*, 258–9, 262).

[95] See H. L. Oppenheim, "Brooke, Gustavus Vaughan (1818–1866)," *Australian Dictionary of Biography*, National Centre of Biography, Australian National University, 17 March 2017. http://adb.anu.edu.au/biography/brooke-gustavus-vaughan-3064/text4519.

[96] Holloway, *Playing the Empire*, 88.

ceaseless rocking. Matheson Lang expressed little concern for the ship's non-European passengers, who were confined among the baggage; in fact, Lang thought their proximity to the company's set pieces produced something of a miracle, straight out of one of Shakespeare's romances: "They came up again after what must have been a terrible two or three days apparently smiling and unconcerned—and yet during the worst night of the storm an old man died and a baby was born!"[97] On his voyage to Australia in 1881 around the Cape of Good Hope, Russell Craufurd's ship lost its propeller and began taking on water; luckily, he managed to land at Cape Town.[98] Ward recalls a stormy 960-mile voyage between Hobart and Dunedin in 1884.[99] Kendal remembers an "appalling storm" between Miri and Brunei in Borneo.[100]

When trains were not available for traversing land, stagecoaches were used. When Ward toured in South Africa in 1892, the railroads did not yet connect between all the major cities, so they traveled by coach, which was "frightfully dusty."[101] One of Ward's company, Ms. Josephine St. Ange, was killed in a carriage accident on the veldt; news of her death was delivered during their production of *Hamlet* in Johannesburg, and the company was too distraught to continue the show.[102] Wilkie traveled by stagecoach through New Zealand's Otira Gorge in a snowstorm in 1919.[103] Craufurd went "bushwacking" in the suburbs of Melbourne, taking a stagecoach over terrible roads.[104]

Traveling by train after the monsoon floods in India was always more certain than traveling by bus, since the roads often disappeared underwater.[105] But train travel brought risks too. Frank Benson's South African tour almost ended prematurely when the train car holding their scenery caught fire as it traveled between Cape Town and Johannesburg.[106] On one train ride, Benson's players became stranded when the train was divided into two. Benson's actors passed the time by joining forces with the Steele Payne Bell-Ringers. Together, they performed a concert in an idle dining car. Meanwhile, the first half of the train jumped the tracks, and the next engine that arrived

[97] Lang, *Mr. Wu Looks Back*, 98. John Holloway remembers, in slightly more sympathetic terms, how the deck passengers "had been bundled below decks and battened under hatches, there to fend for themselves in pitch blackness and, of course, without any form of sanitary arrangements" (quoted in Holloway, *Playing the Empire*, 140).
[98] Craufurd, *Ramblings of an Old Mummer*, 117.
[99] Ward and Whiteing, *Both Sides of the Curtain*, 110.
[100] Kendal and Colvin, *The Shakespeare Wallah*, 143.
[101] Ward and Whiteing, *Both Sides of the Curtain*, 172.
[102] Ward and Whiteing, *Both Sides of the Curtain*, 178–9.
[103] Wilkie, *All the World My Stage*, 246–7.
[104] Craufurd, *Ramblings of an Old Mummer*, 128.
[105] Kendal and Colvin, *The Shakespeare Wallah*, 129.
[106] Hardwicke, *A Victorian in Orbit*, 86.

was full of dead and injured passengers.[107] In the Himalayas, companies relied on the mule and the dandy—or "a wooden hammock made exactly like an out-size coffin with the lid off"—which was carried by no fewer than nine men. Wilkie hired a team of 300 men to transport his baggage and scenery to Nainital.[108]

"Where we lay our scene": The Improvised Stages of the British Empire

In a colonial environment, especially in areas where theaters had not yet been built, Shakespearean performances were exposed to a range of ecological factors that could change the effect—and the affect—of the Shakespearean text. Touring in Australia in the nineteenth century often meant visiting places where theaters were improvised spaces of entertainment: "tents, makeshift halls, hotel saloons and dining rooms—these were very often the theatres of the outback."[109] Frank Gerald, one of the founding members of the Gerald and Duff Dramatic Company, once performed in a railway goods yard, where "railway tarpaulins formed the proscenium and the station bell rang the audience in and the curtain up."[110] The company also played *The Lights O' London* on the seventh level of a silver mine in Broken Hill, New South Wales, and on a billiard table in Malvern, Victoria, where G. V. Brooke had once performed *Othello* to a crowd of miners who threw gold nuggets onto the "stage."[111] In Colombo, Daniel Bandmann played in the schoolroom of an army barracks, and Genevieve Ward played on the rickety tables of a club when there was no other platform.[112] In India, Allan Wilkie tried to find public gardens and private houses at which to give performances, and often his hosts would erect tents to function as dressing rooms.[113] At one performance in Lucknow, Wilkie gave a performance in the public gardens, which housed the tombs of the Kings of Oudh. The company used the bat-infested catacombs as their dressing quarters.[114] At one performance of *Hamlet*, staged in the small dining room of a hotel somewhere in South Africa, the actor

---

[107] Hardwicke, *A Victorian in Orbit*, 96–7.   [108] Wilkie, *All the World My Stage*, 146.
[109] Booth and Hackenberg, "Touring the Empire," 53.
[110] Gerald, *A Millionaire in Memories*, 38.
[111] Gerald, *A Millionaire in Memories*, 38–9. W. J. Holloway also played *Macbeth* atop a billiard table in rural Queensland, where gold miners were accustomed to throwing gold nuggets onstage in lieu of admission. Holloway, *Playing the Empire*, 34.
[112] Bandmann, *An Actor's Tour*, 244; Ward and Whiteing, *Both Sides of the Curtain*, 105.
[113] Wilkie, *All the World My Stage*, 149.   [114] Wilkie, *All the World My Stage*, 150.

playing Claudius could not find a place on stage to die: "He thereupon picked his way carefully over the bodies of Gertrude and Laertes and expired with standing room only in the wings."[115] Before there were theaters in the British Caribbean—in Jamaica, Barbados, Antigua, St. Lucia, and Trinidad— performances were given in taverns, in long rooms, or even in "temporary sheds erected to house an audience." Courtyards of plantation houses also functioned as performance venues.[116]

Traveling players also had several opportunities to play in outdoor venues, where weather events and other ecological factors could influence a performance. For example, delivering a Shakespearean monologue may have been second nature to some well-rehearsed actors, but at 8,000 feet above sea level, visitors to Mussoorie had to adapt their craft to the altitude.[117] In Rangoon, when Bandmann asked to see the theater, he was shown "a large open place without walls, with a stage at the end." The walls of this theater had been removed for a ball a few days prior; Bandmann refused to perform in an "invisible hall."[118] Charles Duval, who toured South Africa in the 1880s with his one-man show entitled *Odds and Ends*, describes an open-air theater at the Good Hope Gardens in Cape Town.[119] On Saint Patrick's Day, Duval performed in Pretoria under "canvas awnings through which the rain descended to the detriment of our grog, by watering it too much."[120] In 1846, the 45th regiment at Fort Napier in Natal gave an open-air production of *Arden of Faversham*.[121] The Himalayas formed the backdrop of the Doon School's open-air theater in Dehra Dun, where Kendal's company performed.[122] Ward recalls seeing a Singalese play in Colombo at an open-air theater in the city's gardens. The theater was "octagonal, with columns open to the air, and lighted by coconut shells with oil and a wick in them."[123] In Kanpur, 1912, a dust storm concluded an open-air performance of *The Taming of the Shrew*.[124] Wilkie supposes he was the first to give a "pastoral performance" of *As You*

---

[115] Hardwicke, *A Victorian in Orbit*, 91.

[116] Kole Omotoso, *The Theatrical into Theatre: A Study of Drama and Theatre in the English-Speaking Caribbean* (London: New Beacon Books, 1982), 16–18.

[117] Wilkie, *All the World My Stage*, 151.   [118] Bandmann, *An Actor's Tour*, 254.

[119] Charles Duval, *With a Show Through Southern Africa*, Vol. 1 (London: Tinsley Brothers, 1882), 54.

[120] Charles Duval, *With a Show Through Southern Africa*, Vol. 2 (London: Tinsley Brothers, 1882), 160.

[121] Fletcher, *The Story of Theatre in South Africa*, 81. See also Alan F. Hattersley, *Pietermaritzburg Panorama: A Survey of One Hundred Years of an African City* (Pietermaritzburg: Shuter and Shooter, 1938), 39. *Arden of Faversham* has been attributed to Shakespeare by some scholars.

[122] Kendal and Colvin, *The Shakespeare Wallah*, 92.

[123] Ward and Whiteing, *Both Sides of the Curtain*, 105.

[124] Wilkie, *All the World My Stage*, 150. Wilkie remarks that dust storms are common before the rainy season, but this storm seemed to devastate the performance space: "The dressing tents were

Like It in Melbourne on the grounds of the Federal Government House; he also gave outdoor performances of this play in Lahore and in Nainital.[125] In the latter, the actor playing Touchstone had trouble climbing the nearly perpendicular slope that formed the backdrop of the natural stage, which the actors used to make their exits and entrances. Once he managed to get offstage, Touchstone, exhausted, would fall asleep behind a bush and miss his cues.[126] More recently, in apartheid South Africa, Leslie French's 1972 production of *A Midsummer Night's Dream* performed in the Mannville open-air theater of Port Elizabeth "was punctuated with frequent heavy rain. French was heard to remark, 'I think I was the only dry Bottom at the theatre tonight.'"[127] The record we have of outdoor performances of Shakespeare in the British colonies is far from complete, and the performance history of this theater ecology remains largely undocumented. However, the number of outdoor theaters and improvised venues in the colonies suggests that many performances were subjected to unintended ecological events.

While open-air colonial theaters invited their own set of ecological parameters to each performance, indoor colonial theaters also created conditions that could augment or diminish the effect of a performance. Monkeys, which would climb in the rafters of the Grand Opera House in Calcutta and throw screws and bolts down at the performers below, proved a nuisance to Allan Wilkie. During one performance of *The Merchant of Venice*, Frediswyde Hunter-Watts (Wilkie's wife), who played Portia, had just explained to Shylock, "The quality of mercy is not strained, / It droppeth as a gentle rain from heaven / Upon the place beneath" (4.1.190–2) when a heavy wrench fell to the stage, narrowly missing her head. After the show, a furious Wilkie, who seems to have taken the projectile as a deliberate and malicious criticism (from a monkey!) rather than as an accident, responded accordingly: "I considered that whatever their opinion of her performance, they should at least have some respect for the immortal William. If that was all they thought of Mercy, *I* would have none, and very reluctantly I had one of them shot, when

blown down and our garments scattered to the four winds of heaven were hastily retrieved by our native servants from the neighboring undergrowth, while the audience made a hurried departure."
    [125] Wilkie, *All the World My Stage*, 230, 139, 148.   [126] Wilkie, *All the World My Stage*, 148–9.
    [127] J. B. Hamber and Eugene Olivier (compiled by Laurence Wright and Lin Gubb), "A Tribute to 'Stratford-on-Baakens': Thirty Years of the Port Elizabeth Shakespearean Festival," *Shakespeare in Southern Africa*, Vol. 3 (1989), 5. The authors note that this outdoor theater also has a history of ecological interruptions during the Port Elizabeth Shakespeare Festival: "Birds would flutter and twitter, sometimes appropriately, sometimes not. Once a dog made a guest appearance and on another occasion a frog hopped about the stage doing an unchoreographed dance of his own. There was even a performance during which a burglar tried to escape the long arm of the law by hiding in the shrubs at the side of the show. Such are the perils of open-air theatre."

the others, realizing with Falstaff that discretion was the better part of valour, quickly disappeared to another, and I trust more suitable, roosting place."[128] On a different occasion in Colombo, Wilkie staged "the most beautiful and effective scene I have ever seen in any theater," which (he is humble enough to admit) was "purely accidental and entirely due to Nature's artful aid." Instead of using a painted backdrop, Wilkie decided to open the folding doors at the back of the stage to reveal a beautiful "natural" setting outside: "Palm trees gently stirred against an indigo sky studded with stars and a bright tropical moon was shining, all with an effect of illimitable distance, providing a setting that was utterly beyond the arts of the scene-painter and electrician."[129] Wilkie's description of the theater at Kandy in Ceylon provides another example of the natural world inhabiting the theater: "The lusty jungle growth had shot up underneath the stage and forced it into a series of waves and hollows…Bamboo trees had been allowed to penetrate the floors of the dressing rooms and with their branches trimmed served as clothes pegs."[130] During a performance at the Great Opera House in Brisbane, the Gerald and Duff Dramatic Company was surprised by a flood: "It had rained for weeks, and that night the water poured down a long passage, burst through and flooded the stage and the great Opera House. The footlights were put out, the ladies screamed, the orchestra got a ducking, the show closed down, and we went home by boat."[131] In Kimberley, the Theatre Royal had a roof of galvanized iron; in a light rain, the drizzle could make the loudest of speeches inaudible: "vain is the attempt of singer or speaker to make the voice heard over the

---

[128] Wilkie, *All the World My Stage*, 124. Wilkie seems more bothered that the monkeys interrupted a play by "the immortal William" than he is concerned for his wife's safety. His interpretation of "mercy" is also interesting, because it tells us how he interprets animal agency within a performance space. To Wilkie, these monkeys are not just monkeys but saboteurs, non-human enemies of the immortal bard. He is unwilling to see them as part of the performance but at the same time suggests that they have some kind of malicious theatrical agency. Wilkie does not miss the significance of the wrench falling—violently, not gently—at that particular moment; the wrench embodies mercy, falling upon the place beneath. But at the same time the wrench seems to imbue the monkeys with the agency of a theater critic, it also seems to present monkeys as merciful creatures. At the very moment that Portia shows the law, the bond, and the doctrine of "mercy" to be malleable, this falling wrench makes monkeys merciful; if the audience accepts that the monkeys can throw a wrench deliberately, then perhaps they can accept that they can throw it accurately enough to miss a human target. Wilkie's reaction to these monkeys, by killing one of them unmercifully, ignores the nuances of Portia's speech and the ecological implications of this performance, which make a mockery of mercy, a monkey of a monarch, and perhaps even of "God himself" (4.1.201).

[129] Wilkie, *All the World My Stage*, 157–8. The scene was created for a performance of Wilde's *Salome*.

[130] Wilkie, *All the World My Stage*, 159. Though Wilkie is abhorred by the condition of this theater, his view is not shared by the theater's patrons: "Fortunately the public of Kandy were not deterred by the obvious defects of this extremely primitive temple of the drama and attended our performances in goodly numbers" (159–60).

[131] Gerald, *A Millionaire in Memories*, 44–5.

obnoxious din produced."[132] The same was true of the Theatre Royal in Pietermaritzburg. Morton Tavares's production of *Macbeth* performed there in 1882 was completely inaudible because of the sound of rain on the roof.[133] In February 1782, the New American Company of Comedians played a Shakespearean farce called *Catherine and Petruchio* in Kingston, Jamaica, after which was displayed "A Grand Set of Chinese and Italian Fire-Works." Members of the company had performed a similar display of fireworks in Philadelphia in 1768, where the ceiling of the theater had been opened to allow smoke to escape. Richardson Wright speculates that the theater in Kingston may have also had a retractable or removable roof.[134] When Matheson Lang visited the Scottish Society in Shanghai, they insisted that his company perform *Macbeth*, even though it was not part of their repertoire. The Shanghai Amateur Dramatic Society even offered them a "Skiopticon" for the Witches' scenes, to represent the moon on a stormy evening. The company decided that the effect was too powerful, however: "We started to rehearse with the Skiopticon, but, so effective was it, and so fascinating to watch these angry stormclouds racing across a watery moon, that I very quickly realized that not a word of *Shakespeare* would be listened to or any of the action of the play paid the slightest attention to! In fact, the Skiopticon would have been very much the star of the whole show."[135] In order to keep the projection device from stealing Shakespeare's thunder, it was omitted from the performance.

Fires were also a common hazard of indoor performances. In January 1785, a fire broke out during a performance in Kingston, Jamaica, caused by whale-oil lamps that had been over-filled.[136] A fire at a theater in Geelong almost ruined Allan Wilkie's Shakespearean tour of Australia.[137] During a performance in Tasmania, a dog knocked over an oil lamp and started a small fire, which an audience member managed to extinguish with his coat.[138]

Clearly, performing Shakespeare in the colonies was no picnic for actors and actresses. But each ecological obstacle provided a triumphant scaffolding for Shakespeare's cultural iconicity and apotheosis. Shakespeare's commercial

---

[132] Duval remarks, "the roof of the Kimberley theatre, in a semi-tropical rain shower, would have made the old man [Demosthenes] offer a stout reward for the loan of a speaking-trumpet" (Duval, *With a Show Through Southern Africa*, 90).

[133] Dennis Schauffer, "Shakespeare Performance in Pietermaritzburg, Natal, Prior to 1914," *Shakespeare in Southern Africa*, Vol. 19 (2007), 13–14. See also *Natal Witness*, 3 April 1882.

[134] Wright, *Revels in Jamaica*, 168–9. For a description of the Philadelphia performance by the Douglass Company, see *Pennsylvania Gazette*, 8 December 1766.

[135] Lang, *Mr. Wu Looks Back*, 107.   [136] Wright, *Revels in Jamaica*, 210.

[137] Wilkie, *All the World My Stage*, 281.   [138] Craufurd, *Ramblings of an Old Mummer*, 129.

value to theater patrons, Shakespearean actors, and even to English departments derives in part from this theater history in which non-human nature plays no small part. The more difficult the playing conditions, this history suggests, the greater the payoff, and the more important the performance. Dromgoole's Globe to Globe tour participates in this same theater history, and calls attention to the danger of claims that seek to immortalize William Shakespeare. I do not intend to disparage Shakespeare here; on the contrary, it is my own love for Shakespeare that drives me to be cautious in singing his praises. By entertaining the possibility that Shakespeare's cultural status today could be an accident, if not a mistake, the product of an ecology between an imperial ideology and the natural world, I hope Shakespeareans will be more reflective about the violent colonial and ecological history that has normalized claims regarding Shakespeare's universalism. At the same time, I hope that attending to the non-human agents of Shakespearean performance can illuminate our own capacity for accidents offstage. The colonial history of Shakespeare in performance overlaps with the history of globalization, industrialization, and climate change. In Chapter 5, I focus more closely on the potential for non-human natural agents to affect the meaning of a Shakespearean performance, in the hopes that the unplanned accidents of a given performance can teach us to understand our accidentally acquired geologic agency in a more productive way.

5

Stolen Thunder

Performing Shakespearean Weather Events in the Anthropocene

Chapter 1 of this book ended with a hypothetical question: what if instead of carrying a venereal disease back to Europe, Columbus had brought back something far more deadly? As Fletcher's play suggests, audiences may have been educated enough about the kinds of human and non-human biota traversing the Atlantic to pose such a question. By the late sixteenth century, a similar thought might have crossed the minds of many a mariner, especially those who knew about weather patterns in the Caribbean. How might the history of globalization have altered, the ensuing relationship between Europe and the Americas changed, if, on Columbus's first voyage, his three ships had sailed headlong into a hurricane? That Columbus arrived in the "New World" in early October 1492 is nothing short of miraculous, considering it was the middle of hurricane season.[1]

But rather than entertain the hypothetical scenario of what might have been had Columbus perished in a hurricane on his initial voyage, I raise his good luck in order to foreground the determining role of accident in the last five centuries of European imperialism and globalization. Europe and the global North have overwhelmingly benefited from the redistribution of wealth, labor, and natural resources that Columbian and capital exchange engendered at the expense of the global South. At the heart of Columbus's accident lies another, because this history of exchange has also been the history of the Anthropocene. In Columbus's blind stumbling into the Americas, I find a salient analogy for the accidental discovery that scientists have only recently made: that human behaviors are irreversibly changing the planet, the

---

[1] Stuart B. Schwartz, *Sea of Storms: A History of Hurricanes in the Greater Caribbean from Columbus to Katrina* (Princeton, NJ: Princeton University Press, 2015), 10. Schwartz writes, "Columbus was undoubtedly a skilled mariner, but he was also a very lucky one. About ninety percent of all tropical storms in the Atlantic form between the latitudes of 10° North and 35° North. Yet in September 1492, at the height of the hurricane season, Columbus voyaged uneventfully from the Canary Islands to his landfall in the Bahamas with good weather, sailing as he did along the predominant track of the great Atlantic hurricanes."

Anthropocene Theater and the Shakespearean Stage. William H. Steffen, Oxford University Press.
© William H. Steffen 2023. DOI: 10.1093/oso/9780192871862.003.0006

climate, and even the intensity of weather events. The history of anthropogenic climate change and the history of nature's globalization began with the same stroke of dumb luck—or blind misfortune, depending on where one is standing.

Assisting the Storm: Provincializing the Species Narrative of the Anthropocene

When real weather events participate in Shakespearean performances, audiences in the Anthropocene are confronted with a dubious spectacle. On the one hand, if the weather behaves felicitously with the human performers, it creates the illusion, if only for a moment, that the weather is an intentional part of the show. From this perspective, the audience is invited to see their anthropogenic agency reflected in the weather's on-stage performance; it appears as if the actors on stage are controlling the weather (instead of generically contributing to its changing behavior within a particular climate, which human behaviors are more precisely responsible for altering). And while it is true that audiences do participate in the weather events they might experience or behold, they also do not contribute to them equally or in the same way. Neither will individual audience members interpret the weather in a performance in the same way. In short, the theater showcases the problem with thinking of human agency as a homogenous narrative about the species.

The best way of knowing how audiences are interpreting a play performance with an enhanced ecological element is of course simply to ask them. Evelyn O'Malley's contribution to the special issue of the *Shakespeare Bulletin* (36.3) from the fall of 2018, focusing on Eco-Shakespeare in Performance, employs an ethnographic methodology to her study of performances given at the outdoor Willow Globe "living theater" in Powys, Wales.[2] O'Malley conducted more than 300 interviews of audience members "weathering" performances at the uniquely ecological performance space.[3] Her findings are useful for what they tell us about the conclusions the attendees—who were not necessarily Shakespeare scholars or climate scientists—are drawing from more eco-conscious performances. "Talk of a changing climate was very far from

---

[2] Evelyn O'Malley, "'To Weather A Play': Audiences, Outdoor Shakespeares, and Avant-Garde Nostalgia at The Willow Globe," *Shakespeare Bulletin*, Vol. 36, No. 3 (2018), 413.

[3] O'Malley, "Outdoor Shakespeares," 411. O'Malley prefers this term to "hearing" a play, which is what audiences do, or "seeing" a play, which is what spectators do: "I would like to supplement these actions by proposing 'weathering' as a way of thinking about audiencing at outdoor Shakespeares."

what audience members had to say about the Shakespeares of this study," O'Malley writes.[4] Spectators did, however, note the ways in which the weather was able to complement the performances they attended, and O'Malley finds that "the conditions in which audience members encounter Shakespeare profoundly affect how they respond to the plays."[5] O'Malley also notes a striking number of responses from spectators who felt that these outdoor performances—which were given in a "twenty-sided geometric structure" of willow arches, home to many birds, and which situate spectators adjacent to a meadow full of wildflowers that "would have grown during 'Shakespeare's Day'"—furnished modern spectators with an authentic sixteenth-century playgoing experience.[6] O'Malley draws an inspiring conclusion from her ethnographic research by applying Kate Soper's hermeneutics of an "avant-garde nostalgia." From audience members who express a desire for an "authentic" Shakespearean performance in this outdoor space, O'Malley concludes that what they are actually expressing is "a longing for a more pleasurable, sustainable past (even a romanticized, imagined past that never existed)," which in turn "might prompt desire for a more pleasurable and less environmentally-destructive future."[7] O'Malley's ethnography represents a superb strategy for provincializing human agency, since it documents how individual audience members are taking stock of the network of human and non-human actors contributing to a given performance.

Unfortunately, the limited archive of outdoor Shakespearean performances from the last four centuries makes accessing audience perceptions of a given performance difficult. As Chapter 4 details, many of the Shakespearean performances given in the British colonies are only documented by the performers themselves, who have a vested interest in framing their struggles as victories for Shakespeare and for the Empire. Other accounts of audiences "weathering" outdoor performances of Shakespeare's plays are accessible in the form of newspaper reviews. But these are beset with another kind of bias. Newspaper reviewers tend to sensationalize and prioritize moments when the weather seems to cooperate with the play's agenda. Whereas accounts given from actors tend to highlight the mistakes, mishaps, and struggles of performing Shakespeare in a new environment, newspaper reviewers tend to highlight the magical moments of felicitous ecological coincidence. Our

---

[4] O'Malley, "Outdoor Shakespeares," 411.   [5] O'Malley, "Outdoor Shakespeares," 412.
[6] O'Malley, "Outdoor Shakespeares," 413–14, 416. One spectator commented that "she loved the performance 'because it is outside in the environment which Shakespeare would have experienced,' describing pleasure derived from a perceived getting closer to Shakespeare outdoors" (416).
[7] O'Malley, "Outdoor Shakespeares," 419.

limited access to audience perceptions of outdoor performances, however, is no reason to discount their significance for studying the interplay between Shakespearean performance, "natural" phenomena, and human agency. On the contrary, the archive of audiences "weathering" Shakespearean performances may train future actors, directors, and audience members to apply a more generous ecological gaze to future theatrical mishaps or outdoor performances.

On stage, actors have more agency than passive audience members in making the weather meaningful. This demonstrates, by way of the stage as a metaphor, how the agency that can be attributed to climate change and weather event intensification is not equally distributed among the species. When an actor chooses to engage with the weather within a dramatic space, the action can enhance the performance. During a performance of *The Tempest* at the College of St. Elizabeth by the Shakespeare Theater of New Jersey in 2005, one reviewer noted the weather's felicitous behavior: "At exactly the moment when Trinculo, a drunken jester anticipating foul weather, looked skyward and proclaimed, 'Yond same black cloud, yond huge one,' an ominous dark mass appeared directly above the stage."[8] While this reviewer's remarks lend agency to the "moment" that a cloud "appeared," it is ultimately the actor who chooses to engage with the natural environment of a play's outdoor setting. Furthermore, the illusion created by the weather's performance that "Yond same black cloud" will remain within Prospero's control for the duration of the play creates a contract between the actor, the atmosphere, and the audience that the atmosphere will not sustain for the entire performance.

At the same time, a congenial audience can be the difference between a theatrical disaster and a felicitous performance of the weather. During an 1895 production of *King Lear* at the Standard Theatre in Johannesburg, for example, the Holloway Theatre Company unintentionally appropriated the storm outside into their performance:

> One night they were playing *King Lear* and the rain was pelting down on the tin roof, accompanied by loud thunder and vivid lightning. There was no need to use their own sound effects, though the storm almost succeeded in killing the play: "It was almost a nightly occurrence for the electric light to fail, being newly installed, and the 'thud-thud' of the donkey engine could be plainly heard all over the building...The audience were very

---

[8] Naomi Siegel, "Weather Adds Touch to Outdoor 'Tempest,'" *New York Times*, 5 July 2009, NJ10.

good-natured, taking everything as it came, and indulging in community singing during unavoidable 'accidents.'"[9]

With a "very good-natured audience," almost anything is possible on stage.

Attending to the weather's behavior on stage can help us to see human agency as unequally distributed in the Anthropocene. But a performance theory for Anthropocene theater might be best illustrated by the early modern stage itself. Early modern audiences perceived the weather in terms compatible with attribution and climate science today; in Shakespeare's lifetime, the weather was understood as a reflection of *individual* human agency, rather than as a result of a collective human agency. When we compare the religious and moral meteorology of the sixteenth century with recent developments in climate science, a strange bridge develops between early modern faith and modern scientific logic about the weather. As Stuart Schwartz defines them, early modern weather events, but especially Caribbean hurricanes, were

> set in a social, political, and conceptual frame that made an understanding of this catastrophe [a hurricane] a moment for reflection on human sin and moral failure as the cause of God's anger. That interpretation would change over time from a providentialist view to one that by the eighteenth century emphasized the normal risks of the natural world, and thus no longer made humans the cause of their own suffering. Explanations would then shift again in the late twentieth century to an emphasis on climate change that once more placed the onus for natural disasters on human error, but this time on human decisions and policies, not on sin or moral failures.[10]

Although "sin and moral failures" no longer dictate the hermeneutics of weather events, I suggest that recent developments in "attribution science" revive the ethical considerations of interpreting the weather. Climate science increasingly represents anthropogenic agency as an ethical problem for which people are morally accountable, making it increasingly compatible with an early modern perspective. In short, early modern interpretations of the weather can help us to further provincialize human geologic agency by encouraging modern audiences to see causal explanations in individual human behaviors.

---

[9] Reader's Digest, *South Africa's Yesterdays* (Cape Town: Reader's Digest Association South Africa, 1981), 121.

[10] Schwartz, *Sea of Storms*, 3–4.

One place we might look for a provincial human influence on global ecology and climate in the early modern period is the inaugural phase of European colonialism. Although the starting point of the Anthropocene is still contested among scholars and scientists, I privilege the proposed 1610 start date—also known as the "Orbis Spike"—because it compels us to see the global predicament we face today as the legacy of European colonialism. Simon Lewis and Mark Maslin show with stratigraphic evidence how human behaviors were responsible for a substantial *decrease* in atmospheric carbon dioxide around 1610. The authors speculate that the rapid depopulation of the Americas and the resulting cessation of American farming practices, paired with the increased traffic of European biota across the Atlantic, resulted in floral growth substantial enough to affect atmospheric carbon dioxide levels.[11] As Lewis and Maslin point out, accepting the 1610 start date means accepting a narrative where "colonialism, global trade, and coal brought about the Anthropocene."[12] Furthermore, accepting 1610 as the start date of the Anthropocene foregrounds the economic inequalities between the global North and South, resulting from centuries of ecological imperialism, resource extraction, and human exploitation. Thus, the unequal distribution of human agency in the Anthropocene can also be traced back to the environmentally exploitive practices of the early modern period.

Although attribution science seems compatible with early modern inter-pretations of the weather because they each uphold human behaviors as causal agents of specific weather events, there are two important distinctions to be made. First, whereas attribution science claims that human behaviors exert a direct influence on the atmosphere by way of a slow, progressive climate change, sixteenth-century authors and pamphleteers held the providential view that human action could incite God's judgment to manifest as a more immediate weather event. One author interpreted the flood in Monmouthshire, Wales during January 1607 as a divine expression of God's displeasure with pride, gluttony, drunkenness, and a general "contempt of the Ministerie of the word."[13] Similarly, in *Pericles*, a "fire from heaven" (2.4.9) strikes Antiochus and his daughter dead for their incest; since plague is responsible for the death of Antiochus in the play's source, Shakespeare's amended lightning strike "ensures that Antiochus does not have time for redemption."[14]

---

[11] Lewis and Maslin, "Defining the Anthropocene," 175.

[12] Lewis and Maslin, "Defining the Anthropocene," 177. For a critique of this hypothesis, see Yusoff, *A Billion*, 29–33.

[13] Anonymous, *Lamentable newes out of Monmouthshire in VVales* (London, 1607), C3r.

[14] Jones, *Shakespeare's Storms*, 53.

Secondly, while the narrative of the Anthropocene suggests that the collective human species shares in the geologic agency responsible for intensifying weather events, early modern moralists were inclined to point to specific sins practiced by *some* as the causal force of a storm or a flood, which served as punishment or warning for *all*. A revised more provincial narrative of human agency in the Anthropocene might be framed in similar terms. To one pamphleteer, the overflowing of the Severn was of Biblical proportion, on par with Noah's flood; the resulting inundation seemed "altogether to be a second deluge: or an universal, punishment by Water."[15] To sixteenth-century moralists, it was understood that storms were caused by individual human behaviors rather than by the species as a whole. Lightning was seen as God's "judicial" punishment for blasphemy, sorcery, ambition, adultery, and usury, though it was also thought to teach offenders to fear God, and to warn of greater punishments to come.[16] The "blacke fatall winter" of 1613 was interpreted by one author as a punishment for wealth inequality in London: "we may behold the fury of his high offended power in witnessing the spoiles of stately houses, and the high turrets of great personages, by these unruly winds defaced, and as it were, in their greatest pride torne in sunder."[17] Though the specific sins for which humans were being punished with natural disasters were often vaguely named, interpreters of such disasters agreed that God's intentions were always justified, and were always good.[18] On 21 October 1638 in Devonshire, a lightning storm killed several members of a congregation worshipping at church.[19] A similar incident occurred in a church in Cornwall in 1640. These seemingly natural phenomena were interpreted as signs of God's mercy, even if they also demonstrated God's wrath. An eyewitness account of *The voyce of the Lord in the temple* in 1640 emphasized the redemptive function of such a terrifying display: "you have seene flames scorching, but not consuming: A Ball of Fire shot, and striking, but not killing; yea killing of Beasts, and unreasonable creatures, but sparing the reasonable; casting downe, but not destroying."[20] When lightning struck the steeple of a church in Bletchingley on 17 November 1606, it started a fire that "miraculouslie" did not spread to the rest of the town. Thus, "in the middest of iudgement there shined

---

[15] William Jones, *God's vvarning to his people of England* (London, 1607), A2v.

[16] Simon Harward, *A discourse of the seuerall kinds and causes of lightnings* (London, 1607).

[17] Anonymous, *The vvonders of this windie winter* (London, 1613), B2r.

[18] Alexandra Walsham, *Providence in Early Modern England* (Oxford: Oxford University Press, 1999), 123.

[19] John Taylor, *Newes and strange newes from St. Christophers of a tempestuous spirit, which is called by the Indians a hurry-cano or whirlewind* (London, 1638).

[20] Richard Carew, *The voyce of the Lord in the temple* (London, 1640), B4r.

mercie."[21] Attributing natural disasters and weather events to God's wrath or mercy was so common in early modern England that charges of atheism were cast upon anyone who thought to name nature, chance, or accident as the causal agent behind a tempest, flood, or famine.[22]

In the Americas, the weather was used both to defend and to condemn European colonialism. After a hurricane destroyed the port of Veracruz in New Spain, Father Bartolome Romero offered a standard explanation for the loss: "God…was served to punish us all by the loss of our possessions and homes, and to leave us our lives so we could do penance for our sins."[23] The "sins" of the Spanish were, of course, open to interpretation. Gonzalo Fernandez de Oviedo, on the one hand, saw Spanish colonialism as a virtue, and suggested that hurricanes had become less frequent since the Spanish brought Catholicism to the Americas.[24] On the other hand, Bartolome de Las Casas argued that the frequency and intensity of hurricanes had increased since the Spanish occupation of the Caribbean as divine punishment for the atrocities committed against the indigenous populations.[25]

In addition to thunderstorms and lightning strikes, a handful of other weather-related events such as heavy snowfall, flooding, and harvest failure were also interpreted as signs from God.[26] But interpreting the weather through a lens of human sin carried significant cultural consequences, as Wolfgang Behringer shows. When harvests failed because of poor weather, when there were late frosts, sudden summer hailstorms, or persistent rains— when these weather events occurred too infrequently to be the work of "chance," witchcraft was a popular alternative explanation.[27] Reading the weather as a moral consequence of human sin helped fuel the fires of witch hunts in early modern Europe. Today, witch hunts have a less literal connotation. But in the time since climate scientists have begun to demonstrate the

---

[21] Harward, *A discourse*, B1v. Harward also suggests that God's judgment worked according to a Protestant ideology in this instance. The fire melted and destroyed the church's bells, which were "framed in time of Poperie, so (no doubt) they had the blessing and baptizing at that time vsed, and were hallowed by that praier in the Masse book" (B2r). Although Harward concludes that the "cause indeede why the lightning at this time did preuaile both against bels and steeple, was because it was the good pleasure of God, thus to shew his omnipotent power… [and] to giue vs some taste of his iudgments, to summon vs all to true repentance" (B2r), God's iconoclasm here services a Protestant cause.

[22] Walsham, *Providence in Early Modern England*, 124.

[23] Quoted in Schwartz, *Sea of Storms*, 4.   [24] Schwartz, *Sea of Storms*, 14.

[25] Schwartz, *Sea of Storms*, 21.

[26] Wolfgang Behringer, *A Cultural History of Climate*, trans. Patrick Camiller (Malden, MA: Polity Press, 2010), 121.

[27] Behringer, *A Cultural History of Climate*, 129.

reach of human geologic agency, the sentiment for holding "sinners" account-able for the weather has revived.

How to Do Things with Storms: A Theater of the Anthropocene

On Labor Day weekend 1950, a newly formed theater company in Hamilton, Bermuda performed *The Tempest* for their maiden production. Staged out-doors in a "grassy glen," this particular performance was marked by the felici-tous entrance of an unplanned weather event:

> nature also provided some of the most effective and exciting lightning and off-stage sound effects. At this season South Atlantic hurricanes flirt with the Colony, producing crashes of thunder and flashes of lightning. With such realism the synthetic roar of a wind machine was quite unnecessary. During the last of the three performances the weather cooperated somewhat too well and His Excellency, the dignified and intrepid Governor and Commander in Chief of Bermuda, sat through a thunder shower that realis-tically appeared while Prospero's tempest was raging. Under the circum-stances Trinculo's comments on "the foul weather" drew laughter from the damp audience that Shakespearean humor rarely provokes.[28]

The weather's behavior "on stage" during this performance raises questions about the company's intention, the storm's autonomy, and its effect on the "damp" audience. Perhaps the storm clouds, full of "crashes of thunder and flashes of lightning," even entered on cue with Trinculo's speech, and gave the actor something tangible to point at: "Yond same black cloud, yond huge one, looks like a foul bombard that would shed his liquor. If it should thunder as it did before, I know not where to hide my head: yond same cloud cannot choose but fall by pailfuls" (2.2.21–4). Perhaps an audience in the open air would envy Trinculo, who at least has Caliban's gabardine to shelter himself beneath. For Trinculo, a real storm adds comedy and credibility to his perfor-mance. But what does a real storm do for a character like Prospero, whose power over Ariel, Caliban, Miranda, and Ferdinand seems to depend upon his ability both to "put the wild waters in this roar" and also to "allay them"

---

[28] Mary Johnson Tweedy, "Bermuda 'Tempest': Presentation in Hamilton Recalls Belief That Island Was Scene of Play," *New York Times*, 17 September 1950. ProQuest Historical Newspapers: *The New York Times (1851–2010)*, 111.

(1.2.2)? What happens when an audience sees that Prospero has no control over his storm? The stakes of this question are high, especially at a performance in colonial Bermuda, with "the dignified and intrepid Governor and Commander in Chief" Sir Alexander Hood weathering the storm in the audience. *The Tempest* was one of several works by Shakespeare that functioned as a vehicle for disseminating an imperial ideology throughout the British Empire.[29] If the Walsingham Players intended to stage Prospero's subjugation over Caliban before the governor of Bermuda, then the weather, which "cooperated somewhat too well," may have productively disrupted Prospero's colonial, environmental, and patriarchal display by entering without the magician's permission, and exposing his power as a mere performance. There is no record of Governor Hood's response to the performance; we only know that he sat through it, and that he got wet.

The storm that interrupted *The Tempest* in Hamilton, Bermuda was not an isolated incident; weather events coalesce with Shakespearean performance all the time. The question is: what does the weather *do* to the performance? The spectrum of audience interpretations will range from seeing the weather as an unhappy accident capable of ruining the evening to seeing the weather as a felicitous marriage of Shakespeare and the atmosphere. Reviewers are more inclined to comment when the latter interpretation is available. During a performance of *Macbeth* in Washington Square in the summer of 1966, Duncan entered Macbeth's castle amidst an intensifying downpour. His observation, "This castle hath a pleasant seat: The air / Nimbly and sweetly recommends itself" (1.6.1–2) became all the more ironic in the rain, and earned him a "roar of laughter" from the audience.[30] The Delacourt Theater, established in 1962, has a long history of staging wet productions of Shakespeare in the Park. During a particularly damp season in the summer of 1988, rain interrupted a performance of *Much Ado About Nothing*. After a twenty-five-minute pause, the show restarted with Benedick asking, "Lady Beatrice, have you wept all this while?" (4.1.264)—a quip that, under the circumstances, "brought the house down."[31] Reviewers are quick to notice how the atmosphere can enhance a production of *The Tempest*, which might help to explain this play's popularity in summer Shakespeare Festivals. During one

[29] The play's role in the promoting an imperial ideology is also emphasized by later postcolonial adaptations of the work, such as Aimé Césaire's. See Aimé Césaire, *A Tempest*, trans. Richard Miller (New York: Theatre Communications Group, 1992).

[30] Harry Gilroy, "Rain and Praise Shower on 'Macbeth,'" *New York Times*, 29 June 1966. ProQuest Historical Newspapers: *The New York Times (1851–2010)*, 38.

[31] Richard F. Shepard, "Weather, 'Tis Not Always Nobler at the Delacorte," *New York Times*, 14 August 1988. ProQuest Historical Newspapers: *The New York Times (1851–2010)*, H5.

performance by Connecticut's Flock Theater, "as Prospero was calling up the winds and the rains, there was a storm front moving through, so as luck would have it, you could see little streaks of lightning in the distance and wind rustling through his cloak."[32]

Just as often, however, the weather can altogether ruin a performance. In 2010, the Optimist Theater in Milwaukee staged a production of *The Tempest* where a storm arrived at a different moment: "around the time that Prospero asks Ariel to call on the goddess Juno to bless the coupling he's arranged between daughter Miranda and shipwrecked prince Ferdinand, in which giant puppets from Milwaukee Mask and Puppet Theatre appear—the sky was aglow with lightning and the show was called before the rain came down."[33] In this instance, instead of delighting the audience, the weather stifles the capacity of audience members to suspend their disbelief about Prospero's supposed control over the weather. Because the weather is so capable of destroying the illusion of Prospero's power, it is likely that Shakespeare, who wrote *The Tempest* after his company acquired the Blackfriars Theater, never *intended* his storm-centered play to be performed outdoors.[34] Unlike the open-roofed venues of London's public theaters, the Blackfriars Theater provided a space where Prospero's magic could be effectively stage-managed under the protection of a roof.

Nevertheless, we might think of the weather as a performative event if it meets the right circumstances during a performance. In his discussion of the "appropriate circumstances" which must underpin a performative speech act, J. L. Austin suggests that "a good many other things have as a general rule to be right and to go right if we are to be said to have happily brought off our action."[35] In the same way that a performative utterance must meet certain criteria, such as containing verbs in the "first person singular present indicative active,"[36] so must storms behave in a certain way in order to be perceived as felicitous or meaningful within the action of the play or performance. Austin names "the doctrine of *the things that can be and go wrong* on the occasion of such utterances, the doctrine of the *Infelicities*."[37] Whether or not a storm is infelicitous or felicitous during the performance of a play depends

---

[32] Kristina Dorsey, "'Oh Bugspray, Where Art Thou?': Birds, Drunks, Sirens Conspire to Make Outdoor Shakespeare a Comedy of Errors," *The Day*, 23 July 2002, C2.

[33] Brian Jacobson, "Optimist Theater's *Tempest* Interrupted by Tempest," *Urban Milwaukee*, 20 June 2010. http://urbanmilwaukeedial.com/2010/06/optimist-theatres-tempest-interrupted-by-tempest.

[34] Andrew Gurr, "*The Tempest*'s Tempest at Blackfriars" (1989), in *The Tempest, Norton Critical Edition*, edited by Peter Hulme and William H. Sherman (New York: Norton, 2004), 251.

[35] J. L. Austin, *How to Do Things with Words* (Oxford: Oxford University Press, 1962), 13–14.

[36] Austin, *How to Do Things with Words*, 56.   [37] Austin, *How to Do Things with Words*, 14.

on the intention of the company, the action of the actors, and how the storm is interpreted by the audience. An unplanned or accidental weather event does not necessarily spell failure for the intention behind the production, as Mary Johnson Tweedy's description suggests of the Bermudan tempest, which rendered "the synthetic roar of a wind machine...quite unnecessary." And yet, in the same way that humans cannot always act intentionally where the weather or our geologic agency is concerned, neither can the weather *intend* to behave a certain way. The circumstances of the performance's setting create the illusion that the weather is functioning within the world of the play, rather than the play functioning within an atmosphere altered by human behaviors.

Whether audiences interpret the weather as felicitous or accidental during a performance, they will agree that the weather always acts independently of the intentions of actors and directors. Jody Enders and Baz Kershaw offer helpful reminders that there is always an intention behind a production that, when confronted with an extra-dramatic element—like a drop in barometric pressure, a clap of thunder, or even an actor's death—may nevertheless change the significance of the action on stage in potentially meaningful ways. As Enders argues, "if an utterance and, more importantly, an *action* during a play is *meant* as anything at all, that is because it is both meant and *performed by someone* and understood by someone else."[38] In her book *Murder by Accident*, Enders details the ethical and legal ramifications of determining human intention (or lack thereof) during a performance by looking at examples of real deaths that took place during medieval stage performances. In asking at what point performance becomes murder, Enders suggests that performance can be legally actionable, "but only when the intentions are clear."[39] A similar problem confronts proponents of attribution science. As attribution science moves toward suggesting that nations experiencing both a carbon debt and the brunt of climate change might be justified in pursuing legal action against carbon-surplus nations, or even individual multinational corporations, determining human intention becomes a crucial, but nevertheless murky and difficult, business. Even if CEOs quit denying the anthropogenic reality of climate change, the tools still do not exist to establish legal culpability where climate change or weather event intensification is concerned. On stage, however, an audience can clearly make out the distinction between the intention of the performers and the heavy clouds rolling over the little scene. The arrival of an

[38] Jody Enders, *Murder by Accident: Medieval Theater, Modern Media, Critical Intentions* (Chicago, IL: University of Chicago Press, 2009), 9. Emphasis original.

[39] Enders, *Murder by Accident*, 3.

unintentional weather event gives the actor a choice either to incorporate the weather into the action of the play, or to pretend it isn't happening until the scene ends or the rain ends it.

Recent productions of Shakespearean plays have incorporated ecological elements into the performance in a much more deliberate way. In such cases, ecological elements of performance are much more difficult to read as "accidental," especially when the director encourages the players to embrace them. Rob Conkie, who directed a performance of *King Lear* on the campus of La Trobe University, presented the action of the play in different locations across the bustling campus, which required a mobile audience and a very flexible cast. During one rehearsal, at the moment when the actor playing the fugitive Edgar delivered his line, "No port is free, no place / That guard and most unusual vigilance / Does not attend my taking," a helicopter appeared over the campus, and Conkie encouraged him to use it: "Use the helicopter...They're coming for you!...Don't let them see you!"[40] Conkie also recounts having Regan and Cornwall lean on an illegally parked car (as if they had driven it there) in front of the loading dock that was meant to function as the entrance to Gloucester's home. In another moment, a disgruntled student leaned out the window and shouted at Gloucester's torture procession, "Shut the fuck up!," much to Regan's delight.[41] Clearly, actors and directors can be intentional about how they interact with their environments. But were actors and directors intentional about embracing the ecological elements where they played in colonial settings? One gets the impression from the accounts surveyed in Chapter 4 that the natural world was a nuisance to the Shakespearean actor touring the British Empire, and that Shakespeare was the preferred tool for taming a "wilderness" perceived as unruly.

Baz Kershaw more fully explores the productive potential of a performance straying from a deliberate human agenda. The Shakespearean weather event that occurred in Bermuda in 1950 is an example of what Kershaw calls a "deconstructive spectacle," which "work[s] paradoxically to open up new

---

[40] Rob Conkie, "Nature's Above Art (An Illustrated Guide)," *Shakespeare Bulletin*, Vol. 36, No. 3 (2018), 395.

[41] Conkie, "Nature's Above Art," 395–6. Rebecca Salazar also details some of the more intentionally directed moments of Shakespearean ecology from the 2014 performance of *Hamlet* in Odell Park in Fredericton, New Brunswick. This performance, like Conkie's, was also meant for a mobile audience, who followed the action of the play through the park. To accommodate this performance structure, actors and actresses had to run between the different scenes, often finding their own paths through the woods. But this also allowed the traveling audience to witness scenes through the woods that were normally not staged in the play, including Hamlet's "ungartered" meeting with Ophelia (Salazar 457).

domains for radical revisions of the way things are."[42] In that particular production, setting, and context, the storm's performance potentially undermines
Prospero's authority over his island, as well as Shakespeare's colonial authority
in Bermuda. *The Tempest* has been largely ignored for the political potential
of its non-human players in performance. Kershaw's articulation of theater
ecology usefully acknowledges how a theatrical accident—or the type of
Shakespearean weather event I am interested in analyzing—carries political
significance and great potential as a tool for activism and revolution. Kershaw
traces a modern division between spectacle and "legitimate theater in the
West" from early modern iterations of spectacle, which were divided between
spectacles of the commons on the one hand, where the people's performance
of power in fairs and festivals was centripetal and diffuse, and spectacles of
the court and church on the other, where state power was centrifugally concentrated in the monarch.[43] Over time, as theater architecture and set designs
reinforced a hierarchy of perspective within performance spaces, and as the
technologies of "legitimate theater" created a more contained theatrical space,
pushing the action back behind the proscenium arch and the gas lights,
spectacle came under suspicion for drama critics and theorists.[44] "The
dominant traditions of Western theater," Kershaw argues, "have aimed to
tame spectacle, to incorporate spectacle in a reduced form into its disciplinary

---

[42] Baz Kershaw, *Theatre Ecology: Environments and Performance Events* (Cambridge: Cambridge
University Press, 2007), 219. Kershaw's own example of a deconstructive spectacle is the scene from
Buster Keaton's silent classic *Steamboat Bill Jr.* (1928), where a cyclone causes the one-ton edifice of a
house to collapse onto Keaton, who stands precisely where the top window is located, which miracu-
lously spares his life. Kershaw argues that this scene "resonates with the ambivalent pleasure characteristic of spectacles of deconstruction and paradox" because it makes the world "both contemptuous
and curious, disgusting and alluring" (Kershaw 217–18). He defines the paradox of this moment in
the way that Keaton risks his life for a stunt: "the utter vulnerability on display is heightened because
the distance between Keaton and his character collapses with the wall" (Kershaw 218). Though
Keaton's disaster is staged and premeditated, the collapse between actor and character that his disaster
produces resonates with my understanding of how storms make meaning of theatrical performance
and acquire political agency.

[43] Kershaw, *Theatre Ecology*, 208.

[44] Kershaw, *Theatre Ecology*, 224. See also Una Chaudhuri, "Land/Scape Theory," in *Land/Scape
Theater*, edited by Una Chaudhuri and Elinor Fuchs (Ann Arbor, MI: University of Michigan Press,
2005), 20. Chaudhuri shows how the political valences of perspective fostered by landscape painting
had a significant impact on the stage: "The stage aesthetic that developed rapidly thereafter proved to
be a costly bargain: with the illusion of depth now available to it, set design could supply astonishing
degrees of realism, but only—and always—within the confines of the picture frame, the proscenium
arch. Pushed outside this frame, banished from participating in the life-art dialectic that is theatrical
process, the spectator became a viewer and had to relinquish the unique experiential mode of receiv-
ing art that is offered by this art alone. True, this new mode of spectatorship recast the ideal spectator
as a sovereign, giving him a model of individuality, centrality, and authority to aspire to: the position
in the auditorium from which the perspectival effects were seen to perfection. But the bargain was a
Faustian one: the average spectator's chances of actually sitting in the 'duke's seat' were nil, just as bleak
as his or her chances of actually 'mastering' the social world" (20).

regimes."[45] But anything can happen during a performance, especially when the performance space is located outdoors, beyond the disciplinary architecture of a theater. Outside, a theater's disciplinary structures are far from absolute. A theatrical mishap, or "theatre *in extremis*," gives birth to a different kind of performance, which can create productive sites of political and ecological action.[46] As an example, in Chapter 4 I discuss Shakespeare's cultural status as a consequence of the improvised and often unpredictable playing conditions of British colonial theater. When a real storm converges with a Shakespearean performance, spectacle triumphs. Especially in a colonial environment, where a different kind of environmental and cultural taming was underway, and where Shakespeare was deployed to serve pedagogical and recreational purposes (which were nonetheless disciplinary), the effects of such a spectacle bear significant political weight.

Jane Bennett usefully articulates the benefit of shifting our understanding of who or what has agency during the performance of a play. Proposing a theory of distributive agency, Bennett grounds her discussion of agency "in that tradition that defines [it] as a *moral* capacity" while also dislocating a single (human) subject as the "root cause of an effect."[47] As such, non-human actants become capable of compelling humans to act:

> This understanding of agency does not deny the existence of that thrust called intentionality, but it does see it as less definitive of outcomes. It loosens the connections between efficacy and the moral subject, bringing efficacy closer to the idea of the power to make a difference that calls for response.[48]

---

[45] Kershaw, *Theatre Ecology*, 221. *The Tempest* is actually a great example of a play that was likely written with the "disciplinary regimes" of indoor theater in mind. Shakespeare's theater was meant to constrict spectacle to the realm of the intentional, but perhaps at some cost: "Staging the tempest just dampens it down" (Kershaw 222).

[46] Kershaw, *Theatre Ecology*, 58. In his first chapter, Kershaw offers several examples of what he terms "theatre at the end of its tether" to "show how at the limits of theatre another kind of performance begins" (Kershaw 55). These are moments where "the protocols that create the theatrical frame begins to unravel under the pressure of mishaps" and where "performance that in some crucial sense is *not an intended part of the theatrical frame* has to be called on to preserve it, restore it, or connect it to some other more urgently meaningful domain" (Kershaw 57–8). His explanation helps us negotiate theatrical mishaps as something that may not be intentional from the perspective of the playing company, but that are not altogether unproductive. He also points out that the risk of something going wrong is part of the allure of the theater, which also demonstrates how performance functions as "an ecology that can be very finely tuned" (58). Once we can see performance as an ecology, we can also see how nature is the best example of an unpredictable performance: "nature is awash with unpredictability, even as humans like to think they have 'mastered' it through science and technology...The performance of the climate ultimately answers no one's bidding" (59).

[47] Bennett, *Vibrant Matter*, 31.　　[48] Bennett, *Vibrant Matter*, 32.

Agency may be bound to efficacy, but efficacy need not be tied to human beings exclusively. A storm may not be a moral subject, but that does not mean that a human audience cannot act morally in response to what power the storm embodies or engenders.

Shakespeare's plays are already preoccupied with representing the weather,[49] but accounting for how the *actual* weather functions differently from theatrical representations of weather in performance seems particularly pressing, especially in light of the recent turn to climate change and weather in Shakespeare studies. In *Shakespeare's Storms* (2015), Gwilym Jones reads Shakespeare's representation of storms in context with early modern theatrical traditions, performance practices, and ideas about the weather. He argues that Shakespeare's storms serve the functional purpose of separating characters, but in performance Shakespeare's storms repeatedly subvert audience expectation by distancing theatrical thunder and lightning from their conventional association with supernatural forces.[50] Similarly, Jennifer Mae Hamilton's *This Contentious Storm* (2017) offers a concentrated theater history of the storm scenes from *King Lear* and traces how the storm has transformed from a literal event in the seventeenth century into a psychological metaphor for Lear's inner storm in twentieth-century productions. Hamilton's meteorological theater history shows how "the literal or meteorological is given meaning through design, adaptation and interpretation," which presupposes that the meaning of a storm on stage derives from a presumably human intention provided by actor, set-designer, and director.[51]

But how should audiences interpret Lear's storm when it is represented by the *actual* weather itself? Jones's book begins with his own anecdote of watching a 2008 production of *Lear* from the pit of the Globe when, toward the end

---

[49] In early modern theater, the weather served a very specific function, depending on how it was cued and staged. Prospero's tempest, for example, may have borne only metaphorical significance to its initial audiences. The play's storm scenes are punctuated by stage directions specifically for "thunder and lightning" rather than "storm and tempest," which proliferate throughout other plays. According to Leslie Thomson, executing the former stage direction would have signaled to audiences that something supernatural was occurring on stage, while the latter would have signaled a mere weather event. In a play like *Macbeth* (1606), the stage technology would have supplied additional hints to audiences that something unnatural was unfolding. Squibs—stage explosives made of sulfurous brimstone, coal, and saltpeter—were particularly effective for creating not only the supernatural "thunder and lightning" that opens *Macbeth* but also the "fog and filthy air" (1.1.12) in which the weird sisters first show themselves. The weather in *King Lear*, on the other hand, does not serve a supernatural function; a storm is just a storm in *Lear*, though it remains charged with a symbolic function. See Leslie Thomson, "The Meaning of Thunder and Lightning: Stage Directions and Audience Expectations," *Early Theatre*, Vol. 2 (1999), 11–24. For a discussion of early modern squibs, see chapter 4 in Harris, *Untimely Matter*, 119–40.

[50] Gwilym Jones, *Shakespeare's Storms* (Manchester: Manchester University Press, 2015), 2, 10.

[51] Jennifer Mae Hamilton, *This Contentious Storm: An Ecocritical and Performance History of* King Lear (London: Bloomsbury, 2017), 113.

of act 2, scene 2, "the skies above the open roof begin to darken," just in time for the storm scenes in the following act.[52] Jones suggests that his experience of the rain during an open-roofed performance of *Lear* demonstrates an environmentally inflected "dramatic irony."[53] But beyond offering an interpretation of a felicitous weather event, this dramatic irony and others like it carry important implications for how we understand the function and meaning of weather, and by extension human agency, in Shakespeare's plays.

One thing that a real weather event *does* for a Shakespearean performance is challenge the artifice of weather that Shakespeare's plays and theater embrace and construct. If the portrayal of a realistic weather event was attempted on the early modern stage, it was likely done to emphasize the storm's theatricality. Speculating on the original representation of the storm scenes in *The Tempest*, Jones argues, "everything in the text points towards an attempt to present a theatrical tempest which is as close to a real one as possible. In doing so, the scene works to diminish the obviousness of its own 'aesthetic framework': that is the mechanics of representation which draw attention to the drama's artificiality."[54] While the audience may experience a realistic storm in the opening act of the play, the realism is all in service of revealing the play's aesthetic framework when Miranda asks her father to "allay" the "wild waters" (1.2.2) he has conjured with his stage managing. Similarly, Hamilton shows that when performances of *Lear* began to emphasize the storm scenes as metaphorical representations of Lear's inward psychological state in the twentieth century, the storm scenes lost their elaborate sets and storm machinery. When John Gielgud played Lear in Harley Granville-Barker's 1940 performance at the Old Vic in London, for example, "the storm was evoked quite simply by means of the recorded sound effects of thunder, wind and the occasional flash of light."[55] Even as stage technologies progressed to fashion more realistic weather events on stage, actors and directors of Shakespeare's storms routinely demonstrate that realism is not always the point.

On the other hand, representing the weather on stage has revealed a certain ingenuity among Shakespeareans over the last few centuries, as well as an obsessive concern for maintaining human control over the weather during a performance. In Shakespeare's day, the open courtyard of the Globe Theater probably provided its own storm effects to be felt by the groundlings on occasion, especially during plays like *Macbeth* (1606), *King Lear* (1608), *Pericles*

---

[52] Jones, *Shakespeare's Storms*, 1.   [53] Jones, *Shakespeare's Storms*, 9.
[54] Jones, *Shakespeare's Storms*, 127.   [55] Hamilton, *This Contentious Storm*, 163.

(1609), and *The Winter's Tale* (1609). But early modern playhouses also made use of drums and gunfire to create artificial thunder. Another method involved rolling a ball down a metal trough. Fireworks and rosin could supply lightning flashes when necessary, and were preferred at open-roofed venues because of the smell.[56] Squibs on lines could create the effect of a thunder-bolt.[57] In the early eighteenth century, stage hands would pound mustard seeds in a giant metal bowl to generate stage thunder. In 1709, John Dennis perfected a method that used wooden troughs with stops in them for his revision of John Webster's *Appius and Virginia*.[58] When his play closed, Drury Lane got rid of every trace of his tragedy—except his "thunder run."[59] When Dennis attended a production of *Macbeth* a few weeks later and heard the sound of his own handiwork, he rose from his seat, shook his fist, and inadvertently coined an idiom: "See how these villains use me!" he cried. "They will not let my play run, and yet they steal my thunder!"[60]

As John Dennis's stormy outburst demonstrated, there was more than one way to create thunder inside a theater. When the intention behind stage thunder is to be realistic and to mask the theater's artifice, stage hands have to remain invisible from the audience's scrutinizing gaze. One labor-intensive method involved shaking the lower corner of a large sheet of copper that was suspended by a chain.[61] A stage hand working for the Leonard Rayne Dramatic Company at the Gaiety Theatre in Johannesburg recalls using "a sheet of thin, black iron strung to a beam. The electrician flashed the lights for lightning and I grabbed the bottom of the iron and shook and bent it. A very little practice enabled me to make the thunder roll and die away."[62] Another method used elsewhere involved "rolling to and fro a large empty cask on the floor of the room above the ceiling of the theatre."[63]

But even the intention to control the weather indoors is prone to unforeseeable accidents, and sometimes a "realistic" storm's artifice is unwittingly exposed to the audience. One production of *King Lear* at the Edinburgh Theatre used a wheelbarrow full of nine-pound cannonballs, which was to be

---

[56] Gurr, "*The Tempest*'s Tempest at Blackfriars," 256.

[57] Hamilton, *This Contentious Storm*, 116.

[58] Anonymous, "Foreign Miscellany: Stage Thunder, From *Once a Week*," *New York Times*, 8 July 1866. ProQuest Historical Newspapers: *The New York Times (1851–2010)*, 2. Gurr suggests that rolling balls down troughs was a method used during Shakespeare's time, so it is likely that Dennis was reviving an old method rather than inventing a new one (Gurr 256).

[59] Hamilton, *This Contentious Storm*, 116.   [60] Anonymous, "Foreign Miscellany," 2.

[61] Hamilton, *This Contentious Storm*, 140.

[62] William T. Powell, "Excerpts from the Memoirs of William T. Powell," in *Johannesburg Pioneer Journals, 1888–1909*, edited by Maryna Fraser (Cape Town: Van Riebeeck Society, 1986), 236.

[63] Anonymous, "Foreign Miscellany," 2.

rolled over a ridged surface by a backstage hand. This particular device seemed "ingenious" enough, until the barrow operator's foot slipped, and the barrow tipped over. The cannonballs rolled onto the stage; the ones that the half-naked elderly Lear managed to dance around made their way into the pit and disbanded the orchestra.[64] When audiences are unwittingly exposed to the "I" of the storm in this way, human error is responsible for altering a rehearsed performance of human intention.

In addition to mediating the level of artifice given to the representation of weather, a real storm also reinforces the unpredictability of live theater in a performance. Acknowledging the legitimacy of a storm's agency to debase or enhance a performance grants modern audiences access to the kind of theater ecology that would have been routine for early modern audiences. As Ellen MacKay shows, the history of early modern theater was fraught with theatrical accident and disaster of Biblical proportions; anti-theatricalists were not wrong to see the theater as a place of judgment.[65] But performance also operated according to an ecological principle in the seventeenth century that made audiences more forgiving of theatrical blunders. Tiffany Stern's work on actors' parts demonstrates the degree to which plays were assemblages that came together according to a distributive agency.[66] Because paper was expensive, actors were given only their "parts" and "cues," and thus had to see each line as an essential element to a larger whole. From the early modern parts that survive today, Stern deduces that the speaker of the cues was not named, and the amount of time between each line was not clear to the actor.[67] Each line of the performance completely depended on the line that preceded it. If a player spoke his cue incorrectly, the performance could grind to a halt.[68] And with only a few rehearsals—sometimes just one, and sometimes none at all—before performing in front of an audience, actors retained an organic element with each new performance, listening to their fellow actors—if only for their cue—as though for the first time.[69] A storm during one of Shakespeare's now

---

[64] Anonymous, "Foreign Miscellany," 2.

[65] MacKay argues that anti-theatricalists like Philip Gawdy supply "intriguing testimony of how theater was thought to happen in early modern England: by careening off the course of its expected event and headlong into disaster." See MacKay, *Persecution, Plague, and Fire*, 3.

[66] Jane Bennett proposes a theory of the distributive agency of assemblages by considering an electrical power grid a "good example" of an assemblage with a number of unpredictable actants, including electricity (Bennett 24).

[67] Tiffany Stern, "Actors' Parts," in *The Oxford Handbook of Early Modern Theatre*, edited by Richard Dutton (Oxford: Oxford University Press, 2009), 501.

[68] Stern, "Actors' Parts," 511.

[69] As Rebecca Salazar suggests, the metatheatrical elements of the play rehearsal scenes in *A Midsummer Night's Dream* demonstrate the extent to which Shakespeare understood theater as an ecological undertaking: "It may not be necessary to cast an actor as the moon or as a wall in every

iconic plays can thus reinvigorate the performance with the ecological uncertainty familiar to Shakespeare's players and audiences, who really did not know what would happen next.

Stolen Thunder: Performing Weather Events on the Colonial Stage

Finally, I turn to another example of the weather's potential as a political agent in performance, which allows us to see Shakespearean performance in a wider environmental context, and within the broader temporal frame of the Anthropocene. The two performances I analyze in this chapter demonstrate how the weather can turn a performance space into a site of anti-colonial resistance. But each performance also seems all the more significant from our present vantage in the Anthropocene. The offshore hurricane that provided the scenery for Shakespeare's *Tempest* during a 1950 performance in Hamilton, Bermuda locates the stage at the site of the storm and shipwreck that may have initially inspired the play. It also allows modern audiences to see the history of British colonialism as invariably linked to a history of mid-Atlantic storms, which are increasing in intensity as a result of climate change. Similarly, the performance of *Romeo and Juliet* given by the Brown-Potter and Bellew Company in Cape Town in January 1892 positions the stage at the gates of a different kind of environmental catastrophe, one more explicitly human-made: a South African gold rush. The poison that Romeo purchases with his own gold takes on a new significance during a gold rush, but also when he makes his purchase in a downpour. A chemical innovation in cyanide during the 1890s made gold extraction more efficient, but also more deadly. Rainwater carried noxious chemicals into the groundwater, and transformed the dust of the mine dumps into toxic sands. While *Romeo and Juliet* has not lost its playing power over the last century, the same amount of time has carried slow but irreversible consequences for the environs surrounding the Johannesburg gold mines.

Cora Urquart Brown-Potter and Kyrle Bellew arrived in Cape Town with their own company from England. They "introduced themselves to prospective Cape Town audiences with an 'At Home'" performance of *Romeo and Juliet*, which they gave at the Rhine Villa on Kloof Street. A crowd arrived,

case, but it is helpful to recognize that factors such as moonlight and topographical features will co-act and interact with human actors in order to produce meaning" (Salazar 460).

despite the weather; "it happened to be one of the Peninsula's summer soakers."[70] Mrs. Brown-Potter's Worth of Paris dresses and stage costumes were well advertised wherever she went, and drew largely female audiences to see her.[71] Olga Racster, a historian of the Cape Town stage, summarizes one review of the performance:

> Between praise and pricks, *Romeo and Juliet* came through successfully, though the wind and rain created such a hullabaloo that Romeo and Juliet had to shout at one another, the scenery sagged from the roof, and the Worth dresses "tended to produce contortions of the Javanese dancer." Yet, there was also praise when Mrs. Potter came to the closing tragic scene.[72]

The rainy performance on Kloof Street proved a portentous start to their South African tour; shortly after their season at the Exhibition opened in Cape Town, the theater burned to the ground with all of the company's uninsured property inside. Bellew estimated his losses stood at £1,500.[73]

The performances in Cape Town and Hamilton showcase the weather's role in producing a "deconstructive spectacle" during a performance, but these two theater ecologies are also worth comparing for the intention they share. Despite being two different weather events occurring at two different times and places during two different Shakespearean performances in the British Empire, these events together show how the weather's performative agency demands provincialization; it needs to be located in a specific time, environment, and social context. As I discuss in Chapter 4, Shakespeare played no small part in the cultural and pedagogical project of British colonialism, thanks to touring companies like Bellew and Brown-Potter's. And even though Shakespeare's role in promoting British cultural superiority in the colonies may have been largely accidental and contingent on a host of ecological and environmental factors, it was nonetheless prominent. One could see Shakespeare performed in any corner of the Empire.

Both of these Shakespearean weather events blur the distinction between human intention and natural phenomenon. But as performance events that engage the natural world, they also trouble the predictability and the ephemerality of stage performance. Each performance, I suggest, turns its respective stage into a potential site of anti-colonial resistance by disrupting the political

---

[70] Olga Racster, *Curtain Up!* (Cape Town: Juta & Co., 1951), 76.
[71] Fletcher, *The Story of Theatre in South Africa*, 118.   [72] Racster, *Curtain Up!*, 77.
[73] Racster, *Curtain Up!*, 78.

message of playing Shakespeare in the colonies. If the theatrical frame of the play makes an audience regard the weather on stage differently, then it should also draw attention to how weather performs in a given climate. Hurricanes are not out of the ordinary in Bermuda, especially around Labor Day weekend. The Bermuda performance is all the more ironic for the way it commemorates the tempest on which Shakespeare's play is originally based. Sir William Strachey's *True Reportory of the Wreck and Redemption of Sir Thomas Gates, Knight*, which catalogs the wreck of *The Sea Venture* on Bermuda in 1609, and which served as a source text for Shakespeare's play, acknowledges a kind of "staying power" of storms.[74] Strachey flounders to describe the storm and the strain it caused those aboard the vessel, and can only compare the storm to other storms he has experienced:

> Winds and seas were as mad as fury and rage could make them. For my own part, I had been in some storms before, as well upon the coast of Barbary and Algiers, in the Levant, and once, more distressful, in the Adriatic gulf in a bottom of Candy...Yet all that I had ever suffered gathered together might not hold comparison with this: there was not a moment in which the sudden splitting or instant oversetting of the ship was not expected.[75]

The Walsingham Players' *Tempest* is thus materially and textually linked to previous weather events around Bermuda, including the one that may have inspired Shakespeare to dream up Prospero.

The weather event in Cape Town, 1892 bears a similar resonance, which helps us to see how the storm's consequence—a centuries-long slow violence caused by rainwater mixing with toxic tailing dumps from the gold mines of the Witwatersrand basin—is invariably tied to human behaviors. Bellew and Brown-Potter's *Romeo and Juliet* was performed in spite of an unplanned weather event, but it was also likely staged *because of* a flourishing gold rush. The discovery of gold in the Witwatersrand basin in the Transvaal in 1886 created a frenzy of gold prospectors, many of whom passed though Cape Town, and may have even composed some of the audience at the Kloof Street downpour. Cape Town saw its own gold mining syndicate form around the

---

[74] Rebecca Schneider, *Performing Remains: Art and War in Times of Theatrical Reenactment* (New York: Routledge, 2011), 37. Jonathan Gil Harris and Andrew Sofer articulate similar theories of the staying power of objects in performance. See Harris, *Untimely Matter in the Time of Shakespeare*, 11; Sofer, *The Stage Life of Props*, 2.

[75] William Strachey, *A True Reportory of the Wreck and Redemption of Sir Thomas Gates, Knight* (London, 1625), 7–8.

same time, but its members could not obtain enough capital to keep the operation going, since so much local capital was being invested in the Witwatersrand.[76] The Witwatersrand mines were coveted by the British, and would eventually reignite combat with the Boers in 1899. Almost nothing is known of the actual audience who attended this rainy performance of *Romeo and Juliet*, but it is likely that the quest for gold had impacted their lives in some capacity by 1892. The context of a gold rush may have added further ecological irony to this production of Shakespeare's play, in which gold is only fit to purchase poison. When Romeo receives word of Juliet's death, he quickly visits an apothecary to buy a deadly concoction for himself:

> There is thy gold—worse poison to men's souls,
> Doing more murder in this loathsome world,
> Than these poor compounds that thou mayst not sell.
> I sell thee poison; thou hast sold me none.
> Farewell, buy food, and get thyself in flesh.
> Come, cordial and not poison, go with me
> To Juliet's grave, for there must I use thee.
>
> (5.1.80–6)

Romeo's exchange of gold for poison and his metaphorical conflation of the two substances may have had an enhanced significance for Bellew's damp Cape Town audience, especially because potassium cyanide became the chemical upon which gold mining syndicates depended in the Witwatersrand. Though the main gold reef was discovered in 1886, by the early 1890s many gold mines had stopped production. In addition to unrestrained and corrupt trading practices in the Johannesburg Stock Exchange, the earth itself presented an obstacle to the continuation of gold mining. The gold of the main reef was stratified in pre-Cambrian slate and quartzite. As the mines grew deeper, miners discovered that the gold was entombed in pyrite, which meant that the amalgamation process for extracting gold from the ore using mercury was no longer viable.[77] However, William and Robert Forrest and John MacArthur had recently patented a new extraction process, which

[76] P. E. Spargo, "The Lion's Head Gold Mine," *Bulletin of the National Library of South Africa*, Vol. 69, No. 1 (2015), 28–40. Spargo shows one figure indicating that as much as £6 million of Cape Town's capital was being invested in the Transvaal Mines (38).

[77] Douglas Fetherling, *The Gold Crusades: A Social History of Gold Rushes, 1849–1929* (Toronto: University of Toronto Press, 2015), 117. Another extracting method, which involved passing chlorine gas over crushed ore to yield a soluble gold chloride that could be dissolved in water, and then extracted using a ferrous sulfate, hydrogen sulfide, or charcoal, had also been used in South Africa

instead of mercury used a weak solution of potassium (or sodium) cyanide—"the same substance," one historian notes, "with which jilted lovers took their lives in shame and despair, if the popular fiction of the day is to be believed."[78] Their process involved dissolving gold in an aerated solution of sodium cyanide, then recovering the gold through zinc precipitation or carbon absorption.[79] Cyanidation made the mining of low-grade ores, like the ore in the Witwatersrand, economically feasible, since it was so efficient.[80] This new process, which was already being tested on the Witwatersrand mines by 1890, not only revived investor confidence in the mining industry but also boosted gold production, and sparked another boom in 1895.[81] South African gold miners thus had an intimate relationship with poison—the effects of which will continue to be felt by generations of South Africans to come.

Cyanidation may have revolutionized the gold mining industry but it has also carried a troubling environmental legacy, made worse by frequent rainfall. Gold mining produces large dumps of crushed ore, which are then exposed to a cyanide solution. The dust from these dumps could be hazardous to miners and to nearby communities. The well-traveled actor John Holloway recalls the nuisance of poisonous dust during his visit to Johannesburg in 1895: "In dry weather, clouds of dust from the mine dumps, charged with cyanide of potassium, swept along, bringing discomfort to all, and death to the unfortunate with weak lungs and throats."[82] More recently, inhalation of quartz dust from mine dumps has been cited as a cause for the high incidence of silicosis and tuberculosis among mining communities in Ghana.[83] Rainwater exacerbates the environmental problem of the ore heaps, even without cyanide. The Witwatersrand ore deposits are rich in pyrite (or iron disulfide), which oxidizes when it comes into contact with oxygenated water.

gold mining before cyanide solutions. See John O. Marsden and C. Iain House, *Chemistry of Gold Extraction*. Edited by John O. Marsden and C. Iain House (Littleton, CO: SME, 2006), 16.

[78] Fetherling, *The Gold Crusades*, 118. I am not suggesting that Romeo would have used potassium cyanide, which Fetherling names here, and which was not discovered until the nineteenth century, or sodium cyanide, which was not discovered until the eighteenth century.

[79] George M. Wong-Chong, David V. Nakles, and David A. Dzombak, "Management of Cyanide in Industrial Process Wastewaters," in *Cyanide in Water and Soil: Chemistry, Risk, Management*, edited by David A. Dzombak, Rajat S. Ghosh, and George M. Wong-Chong (London: Taylor & Francis, 2006), 524. Fetherling notes the process involves potassium cyanide rather than sodium cyanide (Fetherling 118).

[80] Wong-Chong et al. show that cyanide is the most effective lixiviant, or extracting agent. It yields 73 percent of gold from ore samples; it only takes 0.5 to 1.3 grams of the cyanide ion per ton of ore to yield 1.4–5.6 grams of gold (524, 530–2). Marsden and House suggest that cyanidation increased gold recoveries from 70 percent to 95 percent (18).

[81] Fetherling, *The Gold Crusades*, 118.   [82] Holloway, *Playing the Empire*, 68.

[83] Abraham Kumah, "Sustainability and Gold Mining in the Developing World," *Journal of Cleaner Production*, Vol. 14 (2006), 321.

When it rains on the dumps, or when abandoned mines fill with rainwater, the pyrite oxidizes. This process yields ferrous sulfate, ferric hydroxide, and sulfuric acid—a corrosive mineral acid and the main ingredient in some drain cleaners. This environmental hazard of gold mining, better known as acid mine drainage, can have a serious impact on surrounding ecological life, especially when this toxic water seeps into ground and river water. Sulfuric acid also dissolves other heavy metals in the Witwatersrand dumps, including uranium. Acid mine drainage is potentially a centuries-long problem, since the process will only stop when all of the exposed pyrite oxidizes.[84]

Cyanide spills are another devastating consequence of gold mining. Gold mines have been recovering cyanide from their mining processes since the 1930s by using impoundment ponds for treating wastewaters.[85] However, there have also been more than a dozen environmental disasters caused by spills or tailing discharges in the last three decades.[86] For example, in 1994, ten miners were killed by cyanide-laced mud at the Harmony Mine in South Africa.[87] Because many multinational gold mining companies have turned to the mineral-rich deposits in the developing world, these disasters have disproportionately affected poor indigenous communities and women.[88]

---

[84] Terence S. McCarthy, "The Impact of Acid Mine Drainage in South Africa," *South African Journal of Science*, Vol. 107, No. 5 and 6 (2011), 1–7.

[85] Wong-Chong et al., "Management of Cyanide," 533.

[86] Wong-Chong cites several examples: the Brewer Mine in South Carolina and the Summitville Mine in Colorado (1990), the Omai Mine in Guyana (1995), the Gold Quarry Mine in Nevada (1997), the Homestake Mine in South Dakota (1998), the Los Frailes Zinc Mine in Spain (1998), the Aural Mine in Romania (2000), and the Goldfields Ltd. in the Wassa West (2001)—all had cyanide spills (Wong-Chong et al., 529). Kumah adds several to the list. A truck transporting cyanide to Kumtor spilled 2 tons of sodium cyanide in Kyrgyzstan, which killed four and displaced communities in 1998; a helicopter delivering sodium cyanide pellets to the Tolukuma mine in Papua New Guinea in 2000 dropped the 1-ton crate into the rainforest and infected the water system. In Ghana, cyanide spills occurred at the Bogoso Goldfields in 1994, the Teberebie Goldfields in 1996, the Ashanti Goldfields in 1998, and (twice in two weeks) the South African-owned Goldfields in 2001, which resulted in skin rashes, relocations, and devastation to agriculture and wildlife. The Placer Dome tailings disposal in the Philippines between 1975 and 1991 killed aquatic life forms in the Mogpog River and in Calancan Bay; the Grasberg Mine in Indonesia in 1996 spilled 40 million tons of tailings into the Ajkwa River. Freeport acknowledged their dumping of 125,000 tons of toxic rock waste into the Irian Jaya River on a daily basis, and also admitted involvement in human rights abuses (Kumah 319).

[87] Kumah, "Sustainability and Gold Mining," 319.

[88] Kumah, "Sustainability and Gold Mining," 321. In Ghana, the male heads of families are compensated for relocation; sometimes, they abandon their wives and children (Kumah 321). Kumah also explains the paradox of establishing gold mines in developing countries: "whilst an increase in gold mine investment is necessary to propel economies, an expansion of operations is often associated with persistent environmental and socioeconomic problems" (317). Kumah cites a study by Hilson and Murck that demonstrates how multinational corporations use the language of environmental sustainability to promote their developmental plans in the developing world, but because environmental laws in developing countries are "still in their infancy, and...accompanying enforcement programs are far from effective" (317), multinationals can get away with skirting around safety regulations that would be commonplace in the first world. The environmental disasters that result from this type of neoliberal racism might be compared to the atrocities committed by Shell Oil against the Ogani in Nigeria or

Most recently, in 2016, the Canadian-based company Barrick Gold contaminated five rivers in western Argentina with 265,000 gallons of cyanide solution.[89] Thus, while the weather that occurred in Bermuda in 1950 looks backward to the pattern of hurricanes that brought the English to the unpeopled isle in 1609, the rain in Cape Town directs its audience to look west to the Witwatersrand, and to the future, where the environmental damage of gold mining will continue to rehearse Romeo's suicidal purchase. And so when Romeo pays forty gold ducats *in the rain* to commit suicide, he unwittingly exposes an ecological relation between anthropogenic behaviors and a seemingly natural atmospheric weather event. Whereas audiences in 1892 were perhaps unaware of just how closely rainwater, gold mining, and poison were linked, those of us consciously living in the Anthropocene today ought to see the rain, the gold, and Romeo's suicide as an accidental performance of our own eco-cidal ideations.

While little is known about the audience that made up either of these two performances, the political intention of each performance—which the weather's agency obstructs—can be clarified with some historical context. The social climate of Bermuda in 1950 was characterized by racial tension and segregation. The island, which remains a self-governing British territory in 2022, has a long history of slavery and racial inequality, despite its unsuccessful record with growing sugar and tobacco in the seventeenth century. When it was discovered by the Spanish explorer Juan de Bermudez in 1503, the island was uninhabited by human populations.[90] So even though English colonization of the island in 1612 did not displace any native populations, the English began importing African slaves from the West Indies in 1616. About 5,000 slaves were brought to the island before slavery was abolished.[91] After abolition, legislation like the 1834 Voting Act kept power in the hands of

those committed by Dow Chemical against the people of Bhopal. See Rob Nixon, *Slow Violence and the Environmentalism of the Poor* (Cambridge, MA: Harvard University Press, 2011). Kumah notes, "the major environmental and socioeconomic problems caused by gold mining in the developing world include deforestation; acid mine drainage; noise, dust, air and water pollution from arsenic, cyanide and mercury; social disorganization; a loss of livelihoods and mass displacement" (Kumah 317).

[89] Erik Shilling, "Massive Cyanide Spill at Gold Mine Leaked Into 5 Different Rivers," *Atlas Obscura*, 25 February 2016.

[90] Schwartz, *Sea of Storms*, 37. Schwartz suggests that the Spanish decided not to colonize the island because of its hurricanes.

[91] Virginia Bernhard, *Slaves and Slaveholders in Bermuda, 1616–1782* (Columbia, MO: University of Missouri Press, 1999), 17. Bernhard also notes that Bermuda's history with slavery is unique since not all Africans who arrived on the island were slaves, and many possessed privileges in the colony that they would not have possessed elsewhere (Bernhard 28).

Whites through segregation.[92] In 1946, only 7 percent of the adult population was registered to vote in Bermuda, and these were mostly White landowners. In 1949, though the Black population on the island exceeded the White population by more than 10,000, there were 2,290 Whites registered to vote and only 1,920 Blacks.[93] The Walsingham Players likely performed before a segregated, all-White audience. In 1953, the Select Committee on Racial Relations deemed racial segregation to be an economic necessity in the colony. Six years later, in 1959, the successful Theatre Boycott of the Island Theatre chain, organized by the island's Progressive Group of young Black students, compelled the desegregation of Bermuda's hotels, restaurants, and movie theaters in a matter of days.[94]

The Walsingham group was also likely an all-White company. "Composed of Bermudians and resident Englishmen," the company included David Huxley (novelist Aldous Huxley's brother), a schoolboy, David Dill (who played Caliban), and "an elder statesman, W. E. S. Zuill, as Gonzalo."[95] The context of this particular production—a White company performing in 1950 before a segregated audience, which included the governor of Bermuda— reveals the play's intention. This was not a postcolonial reclamation of the play, with a villainous Prospero and a sympathetic Caliban. This was political propaganda, with Prospero modeling for Governor Hood how best to control his island.

In Cape Town, staging Shakespeare in English was part of an aggressive effort to champion British culture and the English language over the prolifer- ation of Afrikaans.[96] Purging the colony of the Dutch-influenced language, as many British colonists in the nineteenth century hoped to do, would prove impossible; the Afrikaans-speaking population was too large. Speaking of Cape Town in the late nineteenth century, one minister recalls, "Out of Cape Town I will venture to say that there are not more than 400 who can converse

[92] Quito Swan, *Black Power in Bermuda: The Struggle for Decolonization* (New York: Palgrave Macmillan, 2009), 11.

[93] Swan, *Black Power in Bermuda*, 17. The population was 36,770, with 13,310 Whites and 23,460 Blacks. In 1950, the Black population was 22,638 and the White was 14,765.

[94] Swan, *Black Power in Bermuda*, 14–15.

[95] Tweedy, "Bermuda 'Tempest,'" 111. The play was also produced by John Rosewarne, with Dr. Simon Frazer as Prospero, Sylvia Ware as Miranda, Penelope Fisher as Ariel, and John Hart as Antonio. The production was directed by Arthur and Gilbert Cooper and made use of Elizabethan- style costumes, handmade by a committee headed by Mrs. Bayard Dill. See Lois Bauer, [Unknown Title], *The Bermudian*, October 1950, 31.

[96] Fletcher, *The Story of Theatre in South Africa*, 62–116. Between the beginning of theater in Cape Town and Bellew and Brown-Potter's arrival in 1892, Shakespeare had been intermittently staged with varying degrees of success.

in English, and not 200 who write it or can read it."[97] Nevertheless, British schools relied on corporal punishment and public shaming to discourage students from speaking anything but English.[98] Schools also taught descendants of the Dutch colonists to be "ashamed of their ancestry" and that to be English was the "ultimate bliss"—a sentiment that clearly extended to the indigenous populations of Cape Town as well.[99] Staging Shakespeare served a pedagogical and ideological purpose and helped to fan the flames of British nationalism in the Cape too.[100]

The deconstructive spectacle offered by the weather event in Hamilton, Bermuda carries the potential to undermine both Prospero's authority over "his" island and Governor Hood's colonial authority over Bermuda. To a colonial audience, Prospero's *colonial* authority over his subjects and the natural resources available on his island—symbolized by Caliban and Ariel—depend on his ability to control the weather. When a real storm reveals that Prospero does not in fact control the weather, then all of his power—over Ariel, over Caliban, over Ferdinand, and Miranda—becomes suspect. When an errant storm misses its cue, Prospero's power is compromised. Prospero has two slaves—one human, one sprite—and both seem prematurely disenfranchised in the Hamilton performance. Ariel, who already performs a majority of Prospero's "magic" for him, suddenly appears to be "free / As mountain winds" (1.2.496–7) without Prospero's permission. Although Prospero claims "It was mine art, / When I arrived and heard thee, that made gape / The pine, and let thee out" (1.2.291–3), the audience's fidelity in his "art" hinges upon the control he maintains over the storm in the first scene. Prospero is only sovereign of the cloven pine if he is also sovereign of the storm. Similarly, his enslavement of Caliban, who "serves in offices / that profit us" (1.2.312–13), depends upon Prospero's narrative that Caliban "didst seek to violate / The honor of my child" (1.2.346–7). But if Prospero's art is *not* "of such power, / It would control my dam's god, Setebos, / and make a vassal of him" (1.2.371–3),

[97] Quoted in Fletcher, *The Story of Theatre in South Africa*, 107.

[98] Fletcher, *The Story of Theatre in South Africa*, 106. Professor J. D. du Toit remembers that students who were caught speaking Dutch during school hours had to carry around their necks a piece of wood with nails driven through it. They were then forced to write one hundred times: "I must not speak Dutch and ought to know it by now."

[99] Fletcher, *The Story of Theatre in South Africa*, 107.

[100] Nevertheless, Shakespeare was also performed in Dutch in the 1830s. On 28 May 1836, a performance of *Othello, of De Jaloersche Zwart* (*Othello, or the Jealous Husband*) was performed in Cape Town, and in March 1837 the Dutch-speaking society *Voor Vlyt en Kunst* (For Diligence and Art) gave another performance of *Othello* in Dutch, featuring a "Gentleman lately arrived from India" to play the role of Iago. See Eric Rosenthal, "Early Shakespeare Productions in South Africa," *English Studies in Africa*, Vol. 7, No. 2 (1964), 210.

as Caliban supposes it to be, then Caliban's final words in the play seem to apply as much to the drunken Stephano as to the charlatan Prospero:

> I'll be wise hereafter,
> And seek for grace. What a thrice-double ass
> Was I to take this drunkard for a god,
> And worship this dull fool.
>
> (5.1.294-7)

Furthermore, the errant storm helps to legitimize Caliban's claim to his own private property: "This island's mine by Sycorax my mother, / Which thou tak'st from me" (1.2.331-2). Prospero justifies his enslavement of Caliban with a racial hierarchy, which the real storm undoes: "Thy vile race, / Though thou didst learn, had that in't which good natures / Could not abide to be with" (1.2.357-9). Prospero's logic, that his own "good natures" are superior to Caliban's "vile race," falls to pieces if he is not master of the storm. An amateur production with a White cast and an all-White, segregated audience in colonial Bermuda reinforces the same racist logic—which the storm denies. Prospero's power depends on his ability to manage his stage, especially for Miranda, who must be assured that no one was harmed in the making of this tempest:

> The direful spectacle of the wrack, which touched
> The very virtue of compassion in thee,
> I have with such provision in mine art
> So safely ordered that there is no soul—
> No, not so much perdition as an hair
> Betid to any creature in the vessel
> Which thou heard'st cry, which thou saw'st sink.
>
> (1.2.26-32)

Because Prospero summons a storm in part to secure "an hair" or "an heir"— early modern homophones—for Miranda through Ferdinand, he requires the safety of all the passengers on board.[101] But with a second, unplanned storm, spectators see the extent to which Prospero's lineage lies not in his control but at the mercy of the winds. The Walsingham Players' storm-tossed *Tempest* thus potentially turns a play about human dominion over nature into a performance of nature's dynamic community with humanity. Furthermore, it

---

[101] Harris, *Sick Economies*, 47.

makes the performance itself sovereign over the players' intent to situate Shakespeare's play within an imperialist framework.

Although British players in the Cape Colony built up Shakespeare's colonial authority during the nineteenth century, that authority was also potentially subverted in the context of the deconstructive spectacle offered by this rainy performance of *Romeo and Juliet* in 1892. Shakespeare, as the symbol of British cultural superiority and the apogee of the English language, signifies something else when Romeo and Juliet have to "shout at one another" over the noise of the wind and the rain. If Romeo must shout at Juliet—during the balcony scene, perhaps—then his plea, "O, wilt thou leave me so unsatisfied?" (2.1.167), runs the risk of sounding like an angry threat. Juliet's metaphorical despair might seem either weakly expressed or too powerful in poor weather:

> I have no joy of this contract tonight.
> It is too rash, too unadvised, too sudden,
> Too like the lightning, which doth cease to be
> Ere one can say it lightens.

> (2.1.159–62)

In a rainstorm, Romeo can add weight to his conceits regarding Juliet, especially if she is on some sort of covered balcony: "But, soft! what light through yonder window breaks? / It is the east, and Juliet is the sun. / Arise, fair sun..." (2.1.44–6). While a stormy production of *Romeo and Juliet* provides opportunities for felicitous moments, the weather also exposes the artifice of theater—the extent to which it is little more than a human endeavor. The distance between actor and character, actor and audience, reality and performance, becomes blurred by the rain, the crumbling set, and Brown-Potter's "contortions" in her wet costume. When this play is performed indoors, Romeo and Juliet can invent the dawn with their language alone, without even an elaborate set or technical lighting; they use imagery to tell the audience what to see. The same task seems tragically pointless, or perhaps playfully ironic, when the weather is so glaringly unsunny. Romeo directs Juliet's attention to a morning sun that simply is not there on Kloof Street:

> Look, love, what envious streaks
> Do lace the severing clouds in yonder east.
> Night's candles are burnt out, and jocund day
> Stands tiptoe on the misty mountain tops.

> (3.5.7–10)

Juliet, on the other hand, invites audiences to regard the light differently:

> Yon light is not daylight; I know it, I.
> It is some meteor that the sun exhaled
> To be to thee this night a torchbearer,
> And light thee on thy way to Mantua.

(3.5.12–15)

In this performance, these lines have the potential to showcase the innocent and hopeful projections of these two young lovers, who mistake rain and wind for "jocund day." On the other hand, rain and clouds offer a felicitous stage for the prince's final dark observation: "A glooming peace this morning with it brings. / The sun for sorrow will not show his head" (5.3.304–5). Though it is entirely possible that these references to the physical environment were simply omitted during this staging—full of such "hullabaloo" as it was—the agency of non-human actors is hardly negligible in this performance. Non-human actors retain the potential to exert agency in Shakespearean performances, and to wrest control away from an intentional imperialist human agenda.

A broader ecological theater history of Shakespearean performance in the British colonies might prove useful to the project of provincializing "our" geologic agency in the Anthropocene, both on and offstage. It supplies a more thorough archive of performance documentation than performance records from early modern England, while also cataloging performances where British actors were confronting new environments and frequently playing Shakespeare outside. Furthermore, insofar as the history of British colonialism functions as a narrative of the global North acquiring geologic agency at the expense of the global South, this performance archive allows us to revisit the history of European colonialism through the lens of the Anthropocene. When a real storm upsets a dramatic performance, the human intention behind the performance is thrown into crisis, which rehearses our crisis in the Anthropocene of acquiring geologic agency without *meaning* to. Early modern theater may seem an unlikely ally as we confront a future of global warming, sea-level rise, mass extinction, and other imminent threats shaped by anthropogenic climate change. But it would be a mistake to think that Shakespeare's globe was not also facing a dubious future due to human behaviors. In addition to offering accidentally postcolonial stagings, the Shakespearean weather events in Hamilton and Cape Town also anticipate our predicament in the Anthropocene of knowing the extent of our impact on the global environment. The stage teaches us that the climate, like a performance, involves different degrees of audience participation. I suggest this knowledge is a virtue because unlike early modern providentialist thinking or proposed policy solutions for repaying climate debtors, the theater does not aim to hold us accountable for our "sins." Instead, the natural agency of a Shakespearean weather event leaves our individual human agency intact. The theater does not punish its audience. Rather, it can help remind us of the impact of our decisions on the non-human world. Our thoughts are still ours, even if their ends are none of our own. The virtue of the theater's hybrid agency between humans and nature is that it nurtures a greater capacity for both ecological thinking and reflection on the consequences of our agency.

PART III

DISTRIBUTIVE JUSTICE
IN THE *OIKEIOS*

The final part of this book addresses the third element of a theater of the Anthropocene, which positions the stage as a resource for audiences experiencing a global ecological crisis. The first two parts of this book have established the ways in which the properties of the stage and Shakespearean performance itself function as commodities in a global marketplace where human behaviors are changing the global environment. The previous chapters have also showcased how ecological elements and the physical properties of performance exert agency in ways that can be aesthetically and politically productive, especially when they disrupt human intentions. Thus far, this book has attempted to provincialize the homogeneous narrative of the Anthropocene through offering an analysis of the relationship between theatrical commodities and a global marketplace. It has also, up to this point, sought to decenter Shakespeare from the Shakespearean stage by focusing instead on stage properties and the ecological elements of performance.

But Shakespeare deserves credit for shaping early modern theater into an ecological resource. British colonial discourse and the ecological elements of colonial performance may have propelled Shakespeare into his current cultural status, but we should also recognize that Shakespeare's plays were written for an audience in ecological crisis. In *King Lear*, Shakespeare seems to pose a unique question: how can nature itself help us to think through the crises caused by human behaviors under an emergent form of capitalism?

The answer seems to be that the non-human world can model a distributive sense of justice. In this part, provincializing the Anthropocene means flattening the hierarchies between kings and subjects, between patriarchs and heirs, between humans and nature. *Lear* shows how social inequalities are inextricably linked to inequalities in nature, some of which are only visible through a geologic or "deep" timescale. To conclude this book, I discuss nature's agency as a potential corrective measure to the (partially) human-generated imbalances discussed in the previous chapters. The imbalance of wealth, natural resources, and carbon dioxide between the global North and South is one of the legacies of British imperialism in the Anthropocene. But even before Britain had an empire, the stage was rehearsing strategies for allowing the non-human world to correct ecological and economic faults. Regarding the non-human world as an ally in correcting human error has arguably never been more important than it is today.

6

Shaking the Superflux

Sin and Redemption Along Geological
Faults in *King Lear*

Early modern English culture was preoccupied with reading natural events—like storms, floods, or earthquakes—as divine prescriptions for altering sinful behaviors. In Shakespeare's England, the crown, the pulpit, and the classroom each offered an overwhelmingly disciplinary message of retribution for sin or disobedience, one where the general sinning population was trained to see the natural world as a reflection of their own earthly offenses. Even before theaters became a commercial institution in London, the mystery play cycles performed throughout rural parts of England promoted the same message. Much of Shakespeare's early life remains a mystery to modern scholars, but there are two places I want to imagine a young Shakespeare before turning to his dramatic conception of nature's balancing act. The first is in Coventry, or perhaps Warwickshire—each only about twenty miles from Stratford—when Shakespeare was an eleven-year-old. Both were sites where he might have been able to watch a mystery cycle in full.[1]

Scholarship regarding the influence of the medieval mystery play cycles on Shakespeare's tragedies has been extensive, but an analysis of Shakespeare's contribution to an emerging notion of ecological and economic balance begs a return to the playwright's medieval religious sources.[2] Shakespeare's reliance on the Noah's flood plays, for example, have been overlooked as an influence on *King Lear* (c. 1605–6). Three of the five extant flood plays depict Noah's wife refusing to board the ark amidst the apocalyptic downpour. In the Chester play, Noah commands, "Now come, a God's name, time it were / For

---

[1] R. Chris Hassel, Jr. speculates that Shakespeare may have seen a mystery cycle at Coventry or Warwickshire as late as 1575. See R. Chris Hassel, Jr., "Shakespeare's 'Removed Mysteries,'" *Connotations*, Vol. 7, No. 3 (1997), 355.

[2] As a sample, see Hassel, Jr., "'Removed Mysteries,'" 355; Emrys Jones, *The Origins of Shakespeare* (Oxford: Clarendon Press, 1978); Glynne William Gladstone Wickham, *Shakespeare's Dramatic Heritage: Collected Studies in Medieval, Tudor, and Shakespearean Drama* (London: Routledge & K. Paul, 1969); Cherrell Guilfoyle, *Shakespeare's Play Within Play: Medieval Imagery and Scenic Form in* Hamlet, Othello, *and* King Lear (Kalamazoo, MI: Western Michigan University Press, 1990); Maurice Hunt, "Old England, Nostalgia, and the 'Warwickshire' of Shakespeare's Mind," *Connotations*, Vol. 1, No. 2 (1997), 159–80.

Anthropocene Theater and the Shakespearean Stage. William H. Steffen, Oxford University Press.
© William H. Steffen 2023. DOI: 10.1093/oso/9780192871862.003.0007

fear lest we drown." His wife refuses because she is unwilling to abandon her friends: "I will not out of our town. / For I have my gossips everyone."[3] Her duty is not to her husband: "So row you forth, Noah, when you list / And get thee a new wife."[4] In the York play, Noah similarly implores his wife, "Come hither fast, dame, I thee pray" (ll. 76); but even after "forty days are near-hand past / And gone since it began to rain" (ll. 85–6), his wife refuses to board the ark.[5] In the Towneley play, even after the "cataracts all / That are open full even" bring "That deluge about," Noah's wife refuses to "come in the ship fast." In this play, she does not want to leave her spinning.[6] In all three plays, Noah's wife must be forced on board with violence, where she subsequently turns obedient, submissive, and docile. The flood plays bear a strong resemblance to 3.2 of *Lear*, when the fool implores his king to seek shelter from the storm: "O nuncle, court holy water in a dry house is better than this rainwater out o' door. Good nuncle, in. Ask thy daughters' blessing. Here's a night pities neither wise men nor fools" (3.2.12–15). In 3.4, too, Kent brings Lear to a hovel and begs him to go inside: "Here is the place, my lord. Good my lord, enter. / The tyranny of the open night's too rough / For nature to endure" (3.4.1–3). But like Noah's wife, Lear stands in the rain as long as he can:

> Rumble thy bellyful! Spit, fire! Spout, rain!
> Nor rain, wind, thunder, fire are my daughters.
> I tax you not, you elements, with unkindness.
> I never gave you kingdom, called you children;
> You owe me no subscription
>
> (3.2.16–20)

Critics have read the obstinacy of Noah's wife as a rehearsal of the fall, as a comic interlude, and as a feminist posturing for both her rejection of patriarchal subjugation, and her independence as a worker.[7] Allegorical interpretations of the flood plays position Noah's wife as the "recalcitrant sinner" who waits until the final possible moment to enter the Church or to accept Christ.[8]

[3] Maurice Hussey, ed., *The Chester Mystery Plays: Sixteen Pageant Plays from the Chester Craft Cycle* (London: W. Heinemann, 1957).

[4] Hussey, *The Chester Mystery Plays*.

[5] Richard Beadle and Pamela M. King, eds., *York Mystery Plays: A Selection in Modern Spelling* (Oxford: Oxford University Press, 2009), 76.

[6] Garrett P. J. Epp, *The Towneley Plays* (Kalamazoo, MI: Western Michigan University, 2017), 99.

[7] Katie Normington, *Gender and Medieval Drama* (Woodbridge: D.S. Brewer, 2004), 124–5.

[8] Woolf, quoted in Normington, *Gender and Medieval Drama*, 125. See Rosemary Woolf, *The English Mystery Plays* (Berkeley, CA: University of California Press, 1972). See also Beadle and King, *York Mystery Plays*, 21.

Shakespeare's appropriation of Mrs. Noah in *Lear*, however, betrays an interest in the future she is willing and able to imagine on earth before it is destroyed—an interest that humans living in the age of anthropogenic climate change are compelled to share.

In this chapter, I suggest that *Lear* overturns a religious model of redemption offered by the medieval flood plays—where human sin is punished with divine retribution and global deluge—in favor of a more secular model of redemption, where self-correcting imbalances in nature provide solutions to economic imbalances between kingly pomp and houseless poverty. Gloucester and Lear each seek redemption in this play. Lear, who hopes Goneril and Regan will pay him "subscription" for giving them "kingdom" and for calling them "children," seeks (like blind Gloucester) to atone for the "fault" (1.4.277) of doubting the credit of his faithful child. But whereas "faults" are recognizable as human sins in the flood plays, they are also in *Lear* the geological fault-lines by which nature achieves balance. This play sediments a link between the circulation of wealth among humans, where fortunes can be made or reversed in an instant, and the imperceptibly slow processes of geology within the *oikeios*.

The second place I am trying to imagine a young, now fifteen-year-old William Shakespeare is where he might have been during Easter of 1580, when the greater part of southern England was rocked by a massive earthquake. If Shakespeare was in Stratford, he may have felt the quake in its full force. But if he was in Lancashire during this time, as E. A. J. Honingmann suggests he may have been, he may have only been able to read about it after the fact.[9] Seismologists now know that the epicenter of the quake was along a fault line somewhere between Dover and Calais. So while moralizing pamphleteers may have located the cause of the quake in human behaviors and sins, seismologists today are able to pinpoint the cause at an active fault between two bodies of land that were once connected by a land bridge. And it is here, at the cliffs of Dover, where Shakespeare (or Edgar) places Gloucester— where the balancing floods once bulldozed the land bridge between England and France, where the unseen underwater fault rocked the English countryside, and where Gloucester redeems his own unseen faults by giving the remainder of his wealth to Edgar. Although Lear and Gloucester seek atonement through different avenues—Lear through a stormy flood and Gloucester

---

[9] Scholars have debated about where Shakespeare was during his infamous "lost years"; E. A. J. Honingmann suggests Shakespeare may have been in Lancashire in 1580, about 300 miles from the epicenter of the quake. See E. A. J. Honingmann, *Shakespeare: The "Lost Years"* (Manchester: Manchester University Press, 1998), 1.

on the edge of a cliff—they also both imagine a future in which the debtor/ debtee paradigm of Christian redemption, the zero-sum scheme in which one's "pomp" (3.4.37) is necessarily another's "houseless poverty" (3.4.30), is replaced by a more distributive justice. As Lear realizes that he "may'st shake the superflux" and "show the heavens more just" (3.4.40–1), Gloucester hopes that "distribution should undo excess, / And each man have enough" (4.1.80–1). The future conditional of Lear's "mayst" and Gloucester's "should" overturns the apocalyptic scenario of the flood plays in order to imagine instead what J. K. Barret calls "an earthly future shaped by the activity of human beings rather than classical precedent or divine providence."[10] The play's abdication of religious redemption depends on two key non-human properties, the storm and the cliffs, which are both present and absent on stage at once. I suggest that the storm and the cliffs allow Lear to see his kingly past from his present vantage of Uxor Noah in the storm; they also allow Gloucester, who cannot see at all, to relive his own "fall" through his theatrical perception of the phantom Dover cliffs.

In this way, the play registers a contemporary antiquarian interest in an emergent form of "natural history," which developed in part when scholars began to supplement historical texts and documents with artifacts and evidence from the physical world.[11] One antiquarian, Richard Verstegan, imagined that the white cliffs of Dover had formed as the result of a superflux finding its balance in nature, a theory that informs the white cliffs as the site of Gloucester's economic redistribution. Both storm and cliffs are central to the action of the play because they suggest that the play's economic imbalances might be restored not with God but with the help of the earth's restoration of natural imbalances. Lear's fault to Cordelia and Gloucester's fault to Edgar are economic because they do not bestow upon their children the riches they deserve. But Cordelia and Edgar are redeemed by their fathers, not through a rehearsal of Adam's fall or Noah's flood, but through a plunge more secular, a deluge more natural.

In the age of anthropogenic climate change, where science has proven the damaging global reach of human behaviors, Lear's lesson has never been more important. We need to learn to see economic imbalance as resolvable

[10] J. K. Barret, *Untold Futures: Time and Literary Culture in Renaissance England* (Ithaca, NY: Cornell University Press, 2016), 8.

[11] Martin J. S. Rudwick, *Earth's Deep History: How It Was Discovered and Why It Matters* (Chicago, IL: University of Chicago Press, 2014), 31; Paolo Rossi, *The Dark Abyss of Time: The History of the Earth and the History of Nations from Hooke to Vico* (Chicago, IL: University of Chicago Press, 1984), 4.

not through God's divine grace but through the distributive justice made possible by an alliance between human and natural agency. Even in *Lear*'s ancient England, the legacies of capitalism figure (however anachronistically) in the economic imbalances created by a long history of human (and geologic) "faults."

"Bond of Childhood": Lear and Gloucester's Unbalanced Family Accounts

Lear and Gloucester both feel they are owed a debt by their children, and each seeks in vain for a balancing of their familial accounts. When Cordelia tells her father she loves him "according to [her] bond, no more nor less" (1.1.101), she underlines the bad math her sisters commit with their flattery: "Why have my sisters husbands if they say / They love you all?...Sure I shall never marry like my sisters, / To love my father all" (1.1.109–15). By portioning out the "largest bounty" (1.1.57) of the kingdom to his daughters according to their professed affections, Lear assigns a tangible value to their love, which leaves him vulnerable to Regan's subtracting negotiations. To Lear, the number of knights he is allowed to keep quantifies the affection he reciprocates for his daughters, and he tells Goneril, "Thy fifty yet doth double five-and-twenty, / And thou art twice her love" (2.4.299–300). Lear speaks an economic language (familiar to the heroes of revenge tragedy and tragicomedy) of balance, repayment, and redemption.[12] He reminds Regan, "I gave you all" (2.4.287), and urges her to remember her debt:

> Thou better know'st
> The offices of nature, bond of childhood,
> Effects of courtesy, dues of gratitude.
> Thy half o' th' kingdom hast thou not forgot,
> Wherein I thee endowed.
>
> (2.4.201–5)

For Lear, fatherhood has been an economic investment, and a bad one where Goneril and Regan are concerned. Their "bond" and "dues" to him will not be repaid.

Like Lear, Gloucester imagines his child's alleged offense to be all the more sinister for the economic imbalance it reflects between a father who has

---

[12] Forman, *Tragicomic Redemptions*, 8; Woodbridge, *English Revenge Drama*, 61.

imparted his wealth onto his ungrateful son. Gloucester can hardly fathom Edgar's ingratitude against his own father, "that so *tenderly* and *entirely* loves him!" (1.2.101–2, emphasis added). The love that Gloucester tenders "entirely" to his legitimate son helps to sow the seeds of Edmund's jealous revenge; it demonstrates that Gloucester's money is hardly distributed evenly between his two sons. Much like Lear, Gloucester imagines he is owed for providing his sons with childhood; Edgar's alleged offense is an economic affront, a defaulted loan, a "bond cracked 'twixt son and father" (1.2.114–15). For both Lear and Gloucester, paternal love is an overbalanced account in need of reckoning.

But the economics of *King Lear* differ from revenge tragedy (where blood repays blood) and tragicomedy (where losses are redeemed with interest) in part because Lear and Gloucester possess enough introspection to confront their own debts and imbalances. At the same time that Lear seeks repayment from Goneril and Regan, he also wants to atone for his mistreatment of Cordelia. When he is finally reunited with Cordelia, Lear tells her, "If you have poison for me, I will drink it" (4.7.82). He acknowledges that she, unlike her sisters, may have "some cause" (4.7.85) not to love him. In the stocks, Kent imagines Cordelia as the play's great redeemer; he hopes she will "find time...to give / losses their remedies" (2.3.183–5). She does remedy her father's madness, but Lear's redemption is short-lived. Having just acquired his daughter's forgiveness, Lear is quickly burdened with responsibility for her death. Though he slays her murderer, Lear blames himself for Cordelia's demise: "I might have saved her" (5.3.326). Lear hopes in vain that she might be left alive, "a chance which does *redeem* all sorrows / That ever I have felt" (5.3.320–1, emphasis added). But the play repeatedly denies his redemption; he dies waiting for her to breathe. If the storm teaches Lear how he has misestimated the fidelity of his daughters, it also teaches him to see his wealth as a grossly overbalanced account. Lear admits, "I have ta'en / too little care of this" (3.4.36–7).

Similarly, Gloucester's blindness—along with Edgar's costumed performance of poverty and the illusory cliffs of Dover—illuminate the fault of the unfair distribution of wealth in the realm. Gloucester, a self-proclaimed "superfluous and lust-dieted man" (4.1.77), might agree with Edgar's didactic estimation of him, that "the dark and vicious place where [Edmund] he got / Cost him his eyes" (5.3.206–7). Gloucester and Lear each perceive their superfluity, their excess, their overdrawn accounts only when they are suffering; they are not without vices of their own, and each ponders the equity of their trials. But the future conditional that both Gloucester and Lear are able to imagine as an alternative for an inadequate redemption is an environmental concern for Shakespeare as much as a temporal one. In other words, a future in which the superflux is shaken—when both Lear's wealth and his current "overflow of water"[13] are more evenly distributed, less concentrated, and when distribution undoes excess and superfluity—is only perceptible to the audience if they can see the water through which Lear wades in the present, and the cliff which Gloucester thinks he stands on.

"O most small fault!": Economic Imbalances and Geological Redemptions

By appropriating the medieval flood plays in *King Lear*, Shakespeare maps the economic and emotional registers of redemption sought by Lear and Gloucester onto the flood's parable of spiritual redemption. Lear's epiphany in the storm—his pivot from perceiving himself as a man "more sinned against than sinning" (3.2.63) into acknowledging himself as a king with enough economic agency to redeem the poor, to "shake the superflux," and to "show the heavens more just"—participates in a shifting discourse about the meaning of redemption on the English stage. Even before the Reformation, Christian redemption was understood as a kind of spiritual economics. As Valerie Forman describes it, "man owes an infinite and ultimately unpayable debt to God for an original sin understood as the result of defrauding God." However, this debt is repaid, "even overpaid, by Christ, who is both man and God and whose life has infinite value."[14] Christ's redemption for man's fall is the great theme of the mystery plays. God's salvation of Noah and his family from the flood anticipates the second, more important redemption later in the cycle. Forman shows how the productive potential of Christ's redemption for human debts, sins, and losses found purchase on the Renaissance stage through the genre of tragicomedy, especially after an economic debate erupted between mercantilists over the causes of and remedies for England's depleting store of bullion in the early seventeenth century.

Lear was written shortly after the mercantilist George Malynes diagnosed the depletion of bullion as England's economic "disease" in his 1601 pamphlet, *A treatise of the canker of Englands common wealth*.[15] A few years later, the economic treatises of Edward Misselden and Thomas Mun would propose

---

[13] *Oxford English Dictionary*, "superflux," n. 2.   [14] Forman, *Tragicomic Redemptions*, 11.
[15] George Malynes, *A treatise of the canker of Englands common wealth* (London, 1601), B1r.

that English merchants could restore an upset "balance of trade" through exporting more than they imported, and offered an early theorization of the interchangeability between money and commodities.[16] Scholars who have addressed the impact of the economic debates between Malynes, Misselden, and Mun on the English stage have overlooked *Lear* with good reason. As a tragedy, the play hardly explores the productive potential of the play's initial losses.[17] But these competing economic and spiritual registers of redemption and "balance" are not wholly irrelevant to the economy of *Lear*'s "physic." They are, however, incomplete without a consideration of the play's central restorative agent of economic imbalance: nature.

Lear demonstrates how economic imbalances are inextricably linked to imbalances in nature. The play also models tragedy as a genre of economic and ecological imbalances. The mislaid fortunes of Edgar and Cordelia later beget the squalor of their fathers, Lear and Gloucester. The imbalance of wealth in the kingdom, represented by the play's destitute wanderers, is reflected in the play's unbalanced environments. An excess of water exacerbates Lear's poverty, and a crooked drop at the imaginary cliffs of Dover—also formed by an excess of water—positions Gloucester on the brink of a suicidal despair. As Jennifer Mae Hamilton argues, the play is "not only about seeking shelter in a pragmatic sense, it also offers a rich and complex ethical and political enquiry into the tensions between privileged excess and base necessity in relation to exposure."[18] This tragic convention of unbalanced excess of both the economy of the state and the ecology of the country might also identify a convention of Anthropocene theater, which shows audiences that their own behaviors have taken them to a point where redemption by human hands may be out of reach.

Lear's vision of a shaken superflux anticipates the economic debates of the 1620s because of the way Lear understands the potential for the crown to correct economic imbalances. Although Mun and Misselden disagreed with Malynes on what to do about the depleting bullion, they each "subscribed to a zero-sum conception of global wealth, according to which one nation's gain was almost invariably another's loss."[19] In the storm, Lear shares a zero-sum conception of the wealth circulating *within* his realm; he understands for the first time that his gain has been at someone else's expense. One might be

[16] Ryner, *Performing Economic Thought*, 85.

[17] In tragicomedy, on the other hand, the play's initial losses generate the play's later redemptive gains, which reflects the novel idea of "investment" proposed by Misselden and Mun in the early seventeenth century. See Forman, *Tragicomic Redemptions*, 6.

[18] Hamilton, *This Contentious Storm*, 40.   [19] Harris, *Sick Economies*, 6.

tempted to read Lear as a "bullionist," since he acknowledges the crown's capacity to enforce the value of money and perhaps to determine the flow of wealth to and from the realm as well.[20] He admits, "*I* have ta'en / Too little care of this" (3.4.36–7, emphasis added), and suggests that he, the king (not God), might "feel what wretches feel" (3.4.39), "shake the superflux" (3.4.40), and "show the heavens more just" (3.4.41). If anyone has the power to do something about wealth inequality in Lear's England, it is the king. Or at least it used to be.

Some might also be tempted to read Lear not as a sixteenth-century "bullionist" but as a figure whose madness might be a symptom of his efforts to imagine a post-capitalist system that operates according to a law of balance rather than one of unlimited accumulation. One of the most tragic things about Lear is that his proposal to "show the heavens more just" cannot be taken seriously—not in his kingdom, and not in Shakespeare's. Nor is it likely to be taken seriously in the age of late capitalism. Lear's command to achieve equity among his people through a rebalancing of "superflux" must appear to be wishful thinking even to modern audiences who seek a less drastic imbalance of either wealth between the 1 percent and the 99 percent or else carbon emissions between the global North and the global South. As Peter Sloterdijk points out, the hegemony of capital accumulation makes even the thought of negative growth inconceivable.[21]

Like Lear, Malynes advocated for the crown's intervention to restore economic imbalances. Malynes perceived that bullion was leaving England through trade, through selling English commodities at low prices, and through buying foreign commodities at high prices.[22] The king, however, "(being as it were the father of the family) ought to keep a certaine equality in the trade or trafficke betweixt his realme and other countries, not suffering an ouerballancing of forreine commodities with his home commodities, or in buying more then he selleth."[23] For Malynes, the king managed the commonwealth's "houshold"[24] or *oikos*—which serves as the etymological root for the

---

[20] Ryner, *Performing Economic Thought*, 53.

[21] Sloterdijk, *What Happened*, 19. Sloterdijk writes, "in all of our prognoses and projects for the world of tomorrow, we are today compelled to proceed from the fact that human beings in rich nations consider their affluence and its technological premises to be the irrevocable spoils of conquest. They remain convinced that it is evolution's job to make their material affluence and expressive privileges into global phenomena via continuous growth. They will refuse to put up with a future that is founded on negative growth and restraint."

[22] Malynes, *A treatise of the canker of Englands common wealth*, B2r.

[23] Malynes, *A treatise of the canker of Englands common wealth*, B1v.

[24] Malynes, *A treatise of the canker of Englands common wealth*, B1v.

modern studies of both *economics* and *ecology*.[25] But scholars preoccupied with the economic side of Malynes's *oikos* have overlooked how Malynes also conceived of trade between nations as a necessary human response to an ecological imbalance in nature: "God caused nature to distribute her benefits, or his blessings to seuerall climates, supplying the barenness of some things in our countrey, with the fruitfulnesse and store of other countries, to the ende that enterchangeably one common-weale should liue with another."[26] For Malynes, then, international trade is a strategy for redistributing a natural disproportion of commodities (and wealth) more evenly among nations, so that each might, in Gloucester's words, "have enough."

Though Malynes predates the modern fields of economics and ecology, he was not the only theorist of the balance within nature's household who has bearing on Lear's vision of a "just" economic future in England. The economic and spiritual redemption that Lear and Gloucester seek and then abjure has roots in the emergence of the medieval notion of balance as well. Equity and balance were not just economic or religious concerns of the early modern period; they were, as Joel Kaye points out, ideas that emerged in the medieval period under the discipline of natural philosophy. Jean Buridan, the thirteenth-century Parisian natural philosopher, for example, investigated the question of why the proportion of dry land and water on earth should remain constant in an Aristotilian universe (which is eternal). The problem, as Buridan saw it, was that given enough time, "the whole depth of the sea ought to be filled with the earth, thus consuming the [portion of] earth that was elevated…Therefore, nothing ought to remain habitable."[27] Buridan's solution to this problem was to imagine a dynamic, dual-centered earth, which was responsible for pushing land out of the sea in a balanced proportion to the land swallowed beneath the waves.[28]

Lear was also written around the same time that Francis Bacon was conceptualizing what ecologists would later view as an "imperial" view of nature,

---

[25] Natasha Korda discusses the gendered labor of the early modern English household through the etymology of the term "oeconomy," from the Greek "oikos," or house, and "nomos," or law. "The housewife's oeconomy," she concludes, "thus positioned her in an active, managerial role that required her not only to keep or hold goods, but to deal out, distribute and dispense them, and thereby to 'govern' the household economy." See Natasha Korda, *Shakespeare's Domestic Economies: Gender and Property in Early Modern England* (Philadelphia, PA: University of Pennsylvania Press, 2002), 27.

[26] Malynes, *A treatise of the canker of Englands common wealth*, B3v.

[27] Quoted in Joel Kaye, "The (Re)Balance of Nature, ca. 1250–1350," in *Engaging with Nature: Essays on the Natural World in Medieval and Early Modern Europe*, edited by Barbara J. Hanawalt and Lisa J. Kiser (Notre Dame, IN: University of Notre Dame Press, 2008), 95.

[28] Kaye, "The (Re)Balance of Nature," 96.

which was influenced by Christian and pastoral ideas. Under this view, "nature was [man's] domain, to be altered and rearranged more or less as he chose."[29] For Bacon, nature might never be out of balance if humans had complete control over it. In his *New Atlantis* (1627), Bacon envisions a society dedicated to the scientific probing of nature, which allows for the "enlarging of the bounds of Human Empire, to the effecting of all things possible."[30] His fictive society of "Salomon's House" on the utopic isle of Bensalem is in part dedicated to the "prevention and remedy" of "tempests, earthquakes, [and] great inundations."[31] In the same way that Buridan anxiously strives to justify the impossibility of another universal deluge, Bacon's commercially isolated islanders also seem particularly worried by the prospect of a flood. The governor of Bensalem explains how the "simple and savage people" of America, or the "great Atlantis," were once host to "proud kingdoms in arms, shipping and riches." They "abounded in tall ships," and "the navigation of the world" was "greater then than now," until "the great Atlantis was utterly lost and destroyed...by a particular deluge or inundation."[32] Bacon, like Malynes, imagines trade as a corrective measure against natural imbalances in commodity distribution between nations; but he prefers to trade in "Light" or knowledge, and to correct superflux by preventing it altogether.[33]

Much like Bacon and Buriden, Shakespeare also ponders nature's balance using flood imagery in *Lear*, which extends to the play's economic imbalances as well. That *King Lear* embraces a redemption coded as natural rather than spiritual is evident, ironically, from the play's engagement with the imagery of the flood plays, and with animal imagery in particular. Lear's similarity to Noah—or Noah's wife, as the case may be—in the storm scenes serves to distance him from the spiritual redemption staged in the mystery cycle plays. The play's animal metaphors conflate human with non-human forms, and situate Lear within a kind of ark. Unlike Uxor Noah of the flood plays, however, who finds grace and redemption (along with patriarchal oppression) aboard the ark, Lear finds only animals. Lear's fool conflates Kent in the stocks with the "cruel garters" worn by animals in an image that reinforces both human domain over beasts, and the indistinction that grows between humans

---

[29] Donald Worster, *Nature's Economy: A History of Ecological Ideas* (Cambridge: Cambridge University Press, 1977), 29.

[30] Francis Bacon, *New Atlantis*, in *Francis Bacon: The Major Works*, edited by Brian Vickers (Oxford: Oxford University Press, 2008), 480.

[31] Bacon, *New Atlantis*, 488.   [32] Bacon, *New Atlantis*, 467–70.

[33] Bacon, *New Atlantis*, 486.

and animals when they are quartered with one another: "Horses are tied by the heads, dogs and bears by th' neck, monkeys by th' loins, and men by th' legs" (2.4.10–12). When Regan proposes that Lear should return to dwell with Goneril, Lear protests that he would rather "be a comrade with the wolf and owl" (2.4.243). Kent learns from a gentleman that Lear is parading "unbonneted" through the storm on a night when "the cub-drawn bear would couch, / The lion and the belly-pinched wolf / Keep their fur dry" (3.1.14–16). Cordelia later uses animal imagery to describe the intensity of the same storm: "Mine enemy's dog, / Though he had bit me, should have stood that night / Against my fire" (4.7.42–4). When Lear is finally persuaded to enter the ark-like hovel, he meets the ragged figure of Edgar, who recounts his sins to Lear using animalistic metaphors, further disintegrating the distinction between human and beast. Edgar confesses that he has been a "hog in sloth, fox in stealth, wolf in greediness, dog in madness, lion in prey" (3.4.99–101). Lear consoles Edgar by reinforcing his community with animals at the same time that he underscores Christian redemption as an outrageous doctrine. It is unthinkable to Lear that a man of such poverty, "such a poor, bare, forked animal" (3.4.111–15) would owe God—or even a worm—a debt: "Thou ow'st the worm no silk, the beast no hide, the sheep no wool, the cat no perfume" (3.4.110–12). There is no redemption aboard this ark; all debts are off, even if economic inequality endures. Furthermore, the hovel Edgar shares with Lear is populated, like Noah's ark, with animals. Their purpose, however, is to sustain human life; Edgar is hardly their custodian, and Lear is no Noah. He tells Lear that he has sustained himself on "the swimming frog, the toad, the tadpole, the wall newt, and the water," on "cow dung," on "the old rat and the ditch-dog," and on "mice and rats and such small deer" (3.4.136–47). Cordelia later asks the slumbering king, "[W]ast thou fain, poor father, / To hovel thee with swine and rogues forlorn / In short and musty straw?" (4.7.44–6). Cordelia beholds the depths to which Lear has fallen, but his time within the hovel affords him no retribution. Finally, when divine grace fails to redeem Cordelia's death, Lear fathoms this inequity by contrasting her death with the lives of animals: "Why should a dog, a horse, a rat have life, / And thou no breath at all?" (5.3.370–1). In the flood plays, Lear's rhetorical question might have an answer: these animals have life because Noah (by God's will) saved them. Sinners, on the other hand, perished. But the spectacle of Lear holding his innocent and faithful daughter dead in his arms invites audiences to reevaluate the Christian notion of redemption because it fails to explain adequately the debt she must repay with her life.

Lear pays dearly for his initial fault. But "faults" in this play are never simply moral mistakes; they metaphorically link the play's concern for economic equity and alternative modes of redemption with the natural (and unnatural) fracturing and dividing of landforms. Although the term "fault"—meaning a "dislocation or break in continuity of the strata or vein"[34]—was not associated with the practice of mining or the study of geology until the late eighteenth century, *Lear* anticipates these valences by confronting moral failings with uneven English topography and geography.

The word "fault" appears eleven times in the conflated text of *Lear*, and often bridges moral mistakes with natural or human-made divisions of land. Gloucester and Lear, for example, each fracture their families by distributing unequal quantities of land to their children. When the play opens, Gloucester inquires whether Kent can detect Edmund's illegitimacy by asking, "Do you smell a fault?" (1.1.16). His question not only reduces Edmund (who is on stage) to an unhappy blunder or error of his past, but also suggests Edmund cannot be his brother's equal. Kent politely replies, "I cannot wish the fault undone, the issue of it being so proper" (1.1.17–18). Though Gloucester admits that Edgar is "no dearer in my account" (1.1.20) than Edmund, Gloucester's premarital "fault" will reap the division of his family, which will only play out after Lear commits a fault of his own with the misestimated geographical division of his kingdom. Gloucester weighs the inequity of his two sons only after considering how Lear will divide the kingdom between Albany and Cornwall: "it appears not which of the dukes he values most, for equalities are so weighed that curiosity in neither can make choice of either's moiety" (1.1.4–7). But by describing Edmund as a "fault" who is also "no dearer in my account" than Edgar, Gloucester betrays his own inability to fairly determine equality between his two sons, and between the two dukes.

Poor judgment of equality is a flaw that Lear shares in hoping to balance the love of his daughters in a rhetorical scale. Once she is bereft of her dowry, Cordelia tells her sisters that she is "most loath to call / Your faults as they are named" (1.1.313–14), but warns them that those "Who cover faults at last with shame derides" (1.1.326). But the "faults" of her sisters also belong to her father, and this scene stages his egregious portioning. When Lear bestows part of his kingdom to Goneril, he emphasizes the geographical line that represents her boundary on the map:

---

[34] *OED*, "fault," n. 9.a.

> Of all these bounds, even from this line to this,
> With shadowy forests and with champains riched,
> With plenteous rivers and wide-skirted meads,
> We make thee lady.
>
> (1.1.69–72)

The border of Goneril's territory may be fixed on the map, but because Goneril's portion contains "plenteous rivers," her dowry seems prone to internal, natural, geological divisions, exacerbated by the increase of water or superflux. It is likely that Lear metonymically associates Goneril with her "champains riched," "plenteous rivers," and "wide-skirted meads," since he later curses her through distorting his vision of her verdant and fertile territory. Using imagery of desertification and drought, Lear calls on nature to prevent her from being "fruitful," to promote her "sterility," to "*Dry* up in her the organs of increase," so that from her body a child may "never *spring*" (1.4.289–95, emphasis added). Conflating her body with her dowry and estate, Lear also transforms her "plenteous rivers" into a curse about excess of water:

> If she must teem,
> Create her child of spleen, that it may live
> And be thwart disnatured torment to her.
> Let it stamp wrinkles in her brow of youth,
> With cadent tears fret channels in her cheeks,
> Turn all her mother's pains and benefits
> To laughter and contempt, that she may feel
> How sharper than a serpent's tooth it is
> To have a thankless child.
>
> (1.4.295–303)

Lear hopes Goneril will wear "channels" on her face if her lands remain fertile. Ingratitude in Goneril incites Lear to curse her issue and the dowry he gave to her. But when it comes from Cordelia, ingratitude, that "most small fault," proves tantamount to an earthquake along a geologic fault; "like an engine," Cordelia's fault "wrenche[s Lear's] frame of nature / From the fixed place" (1.4.278–81). Even in the throes of his anger, Lear acknowledges the devastating destruction that can come from a "small fault." Eventually, he will see his faults—his unjust distribution of land among his daughters, and his unjust distribution of wealth within his kingdom—as his own. But because Lear's moral faults deal a greater offense to the physical makeup of his kingdom and his family than to his God, the play's faults—the kingdom's wealth inequality and the mislaid paternalism of two unhappy fathers—appear more redeemable through a secular and natural avenue than through a spiritual one.

Gloucester's Cliff and Lear's Flood: Nature's Redemptive Dark Matter

Whereas faults register as human sins that can only be redeemed by God in the medieval flood plays, the geologic tenor of faults in *King Lear*—the way landed properties and estates remain (after they have been portioned and distributed) prone to further fracturing and division, either metaphorically or else literally along unseen but active seismic boundaries—suggests that redemption is possible without God. For Gloucester, geologic faults are not only a physical embodiment of the uneven distribution of land promised to his two sons; they also form a necessary step—or fall—in Gloucester's economic rebalancing. I suggest that the white cliffs of Dover from which Gloucester hopes to leap to his death, but which the audience can perceive as a trick of Edgar's theater, function as "dark matter" in the play. According to Andrew Sofer, theatrical dark matter refers to the "invisible phenomena" that "continually structure and focus an audience's theatrical experience"; they are "incorporeal yet are crucial to the performed event."[35] Though Sofer refrains from identifying the play's cliffs as dark matter, I suggest that the Dover cliffs are a central "felt absence" in *King Lear* precisely because of the play's fractured landscapes and economic imbalances.[36]

The cliffs of Dover are also central to Shakespeare's appropriation of the flood plays because of contemporary debates regarding how the earth's topography formed, which pivoted on Noah's deluge as a relatively recent earth-shaping event. While Buridan was able to imagine the earth supplying its own defense against superflux and deluge in an eternal universe, scholars of the seventeenth century harbored a more Biblical temporal conception for the earth's history. Human beings and the earth were each thought to have been only about 6,000 years old, and Noah's flood was thought to be a real historical event, occurring about 1,500 years after creation.[37] The history of the earth, furthermore, was divided into "seven ages" (an idea that Jaques in *As*

---

[35] Andrew Sofer, *Dark Matter: Invisibility in Drama, Theater, and Performance* (Ann Arbor, MI: University of Michigan Press, 2013), 4.
[36] Sofer, *Dark Matter*, 4.   [37] Rudwick, *Earth's Deep History*, 20.

You Like It famously parodies), and the living human "present" was thought to be the last and final age.[38] This conception of time gave rise to three prevailing theories about the earth's topography in the seventeenth century: (1) that it was formed 6,000 years ago by God on the day of Creation *as is*, (2) that it was formed by the deluge that Noah and his family escaped, and (3) that it was formed by post-diluvian earthquakes.[39] Though much of this debate occurred in the latter half of the seventeenth century, decades after *Lear* was first performed, it nevertheless sheds light on how Shakespeare's secular, theatrical construction of time more closely resembles geologic "deep" time than the chronologies imagined by his contemporaries.

Richard Verstegan, a Catholic antiquarian living in exile from Elizabethan England, was one proponent of the third theory, that the universal deluge had shaped most of the earth's topography, but not all of it.[40] In *A Restitution of Decayed Intelligence in Antiquities* (1605), published around the same time that *Lear* was first performed, Verstegan muses on how the island of England formed and considers it unlikely "that there were any Iles before the deluge; and so much may be gathered by the words of the scripture."[41] Verstegan's *Restitution* may have seemed "scientific" because it privileged natural antiquities over the armchair science of his forebears, but his observations about the natural world were also tinted with his own national, racial, and linguistic ideology.[42] Verstegan was bent on proving the Germanic and Saxon origins of the English people, and sought to overturn the popular mythical and historical connections to Rome and Troy by tracing the lineage from a more Biblical genealogy.[43] Instead of suggesting that the flood created England, Verstegan proposed that, long ago, "Albion hath bin continent with Gallia."[44] He suggested that England was once connected to France by "a bridge or Isthmus of land, beeing altogether of chalk and flint,"[45] citing for evidence the "neernes of land between England and France...from the Clifs of Douer, unto the lyke clifs lying between Calis and Bullen," as well as their opposing faces, their similar composition "of chalk and flint," the way they appear "to bee broken of[f] from some more of the same stuf or matter," and their matching length,

---

[38] Rudwick, *Earth's Deep History*, 24. Other temporal schemes imagined that human history spanned three, four, six, or even twelve distinct ages. See Burrow, *The Ages of Man*, 2.

[39] Gordon L. Davies, "Early British Geomorphology," *The Geographical Journal*, Vol. 132, No. 2 (1966), 253–4.

[40] Davies, "Early British Geomorphology," 260.

[41] Richard Verstegan, *A Restitution of Decayed Intelligence in Antiquities* (London, 1605), M4r.

[42] Rudwick, *Earth's Deep History*, 51.

[43] Graham Parry, *The Trophies of Time: English Antiquarians of the Seventeenth Century* (Oxford: Oxford University Press, 1995), 51.

[44] Verstegan, *A Restitution of Decayed Intelligence*, M4v.

[45] Verstegan, *A Restitution of Decayed Intelligence*, N1r.

and the distance between them.[46] Although Verstegan believed that "Almightie God" was "the cause and conductor of Nature" who "in creating the world did leaue no parte of his work imperfect or broken," he was willing to see that the real force that drove England apart from France and created the cliffs of Dover was not God, but a kind of superflux, or the property of water finding its level between two unbalanced bodies:[47]

> That the sea on the west syde of the said Isthmos was lower then the sea on the east syde thereof, is besides this great work thereby wrought, to bee iudged by the sundry flats and shallowes on the east syde, aswel on the coste of England as of Flanders, yea one in a manner lying between Douer and Calis, of about three English myles in length, of some called our Ladyes sand. And contrariwise on the west syde no such flats at all to bee found, whereby may wel bee gathered that as the land vnder the sea remaineth on the one syde lower then one the other, so accordingly did the sea also.[48]

Verstegan believed that the waters of the North Sea stood higher than the waters of the English Channel, and he attempts to show similar imbalances in places where two bodies of water "haue but narrow separations of land between them"—between the higher Red Sea and the lower Mediterranean, and between the higher Pacific Ocean and the lower Atlantic on each side of Panama.[49] Thus, for Verstegan, Dover's white cliffs were not shaped by the original deluge, but stood as a visible monument to water's natural ability to redeem its own imbalances over a long period of time after the flood.

Though Verstegan is perhaps unknown to most marine geologists, his theory has been all but confirmed with modern bathymetry mapping techniques. Recent studies in seismology and geology reveal two features of the Dover cliffs that enhance their "incorporeal yet crucial" status as the site of Gloucester's economic and paternal redemption in *King Lear*: not only were the cliffs partly formed by a catastrophic flooding event, they also lie in close proximity to a nest of active faults, responsible for significant seismic activity in southeast England. As Verstegan observed without any modern scientific instruments, England *was* once connected to the mainland of Europe by a ridge, known by geologists today as the Weald-Artois anticline.[50] Sometime

---

[46] Verstegan, *A Restitution of Decayed Intelligence*, N1r.
[47] Verstegan, *A Restitution of Decayed Intelligence*, N2v.
[48] Verstegan, *A Restitution of Decayed Intelligence*, O3r.
[49] Verstegan, *A Restitution of Decayed Intelligence*, O3r–v.
[50] Sanjeev Gupta et al., "Catastrophic Flooding Origin of Shelf Valley Systems in the English Channel," *Nature*, Vol. 448 (2007), 342.

around 300,000 years ago, a large glacial lake in the southern North Sea over-flowed and caused a "catastrophic breach" of the Weald-Artois barrier.[51] The geology of the sea floor of the English Channel bears the traces of this flood event. Verstegan's hypothesis that the waters of the North Sea stood higher than the waters of the English Channel was thus not incorrect, though the two bodies of water likely achieved their balance during the flood in a much less gradual manner than he imagined. Gloucester may select Dover as the location for his suicide for its convenient proximity. But because it is also the location where he seeks redemption through a redistribution of his wealth, Dover's topographical reminder of a natural redistribution of water also emphasizes a physical model of redemption over a spiritual one.[52] Furthermore, in the same way that Gloucester cannot see his faults until he cannot see at all, his "perspective" from the top of Dover cliffs, even as it is falsely mediated and interpreted by Edgar, affords his audience no visibility of the submarine geologic fault that was responsible for the earthquake of 1580. Earthquakes have been recorded in southeast England in 1133, 1247, 1382, 1449, 1580, 1692, 1776, 1938, and 2007.[53] The earthquakes in 1382, 1449, 1580, and 1776 have each had epicenters in the Dover Strait-Pas de Calais region,[54] and the Sangatte Fault in the Dover Strait has been identified as the source of the significant seismic events in 1580, 1776, and 2007.[55]

The providential discourse surrounding an earthquake that Shakespeare must have read about (if he did not experience it firsthand) helps to establish human error as a cause, and thus establishes a precedent of human and

---

[51] Gupta et al., "Catastrophic Flooding Origin," 344. Gupta et al. hypothesize that the breach caused the decline and eventual disappearance of early human populations in England. Human colonization peaked in England between Marine Isotope Stage 13 (533,000 years ago) and MIS 10 (374,000 years ago), but they began to decline around MIS 8 (300,000 years ago), and disappeared entirely for 100,000 years during MIS 6 (191,000 years ago) (Gupta et al. 344–5).

[52] Jennifer Mae Hamilton suggests that the reason Gloucester sends Lear to Dover is because "there 'the sea,' a metonymy for the French army, led by Cordelia, has the capacity to rise up and change the organization of power in the kingdom" (Hamilton, *This Contentious Storm*, 36). This reading of the sea reinforces a connection between a natural environment correcting the imbalance of power in the kingdom.

[53] G. Neilson, R. M. W. Musson, and P. W. Burton, "The 'London' Earthquake of 1580, April 6," *Engineering Geology*, Vol. 20, No. 1 and 2 (1984), 113. For a more thorough list of earthquakes recorded in the British Isles, see R. M. W. Musson, "British Earthquakes," *Proceedings of the Geologists' Association*, Vol. 118 (2007), 305–37.

[54] C. P. Melville et al., "Historical Seismicity of the Strait of Dover-Pas de Calais," *Terra Nova*, Vol. 8, No. 6 (1996), 644.

[55] D. Garcia Moreno et al., "Fault Activity in the Epicentral Area of the 1580 Dover Strait (Pas-de-Calais) Earthquake (Northwestern Europe)," *Geophysical Journal International*, Vol. 201 (2015), 528–9. Musson discusses some of the problems with trying to determine active faults to predict future seismic activity. For one, the United States Environmental Protection Agency (USEPA) defines an active fault as any fault that has "produced an earthquake in the last 10,000 years." Musson prefers to "scrap the idea of active faults" in favor of determining "controlling faults," or the main expressions of ongoing deformational activity (Musson 334).

geologic faults coalescing. Two and a half weeks before Shakespeare's sixteenth birthday, an earthquake rocked Dover and Calais. The quake of April 6, 1580 occurred three days after Easter, and was felt in London, Paris, and Amsterdam.[56] In London, two apprentices were killed by stones falling from the roof of Christ's Church.[57] In Dover, where the intensity was strongest, a section of the cliff face slid into the sea.[58] Most firsthand accounts of the quake identify human sins as the cause of the quake. Richard Tarlton, the famed clown of the Queen Elizabeth's Men, who is perhaps an ironic source for the type of providential moralizing more likely to be expected from anti-theatricalist Puritans, nevertheless viewed the quake as a demonstration of God's judgment in a publication he shared with Thomas Churchyard. Tarlton recounted how "honest men... were upon a suddain tumbled down with such violence," and "The very waters and diches shooke and frothed wonderfully."[59] The quake caused flooding in Calais and powerful waves in the Dover Strait.[60] Tarlton concluded his account with a prophetic poem, which perhaps antici-pates the tenor (if not the anaphora) of Lear's fool's prophesy that "the realm of Albion" shall "Come to great confusion" (3.3.98–9): "Our health of soules must hang in great suspence / When earth and Sea doo quake for our offence."[61] The quake occurred in the afternoon, when plays were being per-formed at the Theatre and at the Curtain. Spectators "were so shaken,

---

[56] Melville et al., "Historical Seismicity of the Strait of Dover-Pas de Calais," 634.
[57] Nielson et al., "The 'London' Earthquake of 1580," 117.
[58] Melville et al., "Historical Seismicity of the Strait of Dover-Pas de Calais," 636.
[59] Quoted in Lily B. Campbell, "Richard Tarlton and the Earthquake of 1580," *Huntington Library Quarterly*, Vol. 4, No. 3 (1941), 298.
[60] Melville et al., "Historical Seismicity of the Strait of Dover-Pas de Calais," 636. The authors doubt, however, that this "modest" quake would have produced a tsunami, even if its epicenter was in the Strait (636).
[61] Campbell, "Richard Tarlton and the Earthquake of 1580," 300. Tarlton writes:

> When Mountaines mooue as late they did in wales
> great signe it is that nature then is crost:
> When Monsterous Infants tels such doctors tales
> The token shews some fauour hath bin lost...
> When blasing stares, and bloody cloudes doo show
> Then time it is for men too search a new...

(Campbell 299)

Though Robert Armin likely played Lear's Fool, he was an apprentice of Tarlton's. It may not be too farfetched to suggest that Armin and Shakespeare are parodying Tarlton's style here. For comparison, Lear's fool pronounces:

> When priests are more in word than matter;
> When brewers mar their malt with water;
> When nobles are their tailors' tutors;...
> When usurers tell their gold I' the field;
> And bawds and whores do churches build;
> Then shall the realm of Albion
> Come to great confusion.

(3.3.88–99)

especially those that stoode in the highest roomthes and standings, that they were not a little dismayed, considering, that they coulde no waye shifte for themselves, unlesse they woulde, by leaping, hazarde their lives or limes, as some did in deede, leaping fro[m] the lowest standings."[62] Like Tarlton, Churchyard interpreted the event as a sign of God's wrath, and as a precursor to a future apocalyptic quake. At the same time, the quake demonstrated God's love, and invited those who experienced it to reflect on their "faults":

> But those that grace hath toucht within,
> By outward signes will show,
> That hart forethinks foule former faults,
> for feare of greater blowe,
> Than now they feele through Earthquake strange,
> wherin Gods might in knowne,
> And London (if Gods loue had lackt)
> had surely bin orethrowne.[63]

Another pamphleteer viewed the earthquake not only as a premonition of coming war, pestilence, and famine[64] but also as a forewarning of an imminent judgment, tantamount to the destruction Noah escaped: "I thinke if the general day of iudgement had come vpon vs, as this was but a forewarning of it, we had all beene founde no lesse vnprouided, than were they in Noes floud, we had all stoode in the state of condemnation."[65] On the brink of a cliff that only he can see, Gloucester kneels before the "mighty gods." And rather than seeking God's mercy or redemption from a divine source, Gloucester prefers to "shake patiently [his] great affliction off" (4.6.44–6). His rejection of divinity and his botched suicide may add to the list of faults, which, barring only himself, everyone can see. But at the same time, it creates a space to embrace a physical mode of redemption—one that requires blindness to perceive, and one where nature's hidden faults, rather than God's secret will, inspire wonder at our state of condemnation, beckoning us to conclude our "life's a miracle" (4.6.69).

Rather than speculate on Verstegan's *Restitution* as a source for Shakespeare's tragedy, I suggest instead that Shakespeare and Verstegan were

---

[62] Thomas Churchyard, *A warning for the wise, a feare to the fond, a bridle to the lewde, and a glasse to the good* (London, 1580), B2r.

[63] Churchyard, *A warning for the wise*, B3r.

[64] Abraham Fleming, *A bright burning beacon forewarning all wise virgins to trim their lampes against the coming of the Bridegroom* (London, 1580), E1v.

[65] Fleming, *A bright burning beacon*, P1r–v.

each capable of thinking about the effects of time and water on the English landscape in a similar way. Through conceiving of the flood and the cliffs of Dover as present absences, Shakespeare imagines a topographical scheme where the agent changing the earth's surface is not God, but secular forces of excess. When Lear conceives of a future in which he "may'st shake the superflux," he conflates his former excess of wealth with the overflow of water he endures. Lear laments that he was unable to distribute his wealth more evenly before he gave it to his ungrateful daughters. In this way, his tragedy operates according to the forces of excess as well. But Gloucester does manage, at least financially, to undo his excess as he stands atop the cliffs of Dover, which some in Shakespeare's audience may have imagined as the record of a natural imbalance finding stability. In the diluvian narratives of Noah, Lear, and Gloucester, water acts as a great equalizer; water not only erases economic disparity, and cleanses the earth of sin and sinner alike, it also finds its own level. God is the cleansing agent for audiences of the medieval flood plays, but Shakespeare imagines water itself as the agent of natural and economic equity.

Gloucester's decision to commit suicide at the cliffs of Dover dramatizes more than his second fall or his redemption. For Shakespeare, the cliffs model an alternative model of redemption, rooted in nature. As soon as Gloucester gives Poor Tom his purse in an effort to "undo excess," he immediately asks the beggar, "Dost thou know Dover?" (4.1.80–1). For Gloucester, the rocky fault provides a means to economic and moral redemption. "Bring me to the very brim of it," he instructs Poor Tom, "And I'll repair the misery thou dost bear / With something rich about me" (4.1.85–7). Gloucester does not know that Poor Tom's misery is in fact his fault, and Edgar only realizes that his disguise as Poor Tom prevents a proper reconciliation between father and son once it is too late. When Edgar recounts his father's death, he narrates that he "became his guide, / Led him, begged for him, saved him from despair" (5.3.226–7). But he "Never—O fault!—revealed [him]self unto him / Until some half hour past" (5.3.228–9). Edgar's fault gives way to other fractures, cracks, and bucklings: after recounting how Gloucester's heart "burst smilingly" (5.3.235), which leaves Albany "ready to dissolve" (5.3.240), Edgar tells of Kent's confession, which ends when "the strings of life began to crack" (5.3.254–5). It is as if Edgar's well-intentioned jest of leading his father to the edge of a theatrical cliff invites the audience to witness Gloucester's inward rupture as a symptom of the play's ruptured landscapes. When Gloucester, bereft of his sight, is being led to the place from which he "shall no leading need" (4.1.89), the audience is also blind to what Edgar describes. As Erika Lin argues, Edgar is theatrically privileged as a *platea* character in this scene, since he is "aware of the playhouse conventions through which visual, aural, and verbal cues onstage come to signify within the represented fiction."[66] Gloucester's contradictory experience of Edgar's narration lets spectators know that Edgar is exploiting the conventions of theater to "trifle thus with his despair" in order to "cure it" (4.6.42–3):

> *Edgar.*   Look how we labor.
> *Gloucester.* Methinks the ground is even.
> *Edgar.*   Horrible steep.
>   Do you hear the sea?
> *Gloucester.*   No, truly.
>
>   (4.6.2–6)

Edgar's jest here flirts with a kind of ecological nihilism, or "catastrophizing" as Gerard Passannante calls it, that is willing to make "anything of anything," even a cliff out of a barren stage. But if Lear's stunned proclamation to Cordelia, "Nothing will come of nothing" (1.1.88), also embodies this nihilistic despair, perhaps Edgar's more playful staging of the phrase for his blind father moves into a more productive and affirming register.[67] On the other hand, Gloucester believes that he has been brought "within a foot / Of th' extreme verge" (4.6.31–2), even if the audience does not. Edgar's descriptions before and after Gloucester falls—of fishermen who "upon the beach / Appear like mice" (4.6.22–3) from above, and of the "shrill-gorged lark so far / [which] Cannot be seen or heard" (4.6.72–3) from below—are enough to convince Gloucester that his "life's a miracle" (4.6.69) after his small tumble on the stage. Even though the "dread summit of this chalky bourne" (4.6.71) of Dover is physically absent from the play, it *is* present for Gloucester. This scene relies on the audience's knowledge of Dover's topography. Spectators must hold the cliffs of Dover in their minds—both from the top, looking down, and from the bottom, looking up—when they see only a stage. Thus, Edgar's use of this theatrical dark matter solicits his audience into experiencing topographical space in a new way. But because it is on the clifftop where

---

[66] Erika T. Lin, *Shakespeare and the Materiality of Performance* (New York: Palgrave Macmillan, 2012), 35.

[67] Passannante, *Catastrophizing*, 144–5. Passannante traces the proliferation of the phrase "*quidlibet ex quolibet*" throughout the early modern period to contextualize instances of bad interpretation that give way to a catastrophizing impulse. Othello, Gloucester, and Leontes are three examples of catastrophizers in Shakespeare who have a habit of making something out of nothing, or anything of anything. But Passannante recognizes potential for such interpretive violence to be productive as well: "Making *quidlibet ex quolibet* can certainly bring upon ruin and, in Shakespeare's tragedies at least, it does more often than not. But such making needn't always imply disaster. It might even suggest the creative act of making what we call poetry."

Gloucester practices his new economy of "distribution"—giving Edgar "another purse" containing "a jewel / Well worth a poor man's taking" (4.6.35–6)—the cliff becomes a necessary pivot for Gloucester to bring his imagined future into being.

"That things might change or cease":
Imagined Futures and Deep Time

The cliff's centrality to the play's redemption of economic and moral faults is not only spatial. Although Edgar's jest on his disoriented father forces the audience to imagine the cliffs from varying perspectives, the cliffs as dark matter also ask us to see the cliffs through a fluid temporal lens. At the same time that antiquarians like Verstegan were beginning to privilege natural objects over ancient manuscripts, leading to new hypotheses about the age of the earth and the place of the human within it, Shakespeare's play represented England's pre-Christian past for a sixteenth-century audience preoccupied with an apocalyptic future. As Ellen MacKay shows, anti-theatricalist sentiments that viewed the stage as a precursor to doomsday were not without foundation; both early modern and earlier traditions of theatrical performance were understood to be "age-endingly unsustainable."[68] Time in *King Lear* is both forward-looking and anachronistically backward-looking; the play represents time as a secular agent capable of changing the earth's topography, and anticipates the deep timescale by which topographical imbalances are measured and through which they are restored.

The apocalyptic connotations of the storm Lear endures would not have been lost on early modern audiences. Since many believed that they were living during the seventh and final age of man, the end of time is one possible future that the play imagines through the storm. To lookers-on, Lear's raving in the storm may be an attempt to bring about change, though it proves about as fruitful as catching the wind; he "Bids the winds blow the earth into the sea, / Or swell the curled water 'bove the main, / That things might change or cease" (3.1.5–7). The earth will manifest one of these two options; it will either be destroyed by the storm or will bring about a "change"—in the earth, in the kingdom, and in the economy. The storm is a great equalizer; Lear hopes that it will "strike flat the thick rotundity o' the world" (3.2.8). Although one topographical theory held that Noah's flood was a similar leveler, and was

---

[68] MacKay, *Persecution, Plague, and Fire*, 7.

responsible for the creation of plains,[69] Lear's call for flattening the earth's "rotundity" unites his concern for a more just economic distribution with the play's representation of natural redemption. But while the play balances the possible outcomes of the storm, it also represents time anachronistically through the fool's jest (which only appears in the Folio edition, not in the quarto). Immediately after Lear finally enters the hovel, the fool "speak[s] a prophesy" (3.3.86) in which he predicts that "the realm of Albion" will "come to great confusion" (3.3.98–9). That time, he suggests, is now: "Then comes the time, who lives to see't, / That going shall be used with feet" (3.3.101). But because the fool occupies the audience's past, his prophesy about the future is directed toward the audience's present: "This prophecy Merlin shall make; for I live before his time" (3.3.102). Through his prophesy, then, the fool occupies the past, the present, and the future all at once. While his prediction may be only a jest, it is a jest the play asks that we take seriously because it reminds us that our present was someone else's future, and our future will become some-one else's past.

Perhaps more pressing than understanding why Shakespeare's interest in secularizing his religious dramatic sources *matters* is understanding why it matters *today*. Although J. K. Barret's project of recuperating the imagined futures of seventeenth-century literature problematizes the authority of the term "Renaissance" and the deterministic connotation of "early modern,"[70] I believe Shakespeare's imagined futures are precious—especially Lear's—because they offer us a model for how to confront our own uncertain future in the age of anthropogenic climate change. Perhaps the term "early modern" does reduce all potential futures into the certainty "of one particular outcome: modernity."[71] But I also think we as scholars need to begin to see our present and Shakespeare's early "modern" present—or perhaps early "Anthropocene" present—as ecologically connected. For example, whereas Verstegan's *Restitution* used fossils and other natural antiquities to deduce how the white cliffs of Dover formed, scientists have since determined that the white cliffs and "chalky bourne" of Dover, which (do not) appear in Shakespeare's play, are in fact fossils themselves. The cliffs are mostly fossilized phytoplankton, which at one time in earth's history managed the earth's carbon dioxide distri-bution, and served as the basis for all marine ecosystems.[72] Thus, the geology of *King Lear* is important for understanding how the play's theme of wealth

---

[69] Davies, "Early British Geomorphology," 253.   [70] Barret, *Untold Futures*, 6.
[71] Barret, *Untold Futures*, 6.
[72] Russ George, "Origin of White Cliffs of Dover Phytoplankton Ehux Genome Sequenced," *Russ George*, 19 June 2013. http://russgeorge.net/2013/06/19/ehux-genome.

redistribution relates to carbon distribution in the deep past and to human-generated emissions today. Furthermore, the play's unique staging of the cliffs of Dover as dark matter exposes audiences to a spatial and temporal experience of English topography in order to imagine alternative models of redemption and restored economic balance. Because economic imbalances between the earth's seven continents are the legacy of the British empire's exploitation of natural resources, this play's attention to how nature restores economic imbalances makes it uniquely relevant to recent postcolonial projects. As Elizabeth DeLoughrey and George Handley argue, "human political and social inequalities cannot be successfully and sustainably resolved without some engagement with the more-than-human world and with deep time."[73] Whether we read the white cliffs as a tombstone to the atmospheric carbon regulation of the pre-Anthropocene, or as a monument to nature's power to correct its own superfluxes and imbalances and to make life more sustainable on earth, the play invites us to connect the inequalities of nature to the economic imbalances we face in our present and our future. It invites us to make connections between the past histories, present violences, and possible futures of global capitalism in an age of global climate change, intensifying weather events, sea-level rise, and superflux.

---

[73] DeLoughrey and Handley, *Postcolonial Ecologies*, 25.

Epilogue

The Empty Drainpipe

In Margaret Atwood's *Oryx and Crake*, Crake explains how frogs earn a bio-logical advantage through exploiting their human-generated surroundings. He explains that "the male frog, in mating season…makes as much noise as it can. The females are attracted to the male frog with the biggest, deepest voice because it suggests a more powerful frog, one with superior genes. Small male frogs—it's been documented—discover that if they position themselves in empty drainpipes, the pipe acts as a voice amplifier, and the small frog appears much larger than it really is." For Crake, the drainpipe is really a metaphor for aesthetic creation: "that's what art is, for the artist…An empty drainpipe. An amplifier. A stab at getting laid."[1] Crake's chauvinist explanation for the "biological purpose" of "doodling, scribbling, and fiddling" cynically praises artistic production for its eugenic capacity (e.g. through the production of "superior genes"), while simultaneously reducing art to the drab image of "an empty drainpipe."[2] Crake's metaphor calls attention to the mating ritual of an amphibian, a class of the animal kingdom that is rapidly declining as a result of human behaviors and anthropogenic climate change. An empty drainpipe may help an individual male frog during mating season, but it cannot save an entire species. Crake, who nearly succeeds in wiping out the human species in Atwood's novel, raises an important question with his metaphor: what is the purpose—biological or otherwise—of art if it cannot stave off mass extinction or other ecological consequences of human behaviors? While I believe it would be a fatal mistake to endorse Crake's brand of mad science, or to embrace his cynical perspective of the humanities, I am also compelled to follow him in asking: what do the humanities have to offer as we continue to adapt and prepare to live in a changing world?

If what's past is in fact prologue, I would like to sketch out some potential avenues for further exploration where Shakespeare and the Anthropocene are

---

[1] Margaret Atwood, *Oryx and Crake* (New York: Anchor Books, 2004), 168.
[2] Atwood, *Oryx and Crake*, 167–8.

Anthropocene Theater and the Shakespearean Stage. William H. Steffen, Oxford University Press.
© William H. Steffen 2023. DOI: 10.1093/oso/9780192871862.003.0008

concerned. As the history of Shakespearean performance makes clear, the proliferation of early modern drama has played no small part in the human and non-human assemblages that make up the *oikeios*. But beyond Eugene Schieffelin's acclimatization of the European starling to Central Park—a brand of mad science that may have contributed to the extinction of the carrier pigeon and, by extension, the earth's sixth mass-extinction event—how else might we measure the ecological impact of Shakespeare and Bardolotry? Is there a carbon footprint attached to the history of Shakespearean performance that should give us pause? Is such a thing worth measuring, and if so, how should it be measured?

Perhaps a more productive question to pose might ask: where does Shakespeare go from here? Lately, I have begun to ask myself, "Are we in trouble?"—not only as a student of the environmental humanities, but also as a student of Shakespeare, and as an English professor. A 2015 report published by the American Council of Trustees and Alumni found that Shakespeare is a requirement for English majors at only four of fifty-two leading universities and liberal arts colleges.[3] At the same time that some high school teachers are weighing the benefits of cutting Shakespeare from their syllabi altogether, some conservative Republicans (who are reluctant to distance themselves from White supremacists) want to embrace the "Anglo-Saxon political traditions" to which Shakespeare is inextricably tied.[4] In one sense, this book has been an attempt to prevent Shakespeare from falling so easily onto either side of such a black-and-white binary of our post-Trump, cancel-culture era. Shakespeare wrote his plays, of course (though there are those who will debate even that).[5] But as I have tried to show here, those plays have taken on a life of their own since Shakespeare put down his quill in London and strolled back

---

[3] American Council of Trustees and Alumni, "The Unkindest Cut: Shakespeare in Exile 2015." *The Washington Post*. 23 April 2015. Accessed 13 June 2022. http://apps.washingtonpost.com/g/documents/local/the-unkindestcut/1523/?itid=lk_inline_manual_14, p. 3.

[4] Amanda MacGregor, "To Teach or Not to Teach: Is Shakespeare Still Relevant to Today's Students?" *School Library Journal*. 4 January 2021. Accessed 13 Jun 2022. https://www.slj.com/story/to-teach-or-not-to-teach-is-shakespeare-still-relevant-to-todays-students-libraries-classic-literature-canon. MacGregor writes, "Shakespeare's works are full of problematic, outdated ideas, with plenty of misogyny, racism, homophobia, classism, anti-Semitism, and misogynoir." See also Andrew Solender, "Marjorie Taylor Greene Forming Caucus to Promote 'Anglo-Saxon Political Traditions.'" *Forbes*. 16 April 2021. Accessed 13 Jun 2022. https://www.forbes.com/sites/andrewsolender/2021/04/16/marjorie-taylor-greene-forming-caucus-to-promote-anglo-saxon-political-traditions/?sh=2f82b0a25672.

[5] Another opportunity for investigating Shakespeare as an ecological phenomenon would be to give more consideration to Shakespeare as a collaborative author than I have done here. See Linda Shenk and William J. Gutowski, "Mind the Gaps! Climate Scientists Should Heed Lessons in Collaborative Storytelling from William Shakespeare." *WIREs Clim Change*. 14 April 2022. Accessed 14 June 2022. https://wires.onlinelibrary.wiley.com/doi/pdfdirect/10.1002/wcc.783, e783, 1–9.

to Stratford and died. Shakespearean performance operates in a global network in tandem with natural, economic, and even accidental forces over which Shakespeare (the man) never had any control. To "cancel" Shakespeare now would be to shut the book on one of the most unique ecological histories we are privy to, and would only serve to strengthen the divide between the humanities and the sciences.

On the one hand, looking at Shakespeare through a lens of the Anthropocene is one strategy for demonstrating the benefits of cross-disciplinary scholarship between the humanities and the STEM fields. Is there an argument for renaming the Anthropocene the "Shakes-cene," given that the history of Shakespearean performance seems to coincide with the measurable consequences of the Columbian "Exchange," the start of the British Empire, the birth of global capitalism, and the onset of anthropogenic climate change on a global scale? Perhaps. If we look hard enough, we might even be able to identify a "Golden Spike" for such a -cene, maybe even in the daggers wielded by Hamlet or Macbeth.[6] Such an undertaking might help to foster a collaborative ethos between English or theater departments and the STEM fields as the next generation of college graduates moves into a job market that seems increasingly dictated by the realities of a changing climate. But on the other hand, I am reluctant to put the humanities in such a defensive position, or to suggest that the study of literature and performance is only relevant in an academic landscape driven by the profitability of the STEM fields.

It is my hope that this book will not only help actors and directors stage Shakespeare more responsibly but also help audience members consume Shakespeare with more ecological awareness—and with a renewed curiosity. But moving forward, how else might eco-materialist histories and the history of eco-global Shakespeares inform modern productions? There are, admittedly, early modern micro-histories I was not able to address in the pages of this book that perhaps belong here, given their potential implications on the stage. The fascinating insect–plant ecology of cochineal, the scarlet-red insects that live on prickly-pear plants in Mexico, and which were used to make cosmetic rouges and clothing dyes (including the dyes for the infamous "lobster-back" British colonial soldiers during the American Revolution), is one. Ambergris, the mysterious by-product of whales that snack lethally on squid beaks, which their stomachs fail to digest but which early modern beach-combers used for perfume and expensive gravy in spite of not knowing

---

[6] As Yusoff argues, "the Golden Spike is something that spikes or impales" (Yusoff, *A Billion*, 59).

the origin of the fecal matter, is another.[7] But another avenue of further exploration might be to investigate the eco-materialist networks at play when modern stage properties and mediums are used to perform Shakespeare. What kinds of materials are used to stage Shakespeare today, for example, that Shakespeare's audiences did not have access to? What is the ecological footprint of mass-producing Shakespeare on film? How might a performance of *Much Ado About Nothing*, staged entirely through text messages, implicate audiences in the troubling ecological networks and labor practices used by Apple and Foxconn, or cell service providers?[8]

The COVID-19 pandemic also generated new opportunities for performing Shakespeare on a "global stage" like never before. In the early modern period, actors hit the road when the civic theaters shut down because of plague outbreaks. Robert Myles and Sarah Peachey's weekly production of a different Shakespeare play during the spring of 2020 were similar performances of necessity after the theaters closed in March, though they required no physical travel for either player or audience. The Show Must Go Online (TSMGO) generated "a full Zoom production of one Shakespeare play a week, in the order in which they were written (as listed by Wikipedia), featuring actors gathered from multiple time zones on six of the seven continents."[9] Does the geographical anomaly of "sailing" between Verona and Milan in *Two Gents* really matter in a production where Proteus is "Zooming" in from London, and Valentine from Los Angeles? What does a Hollywood Squares version of *Lear* do to Gloucester's "fall" or to Cordelia's death? How does Hamlet's complaint that "the time is out of joint" (1.5.211) register a different grievance when he speaks from a different time zone than the one inhabited by his audience?

---

[7] Raymond L. Lee, "American Cochineal in European Commerce, 1526–1625," *The Journal of Modern History*, Vol. 23, No. 3 (September 1951), 205–24; Karl H. Dannenfeldt, "Ambergris: The Search for Its Origin," *Isis*, Vol. 73, No. 3 (1982), 382–97.

[8] Chloe Rabinowitz, "Found Stages to Present Text Message Shakespearean Play: Much Ado Over Texting!" *Broadway World*. 24 March 2022. Accessed 13 June 2022. https://www.broadwayworld.com/atlanta/article/Found-Stages-to-Present-Text-Message-Shakespearean-Play-MUCH-ADO-OVER-TEXTING-20220324. Rabinowitz describes the Found Stages all-text message production as one that "casts you as best friend to Beatrice, Benedick, and Hero." For more on the slow violence perpetrated by Apple, see Tania Branigan, "Chinese Workers Link Sickness to n-Hexane and Apple iPhone Screens." *The Guardian*. 7 May 2010. Accessed 13 Jun 2022. https://www.theguardian.com/world/2010/may/07/chinese-workers-sickness-hexane-apple-iphone; Joel Johnson, "1 Million Workers. 90 Million iPhones. 17 Suicides. Who's to Blame?" *Wired*. 28 February 2011. Accessed 13 June 2022. https://www.wired.com/2011/02/ff-joelinchina.

[9] Austin Tichenor, "'In the brave squares': The Show Must Go Online." *Shakespeare and Beyond*. 29 September 2020. Accessed 13 June 2022. https://shakespeareandbeyond.folger.edu/2020/09/29/the-show-must-go-online-shakespeare-productions-zoom.

As technological innovation continues to multiply and diversify the ways in which audiences consume theater (and Shakespearean theater in particular), there are also new kinds of assemblages to investigate between human and non-human actors. Accidents will endure in these arenas as well. The effect of a storm during a Zoom performance of *The Tempest* might have an impact on how the play is received and interpreted by the audience, though the effect will likely be completely different from an outdoor production of the same play where actors and audiences are weathering the same storm. On the other hand, digital productions of Shakespeare introduce new ecological players. How might a poor internet connection, an unintentionally muted microphone, or a frozen screen prompt an actor into improvising an unscripted soliloquy? How should audiences understand the effect of a weak connection? Is it the actor's fault for not securing a better location from which to log on and perform? Or is a weak internet connection (and a "bad" performance) the fault of other users who are hogging all the bandwidth? How do digital productions of Shakespeare draw attention to ecology and distributive agency for audiences inhabiting the Anthropocene?

Insofar as my project has privileged the "Orbis Spike" hypothesis about the origins of the Anthropocene, what might other performance-based or Shakespeare-oriented provincializations look like when 1800 or 1950 are given as the preferred points of origin? In some ways, the performance history I have presented in this book overlaps with the Industrial Revolution. But what would a history of Shakespearean performance look like that positions nuclear fallout as a key indicator of anthropogenic agency? How did Hiroshima and Nagasaki change Shakespearean performance on an atomic level? What other kinds of theatrical "dark matter" would help us to negotiate the "felt absences" of the Anthropocene—the mass extinction of species, the loss of biodiversity, the swelling desertification as a result of a warming planet, for example?[10]

Finally, I hope this project opens up further possibilities to explore DeLoughrey and Handley's charge for postcolonial inquiry and the environmental humanities to address how "human political and social inequalities cannot be successfully and sustainably resolved without some engagement with the more-than-human world and with deep time."[11] Beyond the faults of *King Lear*, how else does geologic time function in Shakespeare? How can theater generate an experience of "deep time" for audiences that will help to

---

[10] Sofer, *Dark Matter*, 4.   [11] DeLoughrey and Handley, *Postcolonial Ecologies*, 25.

facilitate a redistribution—of wealth, of carbon, of agency? How else can theater flatten ontological hierarchies?

Orderly, to end where I began, I wish to return to the microscopic gaze of
Primo Levi. In Levi's story about "Silver" in *The Periodic Table*, he recounts
being invited (following his liberation from Auschwitz) to his twenty-fifth
college reunion. Attendees were invited to "celebrate our silver wedding with
Chemistry by telling each other the chemical events of our everyday life."[12] At
the dinner, he reconnects with an old acquaintance, Cerrato, who "had not
been compromised by Fascism, and [who] had reacted well to the reagent of
the racial laws."[13] Cerrato tells Levi the story of working in Germany for the
department that manufactures the paper on which X-rays are produced. After
he had received a number of complaints about bean-shaped splotches appearing on the X-ray paper, Cerrato had to determine the cause of the blemishes.
After interviewing a guard who was having no luck in his weekend fishing
lately, Cerrato realized that the water they were using had been tainted by a
tannery and a laundry facility upstream; the tannins in the water were dissolving the silver bromide on the X-ray paper. After a quick experiment,
Cerrato observes that "the bean effect—*Bohneffekt*—had been reproduced in
full."[14] Levi's goal may be to tell the story of "solitary chemistry, unarmed and
on foot, at the measure of man," but it would be a mistake to ignore how Levi's
microscopic gaze enhances our ability to see not just a chemical reaction, but
an ecology.[15] It matters what is in the water upstream, just like it matters who
is telling the story, and through what political regime this particular river
flows. If this story of the "bean effect" is one in which "stolid matter manifests
a cunning intent upon evil and obstruction," then perhaps the world of matter
can be an ally in helping us negotiate the present crises of the Anthropocene.
Levi understood this, which is perhaps why he chose to depict it not with a
microscope, but with a pen:

> We would keep in contact, and each of us would gather for the other more
> stories like this one, in which stolid matter manifests a cunning intent upon
> evil and obstruction, as if it revolted against the order dear to man: like
> those reckless outcasts, thirsting more for the ruination of others than for

---

[12] Levi, *The Periodic Table*, 200.   [13] Levi, *The Periodic Table*, 202.
[14] Levi, *The Periodic Table*, 209. Levi continues: "when all was said and done, it became obvious
that a few thousand molecules of polyphenol absorbed by the fibers of the overalls during the wash
and carried by an invisible piece of lint from the overalls to the paper were enough to produce
the spots."
[15] Levi, *The Periodic Table*, 203.

their own triumph, who in novels arrive from the ends of the earth to thwart the exploits of positive heroes.[16]

I believe, along with Levi and Miranda, that a gathering of such stories might give us arms against a sea of troubles—and by opposing, at least allay them.

---

[16] Levi, *The Periodic Table*, 210.

Bibliography

Abu-Lughod, Janet L. *Before European Hegemony: The World-System A.D. 1250–1350.* Oxford: Oxford University Press, 1989.

Allen, Myles. "In Defense of the Traditional Null Hypothesis: Remarks on the Trenberth and Curry *WIREs* Opinion Articles." *WIREs Clim Change.* Vol. 2 (2011): 931–4.

American Council of Trustees and Alumni. "The Unkindest Cut: Shakespeare in Exile 2015." *The Washington Post.* 23 April 2015. https://files.eric.ed.gov/fulltext/ED560917.pdf. Accessed 13 June 2022.

Appuhn, Karl Richard. *A Forest on the Sea: Environmental Expertise in Renaissance Venice.* Baltimore, MD: Johns Hopkins University Press, 2009.

Atwood, Margaret. *Oryx and Crake.* New York: Anchor Books, 2004.

Austin, J. L. *How To Do Things with Words.* Oxford: Oxford University Press, 1962.

Bacon, Francis. *New Atlantis.* In *Francis Bacon: The Major Works.* Edited by Brian Vickers. Oxford: Oxford University Press, 2008. 457–90.

Bandmann, Daniel E. *An Actor's Tour, or Seventy Thousand Miles with Shakespeare.* New York: Brentano Brothers, 1886.

Barad, Karen. "Posthumanist Performativity: Toward an Understanding of How Matter Comes to Matter." *Signs: Journal of Women in Culture and Society.* Vol. 28, No. 3 (2003): 801–31.

Barbour, Richmond. *The Third Voyage Journals: Writing and Performance in the London East India Company, 1607–10.* New York: Palgrave Macmillan, 2009.

Barker, Richard. "Sources for Lusitanian Shipbuilding." In *Proceedings of the International Symposium "Archaeology of Medieval and Modern Ships of Iberian- Atlantic Tradition,"* Lisbon (1998): 213–28.

Barlow, William. *Magneticall aduertisements: or Diuers pertinent obseruations, and approued experiments, concerning the natures and properties of the load-stone.* London, 1618.

Barret, J. K. *Untold Futures: Time and Literary Culture in Renaissance England.* Ithaca, NY: Cornell University Press, 2016.

Bartels, Emily C. "Making More of the Moor: Aaron, Othello, and Renaissance Refashionings of Race." *Shakespeare Quarterly.* Vol. 41, No. 4 (1990): 433–54.

Bartels, Emily C. *Speaking of the Moor: From Alcazar to Othello.* Philadelphia, PA: University of Pennsylvania Press, 2008.

Bauer, Lois. [Unknown Title]. *The Bermudian,* October 1950.

Beadle, Richard and Pamela M. King, eds. *York Mystery Plays: A Selection in Modern Spelling.* Oxford: Oxford University Press, 2009.

Becker, Tobias. "Entertaining the Empire: Theatrical Touring Companies and Amateur Dramatics in Colonial India." *The Historical Journal.* Vol. 57, No. 3 (2014): 699–725.

Behringer, Wolfgang. *A Cultural History of Climate.* Translated by Patrick Camiller. Malden, MA: Polity Press, 2010.

Bennett, Jane. *Vibrant Matter: A Political Ecology of Things.* Durham, NC: Duke University Press, 2010.

Berners, Juliana. *The booke of hauking, hunting and fysshyng, with all the properties and medecynes that are necessary to be kept*. London, 1556.

Bernhard, Virginia. *Slaves and Slaveholders in Bermuda, 1616–1782*. Columbia, MO: University of Missouri Press, 1999.

Bhatia, Nandi. *Acts of Authority, Acts of Resistance: Theater and Politics in Colonial and Postcolonial India*. Ann Arbor, MI: University of Michigan Press, 2004.

Blanche, Rosalind. *Life in a Gall: The Biology and Ecology of Insects That Live in Plant Galls*. Collingwood, Vic.: Csiro Publishing, 2012.

Blunt, Richard. "The Evolution of Blackface Cosmetics on the Early Modern Stage." In *The Materiality of Color: The Production, Circulation, and Application of Dyes and Pigments, 1400–1800*. Edited by Andrea Feeser, Maureen Daly Goggin, and Beth Fowkes Tobin. Burlington, VT: Ashgate, 2012. 217–34.

Boehrer, Bruce. *Environmental Degradation in Jacobean Drama*. Cambridge: Cambridge University Press, 2013.

Bogost, Ian. *Alien Phenomenology or What It's Like to Be a Thing*. Minneapolis, MN: University of Minnesota Press, 2012.

Boling, Ronald J. "Fletcher's Satire of Caratach in *Bonduca*." *Comparative Drama*. Vol. 33, No. 3 (1999): 390–406.

Bonoeil, John. *His Maiesties gracious letter to the Earle of South-Hampton, treasurer, and to the Councell and Company of Virginia heere commanding the present setting vp of silke works, and planting of vines in Virginia*. London, 1622.

Booth, Michael R. and Pamela Heckenberg. "Touring the Empire." *Essays in Theatre*. Vol. 6 (1987): 49–60.

Botti, Lorean, Orietta Mantovani, and Daniele Ruggiero. "Calcium Phytate in the Treatment of Corrosion Caused by Iron Gall Inks: Effects on Paper." *Restaurator*. Vol. 26, No. 1 (2005): 44–62.

Branigan, Tania. "Chinese Workers Link Sickness to n-Hexane and Apple iPhone Screens." *The Guardian*. 7 May 2010. https://www.theguardian.com/world/2010/may/07/chinese-workers-sickness-hexane-apple-iphone. Accessed 13 June 2022.

Brayton, Daniel. *Shakespeare's Ocean: An Ecocritical Exploration*. Charlottesville, VA: University of Virginia Press, 2012.

Brenner, Robert. *Merchants and Revolutions: Commercial Change, Political Conflict, and London's Overseas Traders, 1550–1653*. London: Verso, 2003.

Briggs, Jonathan D. "Historical Uses of Plant Galls." *Cecidology*. Vol. 1, No. 1 (1986): 6–7.

Brome, Richard. *The Antipodes* (1636). In *Three Renaissance Travel Plays*. Edited by Anthony Parr. Manchester: Manchester University Press, 1995.

Brookes, Kristen G. "Inhaling the Alien: Race and Tobacco in Early Modern England." In *Global Traffic: Discourses of Trade in English Literature and Culture from 1550–1700*. Edited by Barbara Sebek and Stephen Deng. New York: Palgrave Macmillan, 2008. 157–78.

Brunello, Franco. *The Art of Dyeing in the History of Mankind*. Translated by Bernard Hickey. Vicenza: N. Pozza, 1973.

Burrow, John Anthony. *The Ages of Man: A Study in Medieval Writing and Thought*. Oxford: Clarendon Press, 1988.

Burton, Robert. *The Anatomy of Melancholy* (1621). Edited by Holbrook Jackson. New York: New York Review Books, 2001.

Bushnell, Rebecca. *Green Desire: Imagining Early Modern English Gardens*. Ithaca, NY: Cornell University Press, 2003.

Calder, Alison. "'I am unacquainted with that language, Roman': Male and Female Experiences of War in Fletcher's *Bonduca*." *Medieval and Renaissance Drama in England*. Vol. 8, No. 1 (1996): 211–26.

Calhoun, Joshua. "Ecosystemic Shakespeare: Vegetable Memorabilia in the Sonnets." *Shakespeare Studies*. Vol. 39, No. 1 (2011): 64–73.

Callaghan, Dympna. *Shakespeare Without Women: Representing Gender and Race on the Renaissance Stage*. London: Routledge, 2000.

Campbell, Lily B. "Richard Tarlton and the Earthquake of 1580." *Huntington Library Quarterly*. Vol. 4, No. 3 (1941): 293–301.

Carew, Richard. *The voyce of the Lord in the temple*. London, 1640.

Césaire, Aimé. *A Tempest*. Translated by Richard Miller. New York: Theatre Communications Group, 1992.

Chakrabarty, Dipesh. *Provincializing Europe: Postcolonial Thought and Historical Difference*. Princeton, NJ: Princeton University Press, 2000.

Chakrabarty, Dipesh. "The Climate of History: Four Theses." *Critical Inquiry*. Vol. 35, No. 2 (2009): 197–222.

Chapman, Matthieu. *Anti-Black Racism in Early Modern English Drama: The Other "Other."* New York: Routledge, 2017.

Chasteen, John Charles. *Getting High: Marijuana Through the Ages*. Lanham, MD: Rowman & Littlefield, 2016.

Chaudhuri, Una. "Land/Scape Theory." In *Land/Scape Theater*. Edited by Una Chaudhuri and Elinor Fuchs. Ann Arbor, MI: University of Michigan Press, 2005. 11–29.

Childs, Wendy R. *Anglo-Castilian Trade in the Later Middle Ages*. Manchester: Manchester University Press, 1978.

Childs, Wendy R. "Anglo-Portuguese Trade in the Fifteenth Century." *Transactions of the Royal Historical Society*. Vol. 2 (1992): 195–219.

Churchyard, Thomas. *A warning for the wise, a feare to the fond, a bridle to the lewde, and a glasse to the good*. London, 1580.

Conkie, Rob. "Nature's Above Art (An Illustrated Guide)." *Shakespeare Bulletin*. Vol. 36, No. 3 (2018): 391–408.

Counseil for Virginia (England and Wales). *A true declaration of the estate of the colonie in Virginia*. London, 1610.

Craufurd, Russell. *Ramblings of an Old Mummer*. London: Greening, 1909.

Crawford, Julie. "Fletcher's *The Tragedie of Bonduca* and the Anxieties of the Masculine Government of James I." *Studies in English Literature, 1500–1900*. Vol. 39, No. 2 (2009): 357–81.

Crosby, Alfred W. *Ecological Imperialism: The Biological Expansion of Europe, 900–1900*. Cambridge: Cambridge University Press, 1986.

Crosby, Alfred W. *Germs, Seeds and Animals: Studies in Ecological History*. Armonk: M.E. Sharpe, 1994.

Crosby, Alfred W. *The Columbian Exchange: Biological and Cultural Consequences of 1492*. 30th anniversary edition. London: Praeger, 2003.

Daborne, Robert. *A Christian Turn'd Turk*. In *Three Turk Plays from Early Modern England*. Edited by Daniel J. Vitkus. New York: Columbia University Press, 2000. 149–240.

Dannenfeldt, Karl H. "Ambergris: The Search for Its Origin." *Isis*. Vol. 73, No. 3 (1982): 382–97.

Davies, Gordon L. "Early British Geomorphology." *The Geographical Journal*. Vol. 132, No. 2 (1966): 252–62.

Dekker, Thomas. *Lust's Dominion; or, The Lascivious Queen*. In *The Dramatic Works of Thomas Dekker*, vol. 4. Edited by Fredson Bowers. Cambridge: Cambridge University Press, 1961. 114–230.

DeLoughrey, Elizabeth and George B. Handley. Introduction to *Postcolonial Ecologies: Literatures of the Environment*. Edited by Elizabeth DeLoughrey and George B. Handley. Oxford: Oxford University Press, 2011.

Dobson, Michael. *The Making of a National Poet: Shakespeare, Adaptation, and Authorship, 1660–1769*. Oxford: Clarendon Press, 1992.

Dorsey, Kristina. "'Oh Bugspray, Where Art Thou?': Birds, Drunks, Sirens Conspire to Make Outdoor Shakespeare a Comedy of Errors." *The Day*. 23 July 2002. C1–2.

Drew-Bear, Annette. *Painted Faces on the Renaissance Stage: The Moral Significance of Face-Painting Conventions*. Lewisburg, PA: Bucknell University Press, 1994.

Dromgoole, Dominic. *Hamlet: Globe to Globe*. New York: Grove Press, 2017.

Duval, Charles. *With a Show Through Southern Africa*. Vols. 1 and 2. London: Tinsley Brothers, 1882.

Edelman, Charles, ed. *The Stukeley Plays: The Battle of Alcazar by George Peele; The famous history of the life and death of Captain Thomas Stukeley*. Manchester: Manchester University Press, 2005.

Egan, Gabriel. *Green Shakespeare: From Ecopolitics to Ecocriticism*. London: Routledge, 2006.

Ellerbeck, Erin. "'A Bett'ring of Nature': Grafting and Embryonic Development in *The Duchess of Malfi*." In *The Indistinct Human in Renaissance Literature*. Edited by Jean E. Feerick and Vin Nardizzi. New York: Palgrave Macmillan, 2012. 85–99.

Enders, Jody. *Murder by Accident: Medieval Theater, Modern Media, Critical Intentions*. Chicago, IL: University of Chicago Press, 2009.

Epp, Garrett P. J. *The Towneley Plays*. Kalamazoo, MI: Western Michigan University, 2017.

Estacio, Martin. "Couple Charged with Involuntary Manslaughter in Southern California Fire Sparked by Gender Reveal." *USA Today*. 20 July 2021. https://www.usatoday.com/story/news/nation/2021/07/20/couple-charged-involuntary-manslaughter-southern-california-gender-reveal/8036779002. Accessed 21 July 2020.

Estok, Simon C. "Reading Ecophobia: A Manifesto." *Ecozon@*. Vol. 1, No. 1 (2010): 75–9.

Fagan, Margaret M. "The Uses of Insect Galls." *The American Naturalist*. Vol. 52, No. 614 (1918): 155–76.

Feerick, Jean. "Botanical Shakespeare: The Racial Logic of Plant Life in *Titus Andronicus*." *South Central Review*. Vol. 26, No. 1 and 2 (2009): 82–102.

Feerick, Jean. *Strangers in Blood: Relocating Race in the Renaissance*. Toronto: University of Toronto Press, 2010.

Feerick, Jean and Vin Nardizzi, eds. *The Indistinct Human in Renaissance Literature*. New York: Palgrave Macmillan, 2012.

Fetherling, Douglas. *The Gold Crusades: A Social History of Gold Rushes, 1849–1929*. Toronto: University of Toronto Press, 2015.

Fields, Karen E. and Barbara J. *Racecraft: The Soul of Inequality in American Life*. London: Verso, 2012.

Fleming, Abraham. *A bright burning beacon forewarning all wise virgins to trim their lampes against the coming of the Bridegroom*. London, 1580.

Fletcher, Jill. *The Story of Theatre in South Africa: A Guide to Its History from 1780–1930*. Cape Town: Vlaeberg, 1994.

Fletcher, John. *The Knight of Malta*. In *Comedies and Tragedies*. London, 1647.

Fletcher, John. *Bonduca*. Edited by Cyrus Hoy. In *The Dramatic Works in the Beaumont and Fletcher Canon*. 10 vols. Cambridge: Cambridge University Press, 1979. 4: 149–259.

Floyd-Wilson, Mary. *English Ethnicity and Race in Early Modern Drama*. Cambridge: Cambridge University Press, 2003.

"Foreign Miscellany: Stage Thunder, From *Once a Week*." *New York Times*. 8 July 1866. ProQuest Historical Newspapers: *The New York Times (1851–2010)*: 2.

Forman, Valerie. *Tragicomic Redemptions: Global Economics and the Early Modern English Stage*. Philadelphia, PA: University of Pennsylvania Press, 2008.

Foulkes, Richard. *Performing Shakespeare in the Age of Empire*. Cambridge: Cambridge University Press, 2002.

Freedman, Paul. *Images of the Medieval Peasant*. Stanford, CA: Stanford University Press, 1999.

Frost, Christine Mangala, "30 Rupees for Shakespeare: A Consideration of Imperial Theatre in India." *Modern Drama*. Vol. 35, No. 1 (1992): 90–100.

George, Russ. "Origin of White Cliffs of Dover Phytoplankton Ehux Genome Sequenced." *Russ George*. 19 June 2013. http://russgeorge.net/2013/06/19/ehux-genome.

Geouge, Jennifer C. "Anglo-Portuguese Trade During the Reign of Joao I of Portugal, 1385–1433." In *The New Middle Ages: England and Iberia in the Middle Ages, 12th–15th Century: Cultural and Political Exchanges*. Edited by Maria Bullon-Fernandez. New York: Palgrave Macmillan, 2007. 119–34.

Gerald, Frank. *A Millionaire in Memories*. London: Routledge, 1936.

Gerard, John. *The herball or Generall historie of plantes*. London, 1633.

Gilroy, Harry. "Rain and Praise Shower on 'Macbeth.'" *New York Times*. 29 June 1966. ProQuest Historical Newspapers: *The New York Times (1851–2010)*: 38.

Goldenberg, David. *The Curse of Ham*. Princeton, NJ: Princeton University Press, 2003.

Gollancz, Israel. *A Book of Homage to Shakespeare*. 1916. Oxford: Oxford University Press, *Internet Archive*, 15 October 2009. https://archive.org/details/cu31924013146257/page/338/mode/2up. Accessed 3 June 2022.

Gouwens, Kenneth. "What Posthumanism Isn't: On Humanism and Human Exceptionalism in the Renaissance." In *Renaissance Posthumanism*. Edited by Joseph Campana and Scott Maisano. New York: Fordham University Press, 2016. 37–63.

Grazia, Margreta de. *Hamlet Without Hamlet*. Cambridge: Cambridge University Press, 2007.

Green, Paul D. "Theme and Structure in Fletcher's *Bonduca*." *Studies in English Literature, 1500–1900*. Vol. 22, No. 2 (1982): 305–16.

Greene, Robert. *The historie of Orlando Furioso, one of the twelue pieres of France, As it was plaid before the Queenes Maiestie*. London, 1594.

Grier, Miles P. "Inkface: The Slave Stigma in England's Early Imperial Imagination." In *Scripturalizing the Human: The Written as the Political*. Edited by Vincent L. Wimbush. New York: Routledge, 2015. 193–220.

Grove, Richard H. *Green Imperialism: Colonial Expansion, Tropical Island Edens and the Origins of Environmentalism, 1600–1860*. Cambridge: Cambridge University Press, 1995.

Guattari, Felix. *The Three Ecologies*. London: Athlone Press, 2000.

Guilfoyle, Cherrell. *Shakespeare's Play Within Play: Medieval Imagery and Scenic Form in Hamlet, Othello, and King Lear*. Kalamazoo, MI: Western Michigan University Press, 1990.

Gupta, Sanjeev, Jenny S. Collier, Andy Palmer-Felgate, and Graeme Potter. "Catastrophic Flooding Origin of Shelf Valley Systems in the English Channel." *Nature*. Vol. 448 (2007): 342–6.

Gurr, Andrew. "*The Tempest*'s Tempest at Blackfriars" (1989). In *The Tempest, Norton Critical Edition*. Edited by Peter Hulme and William H. Sherman. New York: Norton, 2004. 250–65.

Hageneder, Fred. *Botanical: Yew*. London: Reaktion, 2013.

Hall, Kim F. *Things of Darkness: Economies of Race and Gender in Early Modern England*. Ithaca, NY: Cornell University Press, 1995.

Hamber, J. B. and Eugene Olivier (compiled by Laurence Wright and Lin Gubb). "A Tribute to 'Stratford-on-Baakens': Thirty Years of the Port Elizabeth Shakespearean Festival." *Shakespeare in Southern Africa*. Vol. 3 (1989): 1–8.

Hamilton, Jennifer Mae. *This Contentious Storm: An Ecocritical and Performance History of King Lear*. London: Bloomsbury, 2017.

Harding, Samuel. *Sicily and Naples, or The Fatal Union: A Tragedy*. London: William Turner, 1640.

Hardwicke, Cedric. *A Victorian in Orbit: The Irreverent Memoirs of Sir Cedric Hardwicke*. Westport, CT: Greenwood Press, 1961.

Hariot, Thomas. "A Description of Virginia." From *A Briefe and True Report*. 1588. In *Captain John Smith: Writings with other Narratives of Roanoke, Jamestown, and the First English Settlement of America*. Edited by James Horn. New York: The Library of America, 2007. 874–905.

Harman, Graham. "The Well-Wrought Broken Hammer: Object-Oriented Literary Criticism." *New Literary History*. Vol. 43, No. 2 (2012): 183–203.

Harris, Jonathan Gil. *Sick Economies: Drama, Mercantilism, and Disease in Shakespeare's England*. Philadelphia, PA: University of Pennsylvania Press, 2004.

Harris, Jonathan Gil. *Untimely Matter in the Time of Shakespeare*. Philadelphia, PA: University of Pennsylvania Press, 2009.

Harris, Mitchell M. "The Expense of Ink and Wastes of Shame: Poetic Generation, Black Ink, and Material Waste in Shakespeare's Sonnets." In *The Materiality of Color: The Production, Circulation, and Application of Dyes and Pigments, 1400–1800*. Edited by Andrea Feeser, Maureen Daly Goggin, and Beth Fowkes Tobin. Burlington, VT: Ashgate, 2012. 65–80.

Harward, Simon. *A discourse of the seuerall kinds and causes of lightnings*. London, 1607.

Hassel, Jr., R. Chris. "Shakespeare's 'Removed Mysteries.'" *Connotations*. Vol. 7, No. 3 (1997): 355–67.

Hatch, Jr., Charles E. "Mulberry Trees and Silkworms: Sericulture in Early Virginia." *The Virginia Magazine of History and Biography*. Vol. 65, No. 1 (1957): 3–61.

Hattersley, Alan F. *Pietermaritzburg Panorama: A Survey of One Hundred Years of an African City*. Pietermaritzburg: Shuter and Shooter, 1938.

Henderson, Campbell. "Touring in the Orient." *The Stage Year Book*, 1920.

Heng, Geraldine. *The Invention of Race in the European Middle Ages*. Cambridge: Cambridge University Press, 2018.

Heywood, Thomas. *The Fair Maid of the West, Parts I and II*. Edited by Robert K. Turner Jr. Lincoln, NE: University of Nebraska Press, 1967.

Hill, Errol. *The Jamaican Stage, 1655–1900: Profile of a Colonial Theatre*. Amherst, MA: University of Massachusetts Press, 1992.

Hiltner, Ken. *What Else Is Pastoral? Renaissance Literature and the Environment*. Ithaca, NY: Cornell University Press, 2011.

Hobhouse, Henry. *Seeds of Change: Six Plants That Transformed Mankind*. Washington, DC: Shoemaker & Hoard, 2005.

Holloway, David. *Playing the Empire: The Acts of the Holloway Touring Theatre Company.* London: Harrap, 1979.

Honingmann, E. A. J. *Shakespeare: The "Lost Years."* Manchester: Manchester University Press, 1998.

Hulme, Mike. "Attributing Weather Extremes to 'Climate Change': A Review." *Progress in Physical Geography.* Vol. 38, No. 4 (2014): 499–511.

Hunt, Maurice. "Old England, Nostalgia, and the 'Warwickshire' of Shakespeare's Mind." *Connotations.* Vol. 1, No. 2 (1997): 159–80.

Hussey, Maurice, ed. *The Chester Mystery Plays: Sixteen Pageant Plays from the Chester Craft Cycle.* London: W. Heinemann, 1957.

Ivory, James, dir. *Shakespeare Wallah*, 1965. DVD.

Jacobson, Brian. "Optimist Theater's *Tempest* Interrupted by Tempest." *Urban Milwaukee.* 20 June 2010. https://urbanmilwaukee.com/2010/06/20/optimist-theatres-tempest-interrupted-by-tempest. Accessed 19 July 2021.

Johnson, Joel. "1 Million Workers. 90 Million iPhones. 17 Suicides. Who's to Blame?" *Wired.* 28 February 2011. https://www.wired.com/2011/02/ff-joelinchina. Accessed 13 June 2022.

Jones, Eldred. *Othello's Countrymen: The African in English Renaissance Drama.* London: Oxford University Press, 1965.

Jones, Emrys. *The Origins of Shakespeare.* Oxford: Clarendon Press, 1978.

Jones, Gwilym. *Shakespeare's Storms.* Manchester: Manchester University Press, 2015.

Jones, William. *God's vvarning to his people of England.* London, 1607.

Jowitt, Claire. *Voyage Drama and Gender Politics, 1589–1642: Real and Imagined Worlds.* Manchester: Manchester University Press, 2003.

Karim-Cooper, Farah. "'This alters not thy beauty': Face-Paint, Gender, and Race in Richard Brome's *The English Moor.*" *Early Theater.* Vol. 10, No. 2 (2007): 140–9.

Kaye, Joel. "The (Re)Balance of Nature, ca. 1250–1350." In *Engaging with Nature: Essays on the Natural World in Medieval and Early Modern Europe.* Edited by Barbara J. Hanawalt and Lisa J. Kiser. Notre Dame, IN: University of Notre Dame Press, 2008. 85–114.

Kendal, Geoffrey and Clare Colvin. *The Shakespeare Wallah: The Autobiography of Geoffrey Kendal.* London: Sidgwick & Jackson, 1986.

Kershaw, Baz. *Theatre Ecology: Environments and Performance Events.* Cambridge: Cambridge University Press, 2007.

Kincaid, Jamaica. *My Garden.* New York: Farrar, Straus, Giroux, 1999.

Kirwan, Peter. "*A Christian Turn'd Turk* (Read Not Dead) @ the Sam Wanamaker Playhouse." 6 October 2014. http://blogs.nottingham.ac.uk/bardathon/2014/10/06/a-christian-turnd-turk-read-not-dead-the-sam-wanamaker-playhouse. Accessed 13 June 2019.

Klein, Naomi. *This Changes Everything: Capitalism vs. the Climate.* New York: Simon & Schuster, 2014.

Kobayashi, Kaori. "Touring in Asia: The Miln Company's Shakespearean Productions in Japan." In *Shakespeare and his Contemporaries in Performance.* Edited by Edward J. Esche. Aldershot: Ashgate, 2000. 53–72.

Korda, Natasha. *Shakespeare's Domestic Economies: Gender and Property in Early Modern England.* Philadelphia, PA: University of Pennsylvania Press, 2002.

Kumah, Abraham. "Sustainability and Gold Mining in the Developing World." *Journal of Cleaner Production.* Vol. 14 (2006): 315–23.

Lamentable newes out of Monmouthshire in VVales. London, 1607.

Lang, Matheson. *Mr. Wu Looks Back: Thoughts and Memories*. London: Stanley Paul & Co., 1941.

Latour, Bruno. *Reassembling the Social: An Introduction to Actor-Network Theory*. Oxford: Oxford University Press, 2005.

Lee, Raymond L. "American Cochineal in European Commerce, 1526–1625," *The Journal of Modern History*. Vol. 23, No. 3 (September 1951): 205–24.

Levi, Primo. *The Periodic Table*. Translated by Raymond Rosenthal. New York: Schocken, 1984.

Lewis, Simon L. and Mark A. Maslin. "Defining the Anthropocene." *Nature*. Vol. 519 (12 March 2015): 171–80. http://www.nature.com/nature/journal/v519/n7542/full/nature14258.html.

Lin, Erika T. *Shakespeare and the Materiality of Performance*. New York: Palgrave Macmillan, 2012.

Linebaugh, Peter and Marcus Rediker. *The Many-Headed Hydra*. Boston, MA: Beacon Press, 1992.

Macaulay, Thomas Babington. "Minute of 2 Feb. 1835." In *Archives of Empire, Volume I: From the East India Company to the Suez Canal*. Edited by Mia Carter and Barbara Harlow. Durham, NC: Duke University Press, 2003. 227–38.

MacGregor, Amanda. "To Teach or Not to Teach: Is Shakespeare Still Relevant to Today's Students?" *School Library Journal*. 4 January 2021. https://www.slj.com/story/to-teach-or-not-to-teach-is-shakespeare-still-relevant-to-todays-students-libraries-classic-literature-canon. Accessed 13 June 2022.

MacKay, Ellen. *Persecution, Plague, and Fire: Fugitive Histories of the Stage in Early Modern England*. Chicago, IL: University of Chicago Press, 2010.

Malpighi, Marcello. *De Gallis: On Galls*. Edited and translated by Margaret Redfern, Alexander J. Cameron, and Kevin Down. London: The Ray Society, 2008.

Malynes, George. *A treatise of the canker of Englands common wealth*. London, 1601.

Malynes, George. *Consuetudo, vel lex mercatoria, or The ancient law-merchant*. London, 1622.

Mani, M. S. *Ecology of Plant Galls*. The Hague: Dr. W. Junk, 1964.

Marsden, John O. and C. Iain House. *Chemistry of Gold Extraction*. Edited by John O. Marsden and C. Iain House. Littleton, CO: SME, 2006.

Marston, John. *The vvonder of vvomen or The tragedie of Sophonisba as it hath beene sundry times acted at the Blacke Friers*. London, 1606.

Martin, Randall and Evelyn O'Malley. "Eco-Shakespeare in Performance: Introduction." *Shakespeare Bulletin*. Vol. 36, No. 3 (2018): 377–90.

Mascall, Leonard. *A booke of the arte and maner, howe to plant and graffe all sortes of trees howe to set stones, and sowe pepines to make wylde trees to graffe on, as also remedies and medicines*. London, 1572.

Mascall, Leonard. *A booke of fishing with hooke & line, and of all other instruments thereunto belonging*. London, 1590.

Massinger, Philip. *The Parliament of Love*. In *The Plays of Philip Massinger, in Four Volumes*. Edited by William Gifford. Vol. 2. London, 1813.

McCall, Timothy. "Materials for Renaissance Fashion." *Renaissance Quarterly*. Vol. 70, No. 4 (2017): 1449–64.

McCarthy, Terence S. "The Impact of Acid Mine Drainage in South Africa." *South African Journal of Science*. Vol. 107, No. 5/6 (2011): 1–7.

McMullan, Gordon. "The Colonization of Early Britain on the Jacobean Stage." In *Reading the Medieval in Early Modern England*. Edited by Gordon McMullan and David Matthews. Cambridge: Cambridge University Press, 2007. 119–40.

McMullan, Gordon. "Goblin's Market: Commemoration, Anti-Semitism, and the Invention of 'Global Shakespeare' in 1916." In *Celebrating Shakespeare: Commemoration and Cultural Memory*. Edited by Clara Calvo and Coppelia Kahn. Cambridge: Cambridge University Press, 2015. 182–201.

McNeill, J. R. "Woods and Warfare in World History." *Environmental History*. Vol. 9, No. 3 (2004): 388–410.

Mclville, C. P., A. Levret, P. Alexandre, J. Lambert, and J. Vogt. "Historical Seismicity of the Strait of Dover-Pas de Calais." *Terra Nova*. Vol. 8, No. 6 (1996): 626–47.

Mendes, Americo M. S. Carvalho and Jose A. R. Graca. "Cork Bottle Stoppers and Other Cork Products." In *Cork Oak Woodlands on the Edge: Ecology, Adaptive Management, and Restoration*. Edited by James Aaronson, Joao S Pereira, and Juli G. Pausas. Washington, DC: Island Press, 2009. 59–69.

Mentz, Steve. *At the Bottom of Shakespeare's Ocean*. London: Continuum, 2009.

Mentz, Steve. *Shipwreck Modernity: Ecologies of Globalization, 1550–1719*. Minneapolis, MN: University of Minnesota Press, 2015.

Mentz, Steve. "The Neologismcene." *Arcade: Literature, the Humanities, and the World*. 1 July 2018. https://arcade.stanford.edu/blogs/neologismcene. Accessed 13 June 2022.

Mikalachki, Jodi. *The Legacy of Boadicea: Gender and Nation in Early Modern England*. London: Routledge, 1998.

Minton, Gretchen E. "'The Season of All Natures': Shakespeare in the Parks' Global Warming *Macbeth*." *Shakespeare Bulletin*. Vol. 36, No. 3 (2018): 429–48.

Monsanto. Monsanto's Commitment to Sustainable Yield. 1 July 2018. http://www.aganytime.com/Documents/DemonstrationReportsPDFs/2013%20Demonstration%20Summaries/MON_GLC_MonsantosCommitmenttoSustainableYield.pdf.

Moore, Jason W. *Capitalism in the Web of Life: Ecology and the Accumulation of Capital*. London: Verso, 2015.

Moreno, D. Garcia, K. Verbeek, T. Camelbeeck, M. De Batist, F. Oggioni, O. Zurita Hurtado, W. Versteeg, H. Jomard, J. S. Collier, S. Gupta, A. Trentesaux, and K. Vanneste. "Fault Activity in the Epicentral Area of the 1580 Dover Strait (Pas-de- Calais) Earthquake (Northwestern Europe)." *Geophysical Journal International*. Vol. 201 (2015): 528–42.

Morris, Martha. "Naval Cordage Procurement in Early Modern England." *International Journal of Maritime History*. Vol. 11, No. 1 (1999): 81–99.

Morton, Timothy. *The Ecological Thought*. Cambridge, MA: Harvard University Press, 2010.

Musson, R. M. W. "British Earthquakes." *Proceedings of the Geologists' Association*. Vol. 118 (2007): 305–37.

Nardizzi, Vin. "Grafted to Falstaff and Compounded with Catherine: Mingling Hal in the Second Tetralogy." In *Queer Renaissance Historiography: Backward Gaze*. Edited by Vin Nardizzi, Stephen Guy-Bray, and Will Stockton. Burlington, VT: Ashgate, 2009.

Nardizzi, Vin. *Wooden Os: Shakespeare's Theatres and England's Trees*. Toronto: University of Toronto Press, 2013.

Natal Witness, 3 April 1882.

Neeson, Eion. "Woodland in History and Culture." In *Nature in Ireland: A Scientific and Cultural History*. Edited by John Wilson Foster. Dublin: The Lilliput Press, 1997. 133–56.

Neil, Kelly. "The Politics of Suicide in John Fletcher's *Tragedie of Bonduca*." *Journal for Early Modern Cultural Studies*. Vol. 14, No. 1 (2014): 88–114.

Neilson, G., R. M. W. Musson, and P. W. Burton. "The 'London' Earthquake of 1580, April 6." *Engineering Geology*. Vol. 20, No. 1 and 2 (1984): 113–41.

Nielsen, Wendy C. "Boadicea Onstage before 1800, a Theatrical and Colonial History." *Studies in English Literature, 1500–1900*. Vol. 49, No. 3 (2009): 595–614.

Nixon, Rob. *Slow Violence and the Environmentalism of the Poor*. Cambridge, MA: Harvard University Press, 2011.

Normington, Katie. *Gender and Medieval Drama*. Woodbridge: D.S. Brewer, 2004.

Nuccitelli, Dana. "Matt Ridley Wants to Gamble the Earth's Future Because He Won't Learn from the Past." *The Guardian*. 21 January 2015. https://www.theguardian.com/environment/climate-consensus-97-per-cent/2015/jan/21/matt-ridley-wants-to-gamble-earths-future-because-wont-learn-from-past. Accessed 1 July 2021.

O'Callaghan-Gordo, Cristina, and Josep M Antó. "COVID-19: The Disease of the Anthropocene." *Environmental Research*. Vol. 187 (2020): 109683. doi:10.1016/j.envres.2020.109683. Accessed 13 June 2022.

O'Malley, Evelyn. "'To Weather a Play': Audiences, Outdoor Shakespeares, and Avant-Garde Nostalgia at The Willow Globe." *Shakespeare Bulletin*. Vol. 36, No. 3 (2018): 409–27.

Omotoso, Kole. *The Theatrical into Theatre: A Study of Drama and Theatre in the English-Speaking Caribbean*. London: New Beacon Books, 1982.

Oppenheim, H. L. "Brooke, Gustavus Vaughan (1818–1866)." *Australian Dictionary of Biography*. National Centre of Biography, Australian National University. 17 March 2017. https://adb.anu.edu.au/biography/brooke-gustavus-vaughan-3064/text4519. Accessed 13 June 2022.

Oppermann, Serpil. "Feminist Ecocriticism: The New Ecofeminist Settlement." *Feminismo/s*. Vol. 22 (December 2013): 65–88.

Ovid. *The Metamorphoses*. Translated by Ian Johnston. http://johnstoniatexts.x10host.com/ovid/ovid2html.html. Accessed 18 December 2019.

Parry, Graham. *The Trophies of Time: English Antiquarians of the Seventeenth Century*. Oxford: Oxford University Press, 1995.

Parsons, James J. "The Cork Oak Forests and the Evolution of the Cork Industry in Southern Spain and Portugal." *Economic Geography*. Vol. 38, No. 3 (1962): 195–214.

Passannante, Gerard. *Catastrophizing: Materialism and the Making of Disaster*. Chicago, IL: University of Chicago Press, 2019.

Pennsylvania Gazette, 8 December 1766.

Pietz, William. "Death of the Deodand: Accursed Objects and the Money Value of Human Life." *Anthropology and Aesthetics*. Vol. 31, No. 1 (1997): 97–108.

Pliny. *The historie of the vvorld Commonly called, the naturall historie of C. Plinius Secundus*. Translated by Philemon Holland. London, 1601.

Poitevin, Kimberly. "Inventing Whiteness: Cosmetics, Race, and Women in Early Modern England." *Journal for Early Modern Cultural Studies*. Vol. 11, No. 1 (2011): 59–89.

Pollard, Tanya. "The Pleasures and Perils of Smoking in Early Modern England." In *Smoke: A Global History of Smoking*. Edited by Sander L. Gilman and Zhou Xun. New York: Reaktion Books, 2004. 38–45.

Powell, William T. "Excerpts from the Memoirs of William T. Powell." In *Johannesburg Pioneer Journals, 1888–1909*. Edited by Maryna Fraser. Cape Town: Van Riebeeck Society, 1986.

Primack, Richard B., Abrahama Miller-Rushing, and Kiruba Dharaneesaran. "Changes in the Flora of Thoreau's Concord." *Biological Conservation*. Vol. 142, No. 3 (2009): 500–8.

Prynne, William. *Histrio-mastix, The players scourge, or, actors tragaedie, divided into two parts*. London, 1633.

Rabinowitz, Chloe. "Found Stages to Present Text Message Shakespearean Play: Much Ado Over Texting!" *Broadway World*. 24 March 2022. https://www.broadwayworld.com/atlanta/article/Found-Stages-to-Present-Text-Message-Shakespearean-Play-MUCH-ADO-OVER-TEXTING-20220324. Accessed 13 June 2022.

Racster, Olga. *Curtain Up!* Cape Town: Juta & Co., 1951.

Reader's Digest. *South Africa's Yesterdays*. Cape Town: Reader's Digest Association South Africa, 1981.

Redfern, Margaret and R. R. Askew. *Plant Galls*. Slough: Richmond Publishing Co., 1992.

Ridley, Matt. "Matt Ridley: My Life as a Climate Change Lukewarmer." *The London Times*. 19 January 2015. https://www.thetimes.co.uk/article/matt-ridley-my-life-as-a-climate-change-lukewarmer-8jwbd8xz6dj. Accessed 1 July 2021.

Roberts, Lewes. *The Merchants Mappe of Commerce*. London, 1638.

Rosenthal, Eric. "Early Shakespeare Productions in South Africa." *English Studies in Africa*. Vol. 7, No. 2 (1964): 202–16.

Rossi, Paolo. *The Dark Abyss of Time: The History of the Earth and the History of Nations from Hooke to Vico*. Chicago, IL: University of Chicago Press, 1984.

Rowlands, Samuel. *More Knaves Yet*. London, 1613.

Rudwick, Martin J. S. *Earth's Deep History: How It Was Discovered and Why It Matters*. Chicago, IL: University of Chicago Press, 2014.

Ruscelli, Girolamo. *The seconde part of the Secretes of Master Alexis of Piemont*. London, 1560.

Rustici, Craig. "The Smoking Girl: Tobacco and the Representation of Mary Frith." *Studies in Philology*. Vol. 96, No. 2 (1999): 159–79.

Ryner, Bradley. *Performing Economic Thought: English Drama and Mercantile Writing, 1600–1642*. Edinburgh: Edinburgh University Press, 2014.

Salazar, Rebecca. "A Rogue and Pleasant Stage: Performing Ecology in Outdoor Shakespeares." *Shakespeare Bulletin*. Vol. 36, No. 3 (2018): 449–66.

Schauffer, Dennis. "Shakespeare Performance in Pietermaritzburg, Natal, Prior to 1914." *Shakespeare in Southern Africa*. Vol. 19 (2007): 9–23.

Schneider, Rebecca. *Performing Remains: Art and War in Times of Theatrical Reenactment*. New York: Routledge, 2011.

Schwartz, Stuart B. *Sea of Storms: A History of Hurricanes in the Greater Caribbean from Columbus to Katrina*. Princeton, NJ: Princeton University Press, 2015.

Seed, Patricia. *Ceremonies of Possession in Europe's Conquest of the New World, 1492–1640*. Cambridge: Cambridge University Press, 1995.

Shakespeare, William. *Romeo and Juliet*. Edited by Barbara A. Mowat and Paul Werstine. New York: Washington Square Press, 1992.

Shakespeare, William. *King Lear*. Edited by Barbara A. Mowat and Paul Werstine. New York: Washington Square Press, 1993.

Shakespeare, William. *The Arden Shakespeare: Titus Andronicus*. Edited by Jonathan Bate. London: Routledge, 1995.

Shakespeare, William. *As You Like It*. Edited by Barbara A. Mowat and Paul Werstine. New York: Washington Square Press, 1997.

Shakespeare, William. *Pericles*. Edited by Barbara A. Mowat and Paul Werstine. New York: Washington Square Press, 2005.

Shakespeare, William. *The Tempest*. Edited by Jonathan Bate and Eric Rasmussen. New York: The Modern Library, 2008.

Shakespeare, William. *Macbeth*. Edited by Jonathan Bate and Eric Rasmussen. New York: The Modern Library, 2009.

Shakespeare, William. *Much Ado About Nothing*. Edited by Jonathan Bate and Eric Rasmussen. New York: The Modern Library, 2009.

Shakespeare, William. *The Merchant of Venice*. Edited by Barbara A. Mowat and Paul Werstine. New York: Washington Square Press, 2010.

Shenk, Linda and William J. Gutowski, "Mind the Gaps! Climate Scientists Should Heed Lessons in Collaborative Storytelling from William Shakespeare." *WIREs Clim Change*. 14 April 2022, e783, 1–9. https://wires.onlinelibrary.wiley.com/doi/pdfdirect/10.1002/wcc.783. Accessed 14 June 2022.

Shepard, Richard F. "Weather, 'Tis Not Always Nobler at the Delacorte." *New York Times*. 14 August 1988. ProQuest Historical Newspapers: *The New York Times (1851–2010)*, H5.

Shilling, Erik. "Massive Cyanide Spill at Gold Mine Leaked Into 5 Different Rivers." *Atlas Obscura*. 25 February 2016. http://www.atlasobscura.com/articles/massive-cyanide-spill-at-gold-mine-leaked-into-5-different-rivers. Accessed 14 June 2022.

Shillington, V. M. and A. B. Wallis Chapman. *The Commercial Relations of England and Portugal*. London: Routledge, 1907.

Siegel, Naomi. "Weather Adds Touch to Outdoor 'Tempest.'" *New York Times*. 5 July 2009. NJ10.

Simpson, H. A. D. "Art in Afghanistan." *The Theatre*. Vol. 4 (1881): 140–3.

Sloterdijk, Peter. *What Happened in the 20th Century?* Cambridge: Polity, 2018.

Smith, Ian. *Race and Rhetoric in the Renaissance: Barbarian Errors*. New York: Palgrave MacMillan, 2009.

Smith, Ian. "Othello's Black Handkerchief." *Shakespeare Quarterly*. Vol. 64, No. 1 (2013): 1–25.

Sofer, Andrew. *The Stage Life of Props*. Ann Arbor, MI: University of Michigan Press, 2003.

Sofer, Andrew. *Dark Matter: Invisibility in Drama, Theater, and Performance*. Ann Arbor, MI: University of Michigan Press, 2013.

Solender, Andrew. "Marjorie Taylor Greene Forming Caucus to Promote 'Anglo-Saxon Political Traditions.'" *Forbes*. 16 April 2021. https://www.forbes.com/sites/andrewsolender/2021/04/16/marjorie-taylor-greene-forming-caucus-to-promote-anglo-saxon-political-traditions/?sh=2f82b0a25672. Accessed 13 June 2022.

Spargo, P. E. "The Lion's Head Gold Mine." *Bulletin of the National Library of South Africa*. Vol. 69, No. 1 (2015): 28–40.

Spivak, Gayatri Chakravorty. *Death of a Discipline*. New York: Columbia University Press, 2003.

Standish, Arthur. *The commons complaint*. London, 1611.

Steffen, Will, Jacques Grinevald, Paul Crutzen, and John McNeill. "The Anthropocene: Conceptual and Historical Perspectives." *Philosophical Transactions of the Royal Society*. Vol. 369 (2011): 842–67.

Stern, Tiffany. "Actors' Parts." In *The Oxford Handbook of Early Modern Theatre*. Edited by Richard Dutton. Oxford: Oxford University Press, 2009. 496–512.

Stevens, Andrea. *Inventions of the Skin: The Painted Body in Early English Drama*. Edinburgh: Edinburgh University Press, 2013.

Strachey, William. *A True Reportory of the Wreck and Redemption of Sir Thomas Gates, Knight*. London, 1625.

Subramanian, Meera. "The City and the Sea." *Orion Magazine*. 2015. https://orionmagazine.org/article/the-city-and-the-sea. Accessed 14 June 2022.

Swan, Quito. *Black Power in Bermuda: The Struggle for Decolonization*. New York: Palgrave Macmillan, 2009.

Sylvester, Joshua. *Tobacco Battered & the Pipes Shattered*. London, 1616.

A table plainly teaching ye making and use of a wetherglas. London, 1631.

Tacitus. *Agricola and Germania*. Translated by Harold Mattingly. New York: Penguin, 2009.

Taylor, Gary. "Hamlet in Africa 1607." In *Travel Knowledge*. New York: Palgrave Macmillan, 2001. 223–48.

Taylor, John. *Newes and strange newes from St. Christophers of a tempestuous spirit, which is called by the Indians a hurry-cano or whirlewind*. London, 1638.

Tenner, Edward. *Why Things Bite Back: Technology and the Revenge of Unintended Consequences*. New York: Vintage, 1997.

Thackeray, Francis. "Shakespeare, Plants, and Chemical Analysis of Early Seventeenth Century Clay 'Tobacco' Pipes from Europe." *South African Journal of Science*. Vol. 111, No. 7 and 8 (2015): 1–2.

Thackeray, Francis, N. J. van der Merwe and T. A. van der Merwe. "Chemical Analysis of Residues from Seventeenth-Century Clay Pipes from Stratford-upon-Avon and Environs." *South African Journal of Science* Vol. 97, No. 1 (2001): 19–21.

"Theatrical Touring in the Far East: By One Who Has Tried It." *The Stage Year Book*, 1917.

Thomas, Keith. *Religion and the Decline of Magic*. New York: Charles Scribner's Sons, 1971.

Thommen, Lukas. *An Environmental History of Ancient Greece and Rome*. Translated by Philip Hill. Cambridge: Cambridge University Press, 2012.

Thompson, Ayanna. *Performing Race and Torture on the Early Modern Stage*. New York: Routledge, 2008.

Thomson, Leslie. "The Meaning of Thunder and Lightning: Stage Directions and Audience Expectations." *Early Theatre*. Vol. 2 (1999): 11–24.

Tichenor, Austin. "'In the brave squares': The Show Must Go Online." *Shakespeare and Beyond*. 29 September 2020. https://shakespeareandbeyond.folger.edu/2020/09/29/the-show-must-go-online-shakespeare-productions-zoom. Accessed 13 June 2022.

Todd, Kim. *Tinkering with Eden: A Natural History of Exotics in America*. New York: W.W. Norton & Co., 2001.

Trenberth, Kevin E. "Attribution of Climate Variations and Trends to Human Influences and Natural Variability." *WIREs Clim Change*. Vol. 2 (2011): 925–30.

Tweedy, Mary Johnson. "Bermuda 'Tempest': Presentation in Hamilton Recalls Belief That Island Was Scene of Play." *New York Times*. 17 September 1950. ProQuest Historical Newspapers: *The New York Times (1851–2010)*: 111.

Vaughan, Virginia Mason. *Performing Blackness on English Stages, 1500–1800*. Cambridge: Cambridge University Press, 2005.

Verstegan, Richard. *A Restitution of Decayed Intelligence in Antiquities*. London, 1605.

The vvonders of this windie winter. London, 1613.

Wall, Wendy. "Renaissance National Husbandry: Gervase Markham and the Publication of England." *The Sixteenth Century Journal*. Vol. 27, No. 3 (1996): 767–85.

Walsham, Alexandra. *Providence in Early Modern England*. Oxford: Oxford University Press, 1999.

Ward, Genevieve and Richard Whiteing. *Both Sides of the Curtain*. London: Cassell and Co., 1918.

Warf, Barney. "High Points: An Historical Geography of Cannabis." *The Geographical Review*. Vol. 104, No. 4 (2014): 414–38.

Wecker, Johann Jacob. *Cosmeticks or, the Beautifying Part of Physick*. London, 1660.

Wecker, Johann Jacob. *Eighteen Books of the Secrets of Art & Nature*. London, 1660.

Whitaker, Cord J. *Black Metaphors: How Modern Racism Emerged from Medieval Race-Thinking*. Philadelphia, PA: University of Pennsylvania Press, 2019.

Wickham, Glynne William Gladstone. *Shakespeare's Dramatic Heritage: Collected Studies in Medieval, Tudor, and Shakespearean Drama*. London: Routledge & K. Paul, 1969.

Wilkie, Allan. *All the World My Stage: The Reminiscences of a Shakespearean Actor-Manager in Five Continents*. Unpublished autobiography. MSS 92 W6825. University of Adelaide Special Collections.

Williams, Edward. *Virginia, more especially the south part thereof, richly and truly valued viz. the fertile Carolana, and no lesse excellent Isle of Roanoak, of latitude from 31 to 37 degr. relating the meanes of raysing infinite profits to the adventurers and planters*. London, 1650.

Wilson, Miranda. "Bastard Grafts, Crafted Fruits: Shakespeare's Planted Families." In *The Indistinct Human in Renaissance Literature*. Edited by Jean E. Feerick and Vin Nardizzi. New York: Palgrave Macmillan, 2012. 103–18.

Woodbridge, Linda. *English Revenge Drama: Money, Resistance, Equality*. Cambridge: Cambridge University Press, 2010.

Wong-Chong, George M., David V. Nakles, and David A. Dzombak, "Management of Cyanide in Industrial Process Wastewaters." In *Cyanide in Water and Soil: Chemistry, Risk, Management*. Edited by David A. Dzombak, Rajat S. Ghosh, and George M. Wong-Chong. London: Taylor & Francis, 2006. 517–70.

Wood, Alfred C. *A History of the Levant Company*. London: Frank Cass & Co., 1964.

Wooley, Hannah. *The accomplish'd ladies delight in preserving, physick, beautifying and cookery*. London, 1683.

Woolf, Rosemary. *The English Mystery Plays*. Berkeley, CA: University of California Press, 1972.

Worster, Donald. *Nature's Economy: A History of Ecological Ideas*. Cambridge: Cambridge University Press, 1977.

Wright, Richardson. *Revels in Jamaica, 1682–1838*. New York: Dodd, Mead & Co., 1937.

Yusoff, Kathryn. *A Billion Black Anthropocenes or None*. Minneapolis, MN: University of Minnesota Press, 2018.

Index

For the benefit of digital users, indexed terms that span two pages (e.g., 52–53) may, on occasion, appear on only one of those pages.